NAB OnLine Trading
stay ahead of the game
To get in front and stay there, you need the right strategy and the right equipment at your fingertips. With **NAB OnLine Trading**, your star investments are just a few clicks away. You can buy and sell ASX listed shares, warrants and exchange traded options online or over the phone, and take advantage of a comprehensive range of features* to help you invest.
• Competitive brokerage rates
• Frequent trader rebates
• Prompt trade executions
• Extensive research and analysis
• Email and SMS alerts
• Customer service support
Take control of your financial future with **NAB OnLine Trading**. To find out more, visit **nab.com.au/trading** or call our Client Service Team on **13 13 80**.
invest in your stars
nab
WINNER Money AWARDS 2006 BANK OF THE YEAR

Top Stocks 2007

A SHAREBUYER'S GUIDE TO 109 LEADING AUSTRALIAN COMPANIES

MARTIN ROTH

Wrightbooks

BICENTENNIAL 1807 WILEY 2007 BICENTENNIAL

The author and publisher would like to thank Aspect Huntley for permission to include the five-year shareholder return figures, and Alan Hull (author of *Active Investing* and *Active Retirement*) for generating the five-year share price graphs <www.alanhull.com>.

This thirteenth edition first published 2007 by Wrightbooks
an imprint of John Wiley & Sons Australia, Ltd
42 McDougall Street, Milton Qld 4064

First edition published as *Top Stocks* by Wrightbooks in 1995
New edition published annually

Typeset in 11.2/11.8 pt Bembo

ISBN: 0 731 405455

Cover design by Rob Cowpe

Cover photos © Photodisc Inc.

All charts © TradeStation Technologies, Inc.

Printed in Australia by Ligare Book Printer

10 9 8 7 6 5 4 3 2 1

Disclaimer

The material in this publication is of the nature of general comment only, and does not represent professional advice. It is not intended to provide specific guidance for particular circumstances and it should not be relied on as the basis for any decision to take action or not take action on any matter which it covers. Readers should obtain professional advice where appropriate, before making any such decision. To the maximum extent permitted by law, the author and publisher disclaim all responsibility and liability to any person, arising directly or indirectly from any person taking or not taking action based upon the information in this publication.

CONTENTS

PART II – THE TABLES

Preface

It's been another excellent year for Australian companies, and 109 have qualified for entry to *Top Stocks 2007*. This should send an important lesson to investors: even when the stock market lacks direction – as seemed to be the case when this book was going to press – there are still many excellent companies around. Regardless of short-term share price performance, a well-considered portfolio of a selection of them would surely make an excellent long-term investment.

An indication of the long-term strength of the stock market came in the Australian Stock Exchange's annual survey of investment returns. Australian shares provided an average annual return of 11.8% in the 10 years to December 2005 (including the reinvestment of dividends) and an annual average of 12.2% over 20 years. Such impressive results came despite some sharp declines during those periods.

Some features of this edition of *Top Stocks* are:

- Twenty new companies, of which 12 have never appeared previously in any edition of *Top Stocks*.
- The great majority of the companies in the book enjoyed higher profits and paid a higher dividend in their latest financial year. This is a testament to the continuing strengths of the domestic economy and of the stock market.
- Eight high-tech stocks are included, up from six in *Top Stocks 2006* and four in *Top Stocks 2005*, and the most in any edition of *Top Stocks*. (Most editions contained none.)
- There are eight healthcare stocks, one more than in *Top Stocks 2006*, and the most ever.
- There are 10 resource stocks, the most of any edition of *Top Stocks,* along with others such as Ausdrill and Monadelphous which make most of their profits from the resources industry.

- For the first time since the *Top Stocks* series began, no wine company made it into the book, reflecting the depression in that industry.
- Also falling by the wayside – for a variety of reasons – are housing developers. None are left in this edition of the book, although Lend Lease, which includes housing development among its diverse activities, made a return to *Top Stocks* after six years' absence.

Australian International Financial Reporting Standards

New international reporting rules, known as the Australian International Financial Reporting Standards (AIFRS), have been introduced for Australian companies, for reporting periods that begin on or after 1 January 2005. That covers the majority of companies in this book, whose latest reporting period began on 1 July 2005.

It has led to some significant changes, and it is important that users of this book be aware of these. The main issues are:

- Changes in accounting guidelines mean that sales and profits may in some cases be higher or lower than they would have been under the previous AGAAP (Australian Generally Accepted Accounting Principles) rules, and some ratios in this book are also different. It has almost certainly led to several companies being excluded from this edition of *Top Stocks*. An example is Timbercorp; its debt-to-equity ratio has soared under the new standards, rendering it ineligible for the book.
- Companies have been obliged to restate their previous year's figures in accordance with the new standards. Thus, say, the 2005 financial year ratios in the tables in this book can be very different from the 2005 financial year ratios that appeared in *Top Stocks 2006*. An extreme example is Metcash. In *Top Stocks 2006* its April 2005 debt-to-equity ratio was 14.5%. In *Top Stocks 2007*, under the new reporting standards, this has become 3575.3%.
- Companies now stress their continuing operations, with those parts of their business that they have sold or closed down treated separately. Thus, when reporting their results in their income statement, the revenues figure is generally for continuing operations only. The profit figures are also for continuing operations, followed by a separate entry for discontinued operations, and then a final 'profit for the year' figure that includes both continuing and discontinued operations.

  After some consideration, I have decided to use only continuing operations in the figures in the tables in *Top Stocks*, to ensure consistency in all the figures presented. In fact, most companies do not have discontinued operations, so the vast majority of stocks in this book are not affected by this change. But several are, and it could mean that profit and EPS (and, hence, PER) figures that appear in *Top Stocks* are somewhat different from those in other investment media.

  An example is Coles Myer, which for its July 2006 financial year reported an after-tax profit from continuing operations of $536.4 million, with an EPS of 43.0 cents. (With the removal of significant items, this became a profit of $787.3 million, with an EPS of 63.2 cents, which are the figures used in this book.) But Coles Myer also made a substantial profit of $627.2 million from the operation and sale of its Myer department store chain, and thus it reported a total after-tax profit for the year – from both continuing and discontinued operations – of $1163.6 million, with an EPS of 93.4 cents.

Who is *Top Stocks* written for?

Top Stocks is written for every investor who has ever wondered:

There are more than 1700 companies on the stock exchange – where do I start?

These investors know that there are many excellent companies out there – companies that seem to prosper through good times and bad – but they are just not sure which ones they are, apart from some obvious names.

Whatever may be happening in the market, the fact remains that there are plenty of good, solid companies with excellent long-term records of regular dividends and capital growth. They may not double or triple in price within the space of months. But so long as a company's business continues to flourish its shares should certainly come to represent good value.

This book is for investors seeking out these stocks.

It is not a how-to book. It does not give step-by-step instructions to 'winning' in the stock market. Rather, it is an independent and objective evaluation of leading companies, based on rigid criteria, with the intention of yielding a large selection of stocks that can become the starting point for investors wishing to do their own research.

A large amount of information is presented on each company, and another key feature of the book is that the data is presented in a common format, to allow readers to make easy comparisons between companies.

It is necessarily a conservative book. All stocks must have been listed for five years to even be considered for inclusion (which is why earlier editions missed the dot-com boom entirely). It is especially suited for those seeking out value stocks for longer term investment.

Yet, perhaps ironically, the book is also increasingly being used by short-term traders seeking a good selection of financially sound and reliable companies whose shares they can trade.

In addition, there are many regular readers who buy the book each year, and to them in particular I express my thanks.

What are the entry criteria?

The criteria for inclusion in *Top Stocks* are strict:

- All companies must be included in the All Ordinaries Index, which comprises Australia's 500 largest stocks (out of more than 1700). The reason for excluding smaller companies is that there is often little investor information available on many of them and some are so thinly traded as to be almost illiquid. In fact, the 500 All Ordinaries companies comprise, by market capitalisation, around 98% of the entire market. (Three companies – Adcorp, CMI and Magna Pacific – are no longer in the All Ordinaries Index, but appeared in *Top Stocks 2006*, so for continuity purposes remain in this latest edition of the book.)
- It was necessary that all companies be publicly listed since at least the end of 2001, and have a five-year record of profits and dividend payouts. An exception is companies de-merged from another company in the All Ordinaries Index. These require just a two-year record of profits and dividend payouts. The only such company in this edition is Rinker Group, formerly part of CSR.
- All companies were required to post a return-on-equity ratio of at least 10% in their latest financial year.
- No company should have a debt-to-equity ratio of more than 70%.

- It must be stressed that share price performance is *not* one of the criteria for inclusion in this book. The purpose is to select companies with good profits and a strong balance sheet. These may not offer the spectacular share price returns of a biotech start-up, but they should also present far less risk. To use an Olympics analogy, the stocks in this book are more like marathon runners than sprinters. They should last the distance, providing solid – if un-flashy – performance over the long term.
- There are several notable exclusions. Investment trusts such as Australian Foundation Investment Company are out, as these mainly buy other shares or investments. Also omitted are property trusts.
- A further exclusion is the foreign stocks listed on the Australian Stock Exchange. There is sometimes a lack of information available about such companies. In addition, their stock prices tend to move on events and trends in their home countries, making it difficult at times for local investors to follow them.

Changes to this edition

A total of 23 companies from *Top Stocks 2006* have been omitted from this new edition. One, Australand Property Group, is now designated as a property trust. Another housing developer, Central Equity, has been privatised, and two companies, Foodland Associated and Patrick Corporation, were acquired and delisted. In a rare occurrence for *Top Stocks*, one company, Portman, was eliminated because it paid no dividend.

Seven companies from *Top Stocks 2006* were excluded because they had debt-to-equity ratios that rose higher than 70%:

- Coffey International
- Collection House
- FKP Property Group
- Funtastic
- Timbercorp
- Toll Holdings
- Willmott Forests.

And a further 11 companies had return-on-equity figures that fell below 10%:

- Angus & Coote*
- Australian Gas Light
- AV Jennings
- Brickworks
- Cellnet Group
- Incitec Pivot
- Integrated Group
- McGuigan Simeon Wines
- Pacifica Group
- Sigma Pharmaceuticals
- Washington H Soul Pattinson.

* Angus & Coote had not formally released its July 2006 results as this book went to press, but had made an official announcement to the stock exchange of its expected profit levels.

As noted, there are 20 new companies in this edition (although eight of them have appeared in earlier editions of the book, but were not in *Top Stocks 2006*). The companies are:

- Ausdrill#
- Beach Petroleum#
- Brambles Industries
- Crane Group
- HPAL#
- Hunter Hall International#
- Jubilee Mines#
- Kingsgate Consolidated#

- Lend Lease
- Macarthur Coal#
- National Can Industries
- Objective Corporation#
- OneSteel#
- Orica
- SDI
- Seven Network#
- Skilled Group#
- Sonic Healthcare
- Tabcorp Holdings
- WHK Group.#

Companies that have not appeared in any previous edition of *Top Stocks*.

Companies in every edition of *Top Stocks*

Fully 11 companies have appeared in every edition of *Top Stocks*. (Incitec Pivot – formerly known as just Incitec – had also been in every edition, but was eliminated from *Top Stocks 2007* for a low return on equity figure.) These companies are:

- ANZ
- Commonwealth Bank of Australia
- CSR
- Harvey Norman
- Hills Industries
- National Australia Bank
- QBE Insurance
- Santos
- Suncorp-Metway
- Wesfarmers
- Westpac Banking.

Once again it is my hope that *Top Stocks 2007* will serve you well.

Martin Roth
Melbourne
October 2006

INTRODUCTION

The 109 companies in this book have been placed as much as possible into a common format, for ease of comparison. Please study the following explanations in order to get as much as possible from the large amount of data.

Each page begins with a brief introduction to the company and its activities. Then follow the highlights of its latest business results. For the majority of the companies these are their June 2006 results, which were issued during July, August and September 2006. Finally, there is a section on the outlook for the company, sometimes including comment on the performance of the shares.

Tables

The tables have been made as concise as possible, though they repay careful study, as they contain large amounts of information. Note that the tables for the banks have been arranged a little differently from the others; details of these are later in this introduction.

At the top of each page is a small table with the following data.

Share price

This is the closing price on 5 September 2006. Also included are the 12-month high and low prices, as of the same date.

Market capitalisation

This is the size of the company, as determined by the stock market. It is the share price (again, as of 5 September 2006) multiplied by the number of shares on issue. All companies in this book must be in the All Ordinaries Index (with just a few exceptions, as discussed in the preface), which comprises Australia's 500 largest stocks, as measured by market capitalisation.

Price-to-net-tangible-assets-per-share ratio

The NTA-per-share figure expresses the worth of a company's net tangible assets – that is, its assets minus its liabilities and intangible assets – for each share of the company. The price-to-NTA-per-share ratio relates this figure to the share price.

A ratio of one means that the company is valued exactly according to the value of its assets. A ratio below one suggests that the shares are a bargain, though usually there is a good reason for this. Profits are more important than assets.

Eight companies in this book – Alesco, Commander Communications, Computershare, John Fairfax Holdings, Metcash, Seven Network, Sonic Healthcare and Tabcorp – have a negative NTA-per-share figure as a result of having intangible assets valued at more than their remaining net assets, and a price-to-NTA-per-share ratio cannot be calculated. See table M, in the second part of this book, for a little more detail on this ratio.

Five-year share price return

This is the total return you could have received from the stock in the five years to September 2006. It includes reinvested dividends, bonus stock, rights issues and capital gain from the stock's appreciation. It is expressed as a compounded annual rate of return. These figures have been supplied by Aspect Huntley.

Price-earnings ratio (PER)

The PER is one of the most popular measures of whether a share is cheap or expensive. It is calculated by dividing the share price – in this case the closing price for 5 September 2006 – by the EPS figure. Obviously the share price is continually changing, so the PER figures in this book are for guidance only. Many newspapers publish each morning the latest PER for every stock.

Dividend yield

This is the latest full-year dividend expressed as a percentage of the share price. Like the PER, it changes as the share price moves. It is a useful figure, especially for investors who are buying shares for income, as it allows you to compare this income with alternative investments, such as a bank term deposit or an investment property.

Sector comparisons

It is often useful to compare a company's price-earnings ratio and its dividend yield with those of its sector. Often the stocks in a sector move together. Thus, if a particular stock is lagging the averages, this may – depending on the reasons – be a buying opportunity.

Figures used in this book are those of the S&P/ASX sectors, again as of 5 September 2006.

Share price chart

Also at the top of each page is a five-year share price chart, provided by Alan Hull (author of *Active Investing* and *Active Retirement*, both published by Wrightbooks).

Website

Most public companies now have websites, and the website addresses of companies in this book are placed under the share price chart.

Be aware that some sites are little more than corporate brochures for the company, with glossy photos and beat-up prose. A few are wildly out of date. But increasingly, public companies are using the internet as a means of providing timely data to shareholders.

Thus, you may now find all the latest ASX company announcements – often placed on the site simultaneously to their ASX release – along with media releases and even, sometimes, speeches and presentations to stock market analysts.

If you are following a particular company it is highly recommended that you become familiar with that company's website.

Main tables

In the main tables you will find the following.

Revenues

These are the company's revenues from its business activities, generally the sale of products or services. It does not usually include additional income from such sources as investments, bank interest or the sale of assets. If the information is available, the revenues figure has been broken down into the major product areas.

From this edition of *Top Stocks*, the revenues figure is for continuing operations only, in line with new accounting standards. Thus, the sales revenues of any businesses that the company sold during the year will not be included. An example is Coles Myer, which in its July 2006 business year sold the Myer chain of department stores. But for the great majority of companies, there is no impact.

Earnings before interest and taxation

Earnings before interest and taxation (EBIT) is the firm's profit from its operations before the payment of interest and tax. This figure is often used by analysts examining a company. The reason is that some companies have borrowed extensively to finance their activities, while others have opted for alternative means. By expressing profits before interest payments it is possible to compare more precisely the performance of these companies. The net interest figure – interest payments minus interest receipts – has been used for this calculation.

EBIT margin

This is the company's EBIT expressed as a percentage of its revenues. It is a gauge of a company's efficiency. A high EBIT margin suggests that a company is achieving success in keeping its costs low.

Gross margin

The gross margin is the company's gross profit as a percentage of its sales. The gross profit is the amount left over after deducting from a company's sales figure its cost of sales: that is, its manufacturing costs or, for a retailer, the cost of purchasing the goods it sells. The cost of goods sold figure does not usually include marketing or administration costs.

As there are different ways of calculating the cost of goods sold figure, this ratio is best used for year-to-year comparisons of a single company's efficiency, rather than in comparing one company with another. Not all companies present a cost of goods sold figure, so a gross margin ratio is not given for every stock in this book. The revenues for some companies include a mix of sales and services. Where a breakdown is possible, the gross profit figure will reflect sales only.

Profit before tax/profit after tax

The profit before tax figure is simply the EBIT figure minus net interest payments. The profit after tax figure is, of course, the company's profit after the payment of tax, and also after the deduction of minority interests. Minority interests are that part of a company's profit that is claimed by outside interests, usually the other shareholders in a subsidiary which is not fully owned by the company. Many companies do not have any minority interests, and for those that do it is generally a tiny figure.

From this edition of *Top Stocks*, the profit figures are for continuing operations only, in line with new accounting standards. Thus, the profit from any businesses that the company sold during the year will not be included. For the great majority of companies, this change will not have any impact.

As much as possible, I have adjusted the profit figures to exclude non-recurring profits and losses, which are called significant items. It is for this reason that the profit figures in *Top Stocks* sometimes differ from those in the financial media or on financial websites, where profit figures normally include significant items.

The significance of significant items

Significant items are those that have an abnormal impact on profits, even though they happen in the normal course of the company's operations. Examples are the profit from the sale of a business, or losses from a business restructuring, the write-down of property, an inventory write-down, a bad-debt loss or a write-off for research and development expenditure.

They were formerly called abnormals, and were part of the statement of financial performance. Now they are simply included among the notes to the statement (and sometimes not even there).

Significant items are controversial. It is often a matter of subjective judgement as to what is included and what is excluded. After analysing the accounts of hundreds of companies, while writing the various editions of this book, it is clear that different companies use quite widely varying interpretations of what is significant.

Further, when they do report a significant item there is no consistency as to whether they use pre-tax figures or after-tax figures. Some report both, making it easy to adjust the profit figures in the tables in this book. But difficulties arise when only one figure – generally pre-tax – is given for significant items. A telephone call to the company usually elicits the other figure, but not always.

Fortunately, most companies do not report significant items. But investors should be aware of this issue. It sometimes causes consternation for readers of *Top Stocks* to find that a particular profit figure in this book is substantially different from that given by some other source. My publisher occasionally receives anguished emails from readers enquiring why a profit figure in this book is so different from that reported elsewhere. In virtually all cases the reason is that I have stripped out a significant item.

Earnings per share

Earnings per share (EPS) is the after-tax profit divided by the number of shares. Because the profit figure is for a 12-month period the number of shares used is a weighted average of those on issue during the year. This number is provided by the company in its annual report and its results announcements.

Cash flow per share

The cash flow per share ratio tells – in theory – how much actual cash the company has generated from its operations.

In fact, the ratio in this book is not exactly a true measure of cash flow. It is simply the company's depreciation and amortisation figures for the year added to the after-tax profit, and then divided by a weighted average of the number of shares. Depreciation and amortisation are expenses that do not actually utilise cash, so can be added back to after-tax profit to give a kind of indication of the company's cash flow.

By contrast, a true cash flow – including such items as newly raised capital and money received from the sale of assets – would require quite complex calculations based on the company's statement of cash flows. However, many analysts use the ratio as I present it, because it is easy to calculate, and it is certainly a useful guide to how much funding the company has available from its operations.

Dividend

The dividend figure is the total for the year, interim and final. Please note that it does not include special dividends. The level of franking is also provided.

Net tangible assets per share

The NTA per share figure tells the theoretical value of the company – per share – if all assets were sold and then all liabilities paid. It is very much a theoretical figure, as there is no guarantee that corporate assets are really worth the price put on them in the balance sheet. Intangible assets such as goodwill, newspaper mastheads and patent rights are excluded because of the difficulty in putting a sales price on them, and also because they may in fact not have much value if separated from the company.

As already noted, eight companies in this book have a negative NTA, due to the fact that their intangible assets are so great, and no figure can be listed for them.

Where a company's most recent financial results are the half-year figures, these are used to calculate this ratio.

Interest cover

The interest cover ratio indicates how many times a company could make its interest payments from its pre-tax profit. A rough rule of thumb says a ratio of at least three times is desirable. Below that and fast-rising interest rates could imperil profits. The ratio is derived by dividing the EBIT figure by net interest payments. Some fortunate companies have interest receipts that are higher than their interest payments, which turns the interest cover into a negative figure, and so it is not listed.

Return on equity

Return on equity (ROE) is the after-tax profit expressed as a percentage of the shareholders' equity. In theory, it is the amount that the company's managers have made for you – the shareholder – on your money. The shareholders' equity figure used is an average for the year.

Debt-to-equity ratio

This ratio is one of the best-known measures of a company's debt levels. It is total borrowings minus the company's cash holdings, expressed as a percentage of the shareholders' equity. Some companies have no debt at all, or their cash position is greater than their level of debt, which results in a negative ratio, so no figure is listed for them.

Where a company's most recent financial results are the half-year figures, these are used to calculate this ratio.

Current ratio

The current ratio is simply the company's current assets divided by its current liabilities. Current assets are cash or assets that can, in theory, be converted quickly into cash. Current liabilities are normally those payable within a year. Thus, the current ratio measures the ability of a company to repay in a hurry its short-term debt, should the need arise. The surplus of current assets over current liabilities is referred to as the company's working capital.

Where a company's most recent financial results are the half-year figures, these are used to calculate this ratio.

Banks

The tables for the banks are somewhat different from those for most other companies. EBIT and debt-to-equity ratios have little relevance for them, as they have such high interest payments (to their customers). Other differences are examined below.

Operating income

Operating income is used instead of sales revenues. Operating income is the bank's net interest income – that is, its total interest income minus its interest expense – plus other income, such as bank fees, fund management fees and income from businesses such as corporate finance and insurance.

Net interest income

Banks borrow money – that is, they accept deposits from savers – and they lend it to businesses, home buyers and other borrowers. They charge the borrowers more than they pay those who deposit money with them, and the difference is known as net interest income.

Operating expenses

These are all the costs of running the bank. Banks have high operating expenses, and one of the keys to profit growth is cutting these expenses. Add the provision for doubtful debts to operating expenses, then deduct the total from operating income, and you get the pre-tax profit.

Non-interest income to total income

Banks have traditionally made most of their income from savers and from lending out money. But increasingly this is becoming a commodity business, with a growing number of entrants offering higher interest rates to savers and lower rates to borrowers. In response the big banks are working to diversify into new fields, and this ratio is an indication of their success.

Cost-to-income ratio

As noted, the banks have high costs – numerous branches, expensive computer systems, many staff, and so on – and they are all striving to reduce these. The cost-to-income ratio expresses their expenses as a percentage of their operating income, and is one of the ratios most often used as a gauge of efficiency. The lower the ratio drops the better.

Return on assets

Banks have enormous assets, in sharp contrast to, say, a high-tech start-up whose main physical assets may be little more than a set of computers. So the return on assets – the after-tax profit expressed as a percentage of the year's average total assets – is another measure of efficiency.

PART I – THE COMPANIES

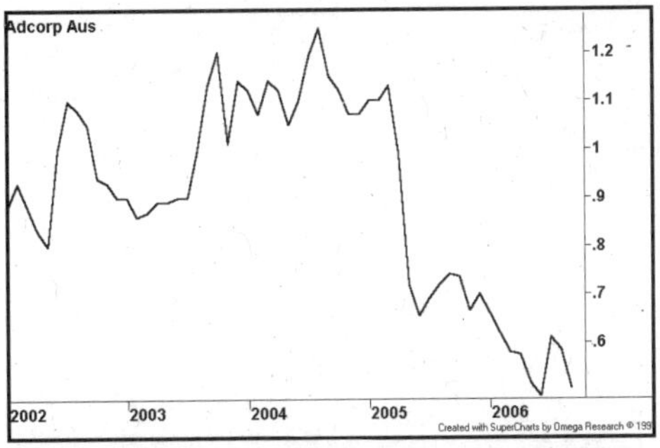

www.adcorp.com.au

ADCORP AUSTRALIA LIMITED

Share price ($)	0.56
12-month high ($)	0.80
12-month low ($)	0.49
Market capitalisation ($mn)	35.6
Price-to-NTA-per-share ratio	3.7
5-year share price return (% p.a.)	–2.6

Sector: Consumer discretionary	Company	Sector
Price-earnings ratio (times)	9.4	18.8
Dividend yield (%)	10.7	4.0

Sydney-based advertising agency services provider Adcorp has its origins in recruitment advertising. It has since grown by acquisition into a leading provider of a wide range of advertising and communications services, specialising in human resources, education, real estate, motor vehicles and auctioneering. The company places a strong emphasis on technology. Adcorp operates from six offices in Australia and four in New Zealand.

Latest business results (June 2006, full year)

Profits fell for the second straight year, with a particularly poor performance from the company's New Zealand operations, as that country's economy started to slow, particularly over the second half. Australia saw good business from the Queensland and South Australian offices, but overall sales fell 3% to $25.9 million, with EBIT down 11%. New Zealand sales revenues declined by 7% to $6.7 million, but EBIT dropped 36%. Nevertheless, although New Zealand operations were responsible for just over 20% of company revenues, they contributed 38% of total EBIT.

Outlook

Adcorp is facing growing competition in its markets and a slowing of demand, and it has said that it is expecting a further decline in its profits in the June 2007 year. It continues the restructuring of its important Victorian and New South Wales operations, including the upgrading of management. Adcorp has no debt and more than $11 million in cash holdings, and it continues to grow by acquisition. During 2005–06 it acquired Streetwise, a specialist motor/retail business based in Sydney, and Cuttriss Dye, a New Zealand–based new-media creative business. In August 2006 it announced the acquisition of a 55% stake in Andrews Advertising, a prominent Sydney retail agency servicing a range of national accounts, and generating annual sales of approximately $10 million. Adcorp will acquire an additional 25% of the equity over three years. In January 2006 the company launched its Connect2 suite of internet-enabled technologies which facilitate artwork generation and drive the ad creation process, thereby reducing turnaround times, improving accuracy and increasing efficiency. By August 2006 Connect2 was being employed by 40 of Adcorp's clients. The company has been achieving success in trimming costs, although it is now experiencing some salary pressures in a tight market for skilled staff.

AAU Year to 30 June	2005	2006
Revenues ($mn)	33.8	32.6
EBIT ($mn)	5.9	4.5
EBIT margin (%)	17.3	13.9
Profit before tax ($mn)	6.4	5.0
Profit after tax ($mn)	3.9	3.6
Earnings per share (¢)	6.3	5.9
Cash flow per share (¢)	8.6	7.5
Dividend (¢)	6.75	6
Percentage franked	100	100
Net tangible assets per share ($)	0.18	0.15
Interest cover (times)	–	–
Return on equity (%)	15.1	14.2
Debt-to-equity ratio (%)	–	–
Current ratio	1.3	1.3

ADELAIDE BANK LIMITED

Share price ($)	13.54	
12-month high ($)	13.75	
12-month low ($)	11.89	
Market capitalisation ($mn)	1443.6	
Price-to-NTA-per-share ratio	2.1	
5-year share price return (% p.a.)	22.1	
Sector: Financials	**Company**	**Sector**
Price-earnings ratio (times)	15.2	15.7
Dividend yield (%)	4.3	4.3

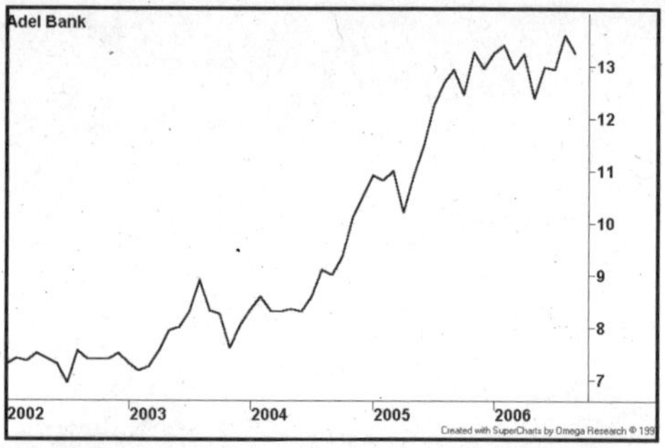

www.adelaidebank.com.au

Adelaide Bank dates back to its establishment as the Cooperative Building Society of South Australia in 1900. It achieved bank status in 1994. It occupies a strong position within South Australia, and is also a prominent home lender in other states. Its Leveraged Equities subsidiary is Australia's second-largest margin lender.

Latest business results (June 2006, full year)

Profits rose strongly, in another excellent result for the bank, despite a slowing housing market and a contraction in the net interest margin. A key factor was cost containment, with the cost-to-income ratio falling. Home loan approvals fell from $8.45 billion to $7.83 billion, with the bank's share of the national mortgage market also down. But business lending was up sharply, from $1.57 billion to $2.17 billion, and the margin lending operation grew strongly, following the 2005 acquisition of the Goldman Sachs JB Were Equity Finance business. The bank reported that the margin lending portfolio increased from $2.64 billion to $3.57 billion, and that this business generated $30 million in pre-tax profit for the year, up from $12.8 million in the previous year. Altogether, the bank's loans under management grew 25% to $23.8 billion.

Outlook

Its strong base in its home state, its ability to contain costs, and its emphasis on the national mortgage market – rather than just serving its home state – continue to hand Adelaide Bank some impressive growth, as well as making it one of the most efficient of the regional banks. It aims at EPS growth of at least 10% in the June 2007 year, and it also believes it is on target to reduce its cost-to-income ratio to 46% by June 2008. It is working to reduce its dependence on home lending, which accounted for 38% of profit in the June 2006 year. In its place the bank expects a greater stream of profit from such activities as margin lending, portfolio funding and business banking, with the latter focused on its areas of expertise, notably aged care, rural lending, commercial property and asset finance. It is also working to boost its managed funds business, with the launch of new investment trusts.

ADB Year to 30 June	**2005**	**2006**
Operating income ($mn)	283.0	311.7
Net interest income ($mn)	223.7	250.1
Operating expenses ($mn)	152.5	161.6
Profit before tax ($mn)	120.0	138.3
Profit after tax ($mn)	83.3	94.4
Earnings per share (¢)	87.1	89.0
Dividend (¢)	53	58
Percentage franked	100	100
Non-interest income to total income (%)	21.0	19.8
Net tangible assets per share ($)	6.69	6.50
Cost-to-income ratio (%)	53.9	51.8
Return on equity (%)	13.5	12.9
Return on assets (%)	0.5	0.4

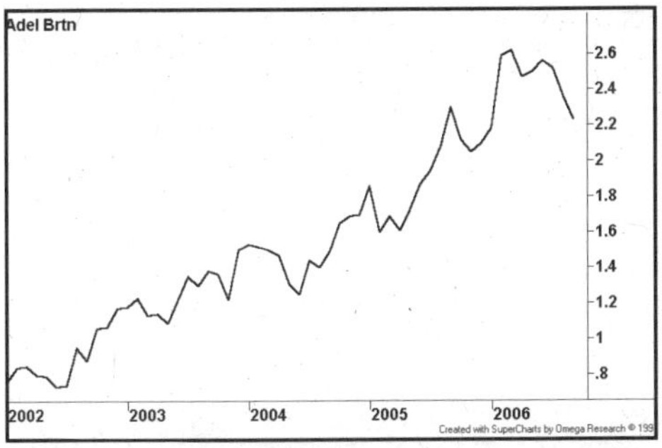

www.adbri.com.au

ADELAIDE BRIGHTON LIMITED

Share price ($)	2.37
12-month high ($)	2.75
12-month low ($)	1.85
Market capitalisation ($mn)	1252.4
Price-to-NTA-per-share ratio	2.7
5-year share price return (% p.a.)	31.7

Sector: Materials	Company	Sector
Price-earnings ratio (times)	14.6	12.3
Dividend yield (%)	4.4	2.3

Adelaide-based Adelaide Brighton, established in 1882, is one of Australia's leaders in the production and supply of construction materials, notably cement, ready-mixed concrete and concrete masonry products. It is a significant supplier to the construction sector, and it also produces lime products for the alumina and steel industries.

Latest business results (June 2006, half year)

Adelaide Brighton overcame mixed market conditions to post a small increase in revenues and after-tax profit. Demand for cement was flat from the previous year, though revenues rose, thanks to price increases in 2005. Lime and concrete product sales fell slightly. However, the successful completion of plant upgrades at the C&M Brick division led to higher profits for the concrete products division. The company announced that it expected a 2006 full-year after-tax profit of $92 million to $96 million.

Outlook

Adelaide Brighton is heavily dependent on the domestic construction industry, and once again the outlook is for continuing strength in the resources, commercial, engineering and infrastructure sectors to offset regional downturns in the housing sector. The company's own forecast is for cement demand to remain little changed over the medium term. It is placing special emphasis on its lime business, and forecasts strong increases in demand from the resources industry over the coming five years, particularly in Western Australia, where Adelaide Brighton is the dominant supplier. It sees great potential in its $28 million Austen Quarry development in New South Wales, which marks its entry into aggregate production and supply. The primary crushing and downhill conveyor stages of the project were commissioned during 2006, with phase two due to be completed in 2007. Aggregate supply is expected to tighten considerably in central New South Wales as the Penrith Lakes quarries move towards exhaustion by the end of the decade. Speculation that Adelaide Brighton could become a takeover target has provided support for the share price.

ABC Year to 31 December	2004	2005
Revenues ($mn)	689.0	723.2
EBIT ($mn)	119.6	134.1
EBIT margin (%)	17.4	18.5
Gross margin (%)	35.5	35.8
Profit before tax ($mn)	104.9	120.2
Profit after tax ($mn)	79.3	87.8
Earnings per share (¢)	14.6	16.2
Cash flow per share (¢)	24.2	25.0
Dividend (¢)	7.5	10.5
Percentage franked	100	100
Interest cover (times)	8.1	9.6
Return on equity (%)	13.8	14.6
Half year to 30 June	**2005**	**2006**
Revenues ($mn)	347.2	363.3
Profit before tax ($mn)	52.5	52.4
Profit after tax ($mn)	38.5	39.7
Earnings per share (¢)	7.1	7.3
Dividend (¢)	4.25	5
Percentage franked	100	100
Net tangible assets per share ($)	0.81	0.87
Debt-to-equity ratio (%)	35.8	40.4
Current ratio	0.6	1.8

ALESCO CORPORATION LIMITED

Share price ($)	8.95
12-month high ($)	10.20
12-month low ($)	7.70
Market capitalisation ($mn)	629.8
Price-to-NTA-per-share ratio	na
5-year share price return (% p.a.)	35.0

Sector: Industrials	Company	Sector
Price-earnings ratio (times)	14.9	13.6
Dividend yield (%)	6.3	4.3

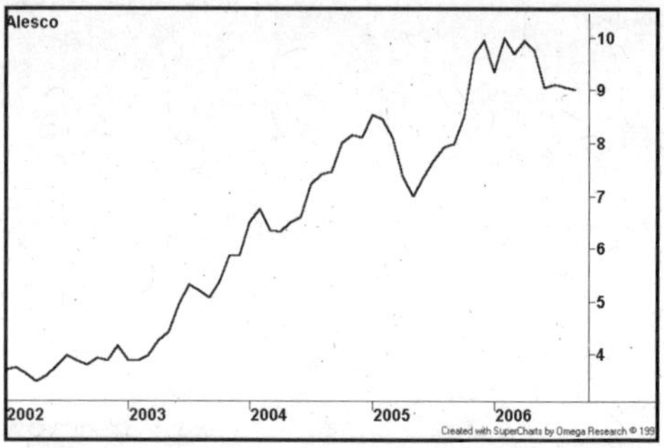

www.alesco.com.au

Alesco has its roots in a general merchant business established in Fremantle in 1896. Today, based in Sydney, it invests in and develops leading industrial brands operating in niche markets. Its B&D garage doors and openers division is Australia's largest manufacturer of garage doors, and a major presence in New Zealand. The kitchen and laundry business comprises Parbury branded building products and the Robinhood kitchen rangehood business. The construction and mining division incorporates Marathon Tyres, which distributes heavy-duty tyres, and Parchem, which manufactures construction chemicals. The scientific and medical division comprises Biolab, a major distributor of scientific and testing equipment.

Latest business results (May 2006, full year)

Profits rose again, thanks in particular to Alesco's exposure to the resources boom. The company's construction and mining division saw earnings before interest, tax and amortisation surge 163% on an 11% rise in sales, boosted by acquisitions and soaring demand. Sales and profits were up for the garage doors business, but this mainly reflected a full year of activity for the New Zealand operation. Otherwise, the business was hurt by a housing and renovations slowdown in both Australia and New Zealand. The Biolab business had a good year, but the kitchen and laundry business operation saw sales and profits down, with weakness in the New South Wales housing market a particular negative.

ALS Year to 31 May	2005	2006
Revenues ($mn)	573.0	600.5
Garage doors & openers (%)	31	34
Construction & mining (%)	27	26
Kitchen & laundry (%)	25	24
Scientific & medical (%)	17	16
EBIT ($mn)	56.7	71.3
EBIT margin (%)	9.9	11.9
Gross margin (%)	33.2	35.0
Profit before tax ($mn)	47.5	60.2
Profit after tax ($mn)	33.7	42.1
Earnings per share (¢)	49.4	60.2
Cash flow per share (¢)	73.4	84.4
Dividend (¢)	45	56
Percentage franked	100	100
Net tangible assets per share ($)	0.33	–
Interest cover (times)	6.2	6.4
Return on equity (%)	12.8	12.9
Debt-to-equity ratio (%)	32.4	46.5
Current ratio	1.5	1.4

Outlook

More than half of Alesco's business is exposed to housing, and trends in this sector will play a major role in the company's outlook. It is undertaking a major restructuring of its garage door business and expects benefits from the 2007 financial year, with the full impact in 2008. It believes a cost reduction program for its kitchen and laundry business will deliver benefits from 2007. Construction and mining is achieving considerable synergy from new acquisitions, and Alesco plans a big rationalisation of this division, to deliver annualised savings of $2 million from the 2009 financial year. Biolab continues to grow, buoyed by the acquisitions during 2006 of the Promedica hospital supplies business and the App-Tek gas detection equipment business.

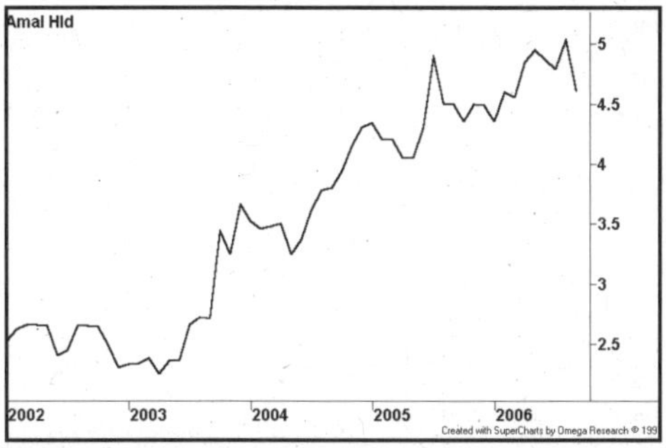

www.ahl.com.au

AMALGAMATED HOLDINGS LIMITED

Share price ($)	4.80
12-month high ($)	5.04
12-month low ($)	4.16
Market capitalisation ($mn)	604.6
Price-to-NTA-per-share ratio	1.4
5-year share price return (% p.a.)	29.2

Sector: Consumer discretionary	**Company**	**Sector**
Price-earnings ratio (times)	10.6	18.8
Dividend yield (%)	5.0	4.0

Sydney-based Amalgamated Holdings, founded in 1910, is one of Australia's leading entertainment, tourism and hotel companies. It divides its businesses into three broad groupings. The entertainment division comprises the Greater Union and the Birch Carroll & Coyle cinema chains, with 475 screens at 57 locations throughout Australia. It also operates 569 screens at 76 locations in Germany, and some others in the Netherlands and the Middle East. The entertainment technology division is centred on the company's 50% stake in the Atlab film processing laboratory, the largest in the southern hemisphere. The hospitality and leisure division includes the Rydges hotel chain and the Thredbo Alpine Resort. The company also owns 50% of Roadshow Distributors, which handles theatrical distribution, TV sales, videos, video games and CD-ROMs. It has sold its loss-making Matilda Cruises business.

Latest business results (June 2006, full year)

Profits nominally fell, due to a big loss in the June 2005 year from the Matilda Cruises business. But as this has become a discontinued business, this loss is stripped from the June 2006 results announcement under new accounting rules, to make comparisons more valid. In fact, strong hotel business and a halving of losses on its overseas cinema business lay behind a rise in profits. The Rydges hotel business saw the average room rate up 10% from the previous year, with hotel management fees up 58%, leading to a 27% EBIT jump. However, Thredbo profits were down, following a decline in days suitable for skiing. A weak first half for the domestic cinema business was followed by a strong second-half recovery, and profits were flat for the year.

Outlook

Amalgamated Holdings occupies leading positions in its areas of activity, yet most of these are volatile, with a string of hit movies needed to generate good cinema business and other major operations quite dependent on levels of domestic and international tourism. Both domestically and overseas it is working to upgrade its movie theatres, through the addition of Gold Class cinemas, expanded food and beverage facilities and larger screens and seats. It is seeing very strong profit growth at its small Mideast cinema business, and is attempting to restructure its loss-making German cinema operation.

AHD Year to 30 June	**2005**	**2006**
Revenues ($mn)	556.5	563.1
Cinema exhibition – international (%)	49	50
Cinema exhibition – domestic (%)	17	18
Hotels (%)	16	18
Thredbo Alpine Resort (%)	8	8
Leisure & attractions (%)	6	3
EBIT ($mn)	85.3	84.5
EBIT margin (%)	15.3	15.0
Profit before tax ($mn)	74.5	74.8
Profit after tax ($mn)	61.2	57.0
Earnings per share (¢)	48.8	45.2
Cash flow per share (¢)	71.3	68.0
Dividend (¢)	18.5	24
Percentage franked	100	100
Net tangible assets per share ($)	3.29	3.54
Interest cover (times)	7.9	8.8
Return on equity (%)	15.4	12.8
Debt-to-equity ratio (%)	42.6	39.6
Current ratio	0.6	0.4

ANZ BANKING GROUP LIMITED

Share price ($)	27.36
12-month high ($)	28.66
12-month low ($)	21.84
Market capitalisation ($mn)	49713.5
Price-to-NTA-per-share ratio	3.4
5-year share price return (% p.a.)	16.8

Sector: Financials	Company	Sector
Price-earnings ratio (times)	16.5	15.7
Dividend yield (%)	4.0	4.3

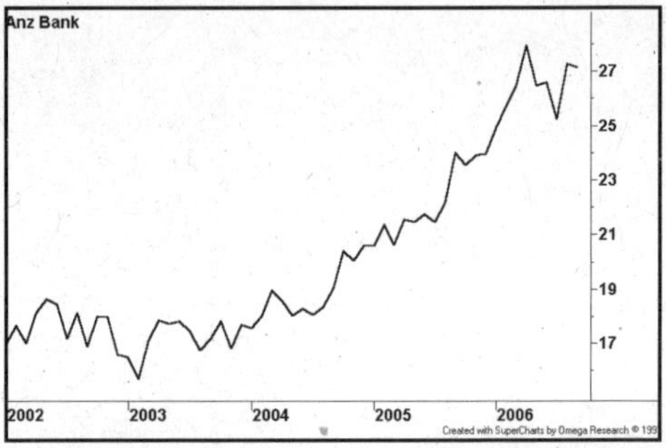

www.anz.com.au

Melbourne-based ANZ has its roots in the establishment of the Bank of Australasia in London in 1835. It is today one of Australia's four banking giants, with significant interests in numerous areas of finance and more than 750 branches nationwide. It owns the finance company Esanda, has a stake in online stockbroker E-Trade Australia, and operates a funds management joint venture with Dutch giant ING. Its ownership of the National Bank of New Zealand (NBNZ) makes it the market leader in New Zealand banking.

Latest business results (March 2006, half year)

Profits rose again, in an excellent result, with strength in most areas of business. Personal banking showed earnings growth of 16%, reflecting new strategies and initiatives. All individual units within personal banking showed double-digit growth, with mortgages up 21% and investment and insurance products up 18%. Institutional banking achieved 8% earnings growth, after adjusting for discontinued businesses, and corporate banking was up 16%, in spite of increasing levels of competition. New Zealand was also strong, and Asia Pacific recorded an 18% increase in profits. However, Esanda saw profits down 20%, affected by lower margins.

ANZ Year to 30 September	2004	2005
Operating income ($mn)	8645.0	9350.0
Net interest income ($mn)	5254.0	5798.0
Operating expenses ($mn)	4026.0	4515.0
Profit before tax ($mn)	3987.0	4255.0
Profit after tax ($mn)	2815.0	3018.0
Earnings per share (¢)	158.7	165.5
Dividend (¢)	101	110
Percentage franked	100	100
Non-interest income to total income (%)	39.2	38.0
Cost-to-income ratio (%)	46.6	48.3
Return on equity (%)	17.8	16.2
Return on assets (%)	1.2	1.1
Half year to 31 March	**2005**	**2006**
Operating income ($mn)	4582.0	4963.0
Profit before tax ($mn)	2146.0	2554.0
Profit after tax ($mn)	1570.0	1811.0
Earnings per share (¢)	83.2	98.4
Dividend (¢)	51	56
Percentage franked	100	100
Net tangible assets per share ($)	7.38	8.00

Outlook

ANZ has been investing heavily to build its domestic operations – including the opening of 22 new branches and 362 ATMs in the year to March 2006 – and is now seeing the benefits. It is devoting more resources to its flagging Esanda business, and expects a turnaround. It is starting to see synergies flow from its $4.9 billion NBNZ acquisition, with a target of annual cost savings of $110 million from 2007. However, the slowing New Zealand economy could delay some of the expected benefits of the acquisition. In mid-2006 it acquired for US$111.5 million a 20% stake in China's Tianjin City Commercial Bank, and it views this investment as offering huge long-term growth potential. In August 2006 ANZ announced that it expected double-digit EPS growth in the September 2006 year.

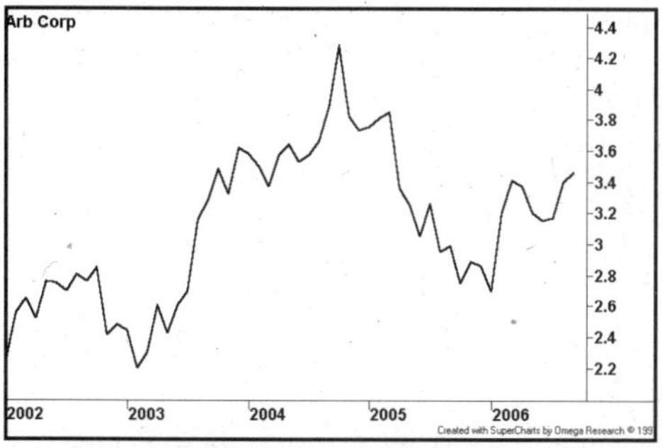

www.arb.com.au

ARB CORPORATION LIMITED

Share price ($)	3.40
12-month high ($)	3.60
12-month low ($)	2.60
Market capitalisation ($mn)	228.3
Price-to-NTA-per-share ratio	4.2
5-year share price return (% p.a.)	18.5

Sector: Consumer discretionary	Company	Sector
Price-earnings ratio (times)	14.3	18.8
Dividend yield (%)	3.4	4.0

Melbourne-based ARB is a small manufacturer of specialty automotive accessories, and is an international leader in the design and production of equipment for four-wheel-drive (4WD) vehicles. Its products are divided into broad groupings: mechanical products, notably the 'air locker' air-operated locking differential system; fabricated metal products, such as bull bars, roof racks and tow bars; the Old Man Emu range of suspension products; ARB canopies; and imported and locally produced 4WD accessories, for which ARB acts as local distributor. ARB exports to numerous countries.

Latest business results (June 2006, full year)

Sales and profits grew modestly, with a strong second half more than offsetting a weak start. However, growth was held back by problems in finding sufficient numbers of skilled workers for the company's Melbourne production facilities. Domestic sales grew only modestly, and the best business was overseas. American sales were up 12% to $19.1 million, with pre-tax profit soaring nearly five times to $1 million. The reported results also include the pre-tax profits on property sales, of $2.5 million in June 2005 and $3.5 million in June 2006. Production began at the company's second factory, in Thailand, in May 2006.

Outlook

ARB has been a big beneficiary of the surging worldwide popularity of 4WD vehicles, and it expects further growth in the June 2007 year. However, rising petrol prices present a challenge, and the company also continues to feel the impact of domestic skill shortages and rising steel prices. In partial response, production will be steadily increased at the new Thai plant, and ARB expects it to break even by March 2007. Another strategy for growth is the establishment of a chain of ARB-brand stores throughout Australia. Five new ones were opened during the June 2006 year, to bring the total to 28, of which nine are company owned. ARB sees particular potential in Western Australia, which, thanks to the mining boom, has a very high density of 4WD vehicles and the highest vehicle growth rate of any state in Australia. ARB has acquired the business of its WA distributor, previously independently owned, to provide a platform for growth in the state.

ARP Year to 30 June	2005	2006
Revenues ($mn)	114.7	125.9
EBIT ($mn)	21.4	22.8
EBIT margin (%)	18.6	18.1
Gross margin (%)	33.9	32.3
Profit before tax ($mn)	20.7	22.5
Profit after tax ($mn)	14.8	15.8
Earnings per share (¢)	22.8	23.7
Cash flow per share (¢)	28.3	29.3
Dividend (¢)	10.5	11.5
Percentage franked	100	100
Net tangible assets per share ($)	0.71	0.81
Interest cover (times)	32.7	86.0
Return on equity (%)	30.5	27.8
Debt-to-equity ratio (%)	29.3	7.0
Current ratio	1.1	1.8

AUSDRILL LIMITED

Share price ($)	1.46
12-month high ($)	1.93
12-month low ($)	0.74
Market capitalisation ($mn)	187.0
Price-to-NTA-per-share ratio	1.4
5-year share price return (% p.a.)	97.1

Sector: Materials	**Company**	**Sector**
Price-earnings ratio (times)	8.7	12.3
Dividend yield (%)	3.6	2.3

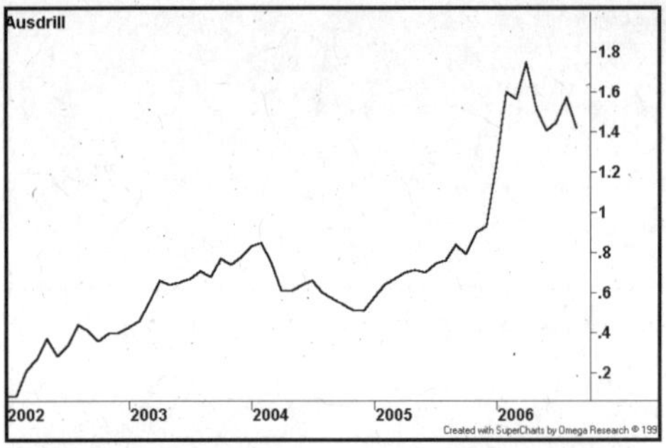

www.ausdrill.com.au

Perth-based Ausdrill, founded in 1987, is a prominent drilling and contract mining company serving the resources industry. Through its Supply Direct subsidiary it is also involved in mining equipment supplies and logistics support, and its Diamond Communications subsidiary is engaged in cable ploughing and the repair and maintenance of communications networks. As well as its domestic activities, it is also active in Africa, particularly Ghana, and it has a small operation in the United Kingdom.

Latest business results (June 2006, full year)

The resources boom handed Ausdrill a big lift in revenues and profits. The contract mining business, representing around three-quarters of turnover, provided the main contribution, with excellent growth. There was also a good result from Supply Direct, which successfully expanded its client base in Africa, Europe and South East Asia. However, the company expressed disappointment in its Diamond Communications operation, which it said had underperformed, despite a recovery in the final few months of the year. Geographically, the company recorded strong business in Africa, which represented about 44% of revenues but 58% of pre-tax profit.

Outlook

Ausdrill has been steadily diversifying away from its roots as a drilling contractor and transforming itself into a diversified mining services company. This is now paying off handsomely, thanks to the continuing boom in the resources industry. More than 60% of turnover is now generated outside the traditional domestic drilling and blasting markets, and the company expects this figure to grow. However, drilling remains important, and the company continues to win long-term contracts with blue-chip clients, including substantial work for BHP Billiton's nickel and iron ore operations in Western Australia. Ausdrill's first full year of total ownership of Ghana-based African Mining Services has led to a big jump in business, notably the award of a $325 million, six-year contract at the country's Damang Gold Mine. Ausdrill also sees significant growth potential in its Supply Direct business, and it expects an improved contribution from Diamond Communications. A share placement has strengthened the balance sheet, and the company has been evaluating a number of acquisition opportunities.

ASL Year to 30 June	2005	2006
Revenues ($mn)	202.8	317.1
EBIT ($mn)	13.2	32.0
EBIT margin (%)	6.5	10.1
Profit before tax ($mn)	12.0	28.2
Profit after tax ($mn)	8.0	19.0
Earnings per share (¢)	7.6	16.7
Cash flow per share (¢)	20.5	35.4
Dividend (¢)	5	5.25
Percentage franked	88	100
Net tangible assets per share ($)	0.83	1.04
Interest cover (times)	10.7	8.4
Return on equity (%)	10.1	16.9
Debt-to-equity ratio (%)	37.3	29.4
Current ratio	1.5	1.8

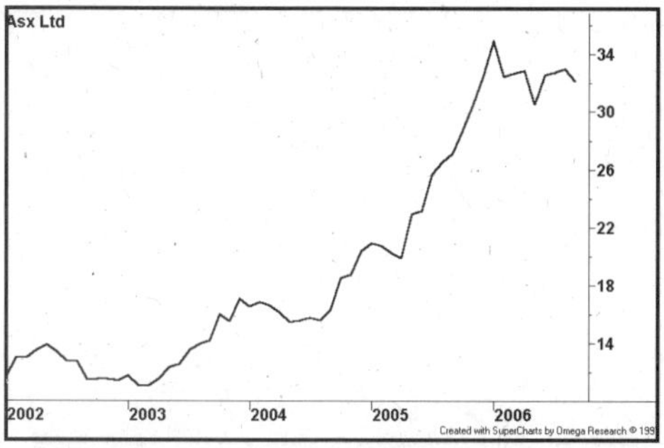

www.asx.com.au

AUSTRALIAN STOCK EXCHANGE LIMITED

Share price ($)	33.88
12-month high ($)	35.90
12-month low ($)	26.00
Market capitalisation ($mn)	5601.7
Price-to-NTA-per-share ratio	10.5
5-year share price return (% p.a.)	29.6

Sector: Financials	**Company**	**Sector**
Price-earnings ratio (times)	25.4	15.7
Dividend yield (%)	3.5	4.3

The Australian Stock Exchange was formed in 1987 through the amalgamation of six independent stock exchanges that formerly operated in the state capital cities. Each of those exchanges had a history of share trading dating back to the 19th century. Though originally a mutual organisation of stockbrokers, in 1998 the ASX became a listed company, with its shares traded on its own market. As well as operating Australia's primary national stock exchange for equities, derivatives and fixed-interest securities, it also provides a comprehensive market data service. In July 2006 it formally merged with SFE Corporation, which manages the Sydney Futures Exchange.

Latest business results (June 2006, full year)

Record equities volumes helped power the ASX to another solid rise in profits. All areas of business were strong. Revenues from equities trading rose 10.7% with an average of 125 047 trades per day, up from 89 178 in the previous year. Revenues from listings were up 7.7%, with 227 new listings, a slight increase on 222 in the June 2005 year. However, several very large new listings – notably SP Ausnet ($2.9 billion), Goodman Fielder ($2.7 billion), Tattersall's ($2.2 billion) and Dyno Nobel ($1.2 billion) – meant that new capital of $23.1 billion was raised, compared to $14.9 billion the year before. Derivatives trading saw revenues up 9.9%, thanks mainly to a sharp rise in the number of new warrants listed, from 3595 in 2004–05 to 4678 in 2005–06. Information services showed an 11.2% increase in revenues.

Outlook

The ASX's profits are highly geared to levels of stock market activity. Much of its business is handled electronically, meaning that relatively small changes in the amount of business handled can deliver quite a substantial swing in profits, and there are concerns that markets have now entered a subdued period. The company is engaged in a three-year project to reduce costs by $15 million to $20 million by mid-2008, and during 2005–06 it achieved savings of $8.6 million. The merger with SFE Corporation is expected to provide potential for future growth and deliver annual cost synergies of $14 million to $18 million, though one-off integration costs could be up to $20 million.

ASX Year to 30 June	2005	2006
Revenues ($mn)	279.5	305.6
Equities trading (%)	42	43
Listings (%)	26	25
Derivatives trading (%)	16	16
Information services (%)	11	12
EBIT ($mn)	145.4	177.6
EBIT margin (%)	52.0	58.1
Profit before tax ($mn)	154.6	194.1
Profit after tax ($mn)	107.3	137.1
Earnings per share (¢)	104.4	133.4
Cash flow per share (¢)	119.9	143.6
Dividend (¢)	95.1	120.1
Percentage franked	100	100
Net tangible assets per share ($)	2.86	3.22
Interest cover (times)	–	–
Return on equity (%)	40.3	41.0
Debt-to-equity ratio (%)	–	–
Current ratio	1.6	1.5

AXA ASIA PACIFIC HOLDINGS LIMITED

Share price ($)	6.68
12-month high ($)	6.81
12-month low ($)	4.51
Market capitalisation ($mn)	11191.8
Price-to-NTA-per-share ratio	5.8
5-year share price return (% p.a.)	24.5

Sector: Financials	**Company**	**Sector**
Price-earnings ratio (times)	21.5	15.7
Dividend yield (%)	2.1	4.3

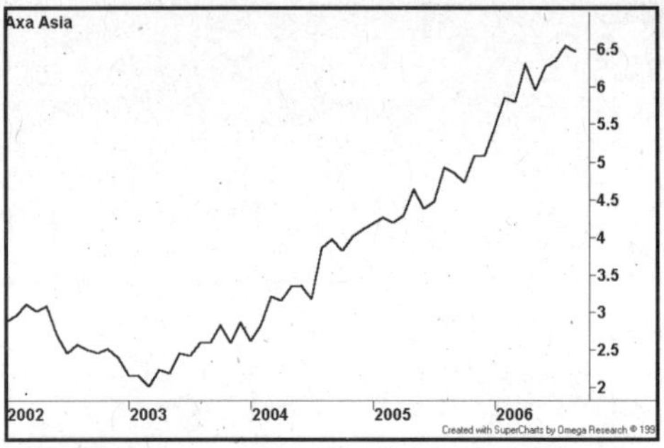

www.axaasiapacific.com.au

AXA Asia Pacific is one of Australia's insurance giants. Established in 1869 as the National Mutual Life Association of Australasia, it is now a 52%-owned subsidiary of the French insurance and financial services giant AXA SA. It is a leading supplier of life insurance and superannuation products in Australia and New Zealand, with a big funds management operation and a growing financial planning business. It has a major business in Hong Kong, responsible for nearly half of company profits, and operations in China, Indonesia, the Philippines, Singapore and Thailand. It is advancing into India.

Latest business results (June 2006, half year)

The company reported another solid mid-year profit gain, with strength across the board. In Australia and New Zealand the strong performance of recent years continued, with operating earnings up 22%. There was a particularly good result from the company's financial protection business, with earnings up 28%, thanks to a favourable claims experience. Hong Kong saw operating earnings up 12% in local currency, with an excellent 82% surge in wealth management earnings. Both regions reported particularly strong growth in new business. Altogether, group funds under management, administration and advice rose 9% to $87.6 billion. The profit gain was aided by continuing cost containment measures, further reducing the company's cost-to-income ratio.

AXA Year to 31 December	**2004**	**2005**
Revenues ($mn)	4940.0	4918.0
Profit before tax ($mn)	584.0	591.0
Profit after tax ($mn)	459.0	542.0
Earnings per share (¢)	26.4	31.1
Dividend (¢)	11.75	14
Percentage franked	23	30
Return on equity (%)	12.7	16.3
Half year to 30 June	**2005**	**2006**
Revenues ($mn)	2139.0	2094.0
Profit before tax ($mn)	282.0	351.0
Profit after tax ($mn)	246.0	304.0
Earnings per share (¢)	10.4	17.4
Dividend (¢)	6.25	7.5
Percentage franked	30	30
Net tangible assets per share ($)	1.15	1.22
Debt-to-equity ratio (%)	–	–

Outlook

In Australia and New Zealand, AXA has become a prominent beneficiary of the boom in wealth management and superannuation markets, and of a buoyant life insurance market, and it should continue to grow while these sectors prosper. It sees great potential in Hong Kong where the retirement savings market is growing strongly, and it is boosting its presence there. The acquisition of MLC insurance businesses in Hong Kong and Indonesia has added 800 agents to AXA's 2400 in Hong Kong and almost doubled its sales force in Indonesia to 2200.

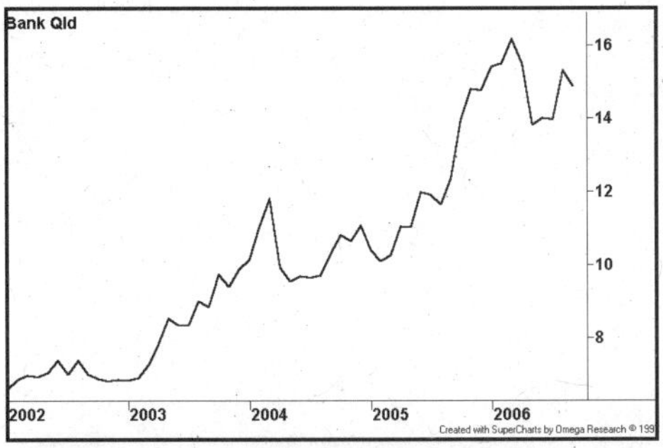

www.boq.com.au

BANK OF QUEENSLAND LIMITED

Share price ($)	15.40
12-month high ($)	16.50
12-month low ($)	11.66
Market capitalisation ($mn)	1602.9
Price-to-NTA-per-share ratio	3.1
5-year share price return (% p.a.)	27.5

Sector: Financials	Company	Sector
Price-earnings ratio (times)	16.6	15.7
Dividend yield (%)	4.1	4.3

The Bank of Queensland was established in 1874 as the Brisbane Permanent Benefit Building and Investment Society, later gaining a banking licence. It has an estimated 6% share of the banking market in Queensland, with 140 branches. In addition, it has more than 70 branches in other states and territories. It owns the equipment finance firm UFJ Finance Australia, and in December 2005 it acquired the debt finance division of Orix Australia.

Latest business results (February 2006, half year)

Bank of Queensland reported another excellent result, as it continued to expand beyond its state borders. Most areas of business were strong, with retail deposits up 18% from February 2005 to $6.4 billion, loan approvals up 28% to $4.5 billion, and loans under management up 19% to $13.5 billion. During the half the bank opened 20 new branches.

Outlook

Bank of Queensland has embarked on an ambitious restructuring and growth program that includes interstate expansion and a new concept of franchised bank branches that are owned and operated by individual managers. It expected to have a total of 215 branches by August 2006, with a target of 250 by August 2007. Most of the growth has been in NSW, Victoria and the ACT, though it has also opened its initial branches in Darwin and Western Australia. In April 2006 it announced an alliance with HBF, Western Australia's biggest health fund, to provide its members with financial products. Also in 2006 it announced an alliance with Genesys Wealth Management to provide financial planning advice to its expanding customer base. It is launching a margin-lending product with Macquarie Bank. The Orix acquisition hands Bank of Queensland 3% of the national debtor finance market, with a concentration in its key growth states of NSW and Victoria, and the scope for significant expansion. In August 2006 Bank of Queensland made a takeover offer for Queensland-based Pioneer Permanent Building Society.

BOQ Year to 31 August	2004	2005
Operating income ($mn)	291.9	356.7
Net interest income ($mn)	183.3	216.7
Operating expenses ($mn)	185.0	213.2
Profit before tax ($mn)	93.3	128.0
Profit after tax ($mn)	64.5	91.7
Earnings per share (¢)	71.9	93.0
Dividend (¢)	43	63
Percentage franked	100	100
Non-interest income to total income (%)	37.2	39.2
Cost-to-income ratio (%)	63.4	59.8
Return on equity (%)	13.1	13.9
Return on assets (%)	0.8	0.9
Half year to 28 February	**2005**	**2006**
Operating income ($mn)	160.1	177.1
Profit before tax ($mn)	49.2	60.2
Profit after tax ($mn)	36.1	40.0
Earnings per share (¢)	33.5	38.5
Dividend (¢)	23	27
Percentage franked	100	100
Net tangible assets per share ($)	6.38	5.01

BEACH PETROLEUM LIMITED

Share price ($)	1.53	
12-month high ($)	1.78	
12-month low ($)	0.71	
Market capitalisation ($mn)	840.5	
Price-to-NTA-per-share ratio	2.9	
5-year share price return (% p.a.)	94.4	
Sector: Energy	**Company**	**Sector**
Price-earnings ratio (times)	15.8	14.8
Dividend yield (%)	1.0	2.6

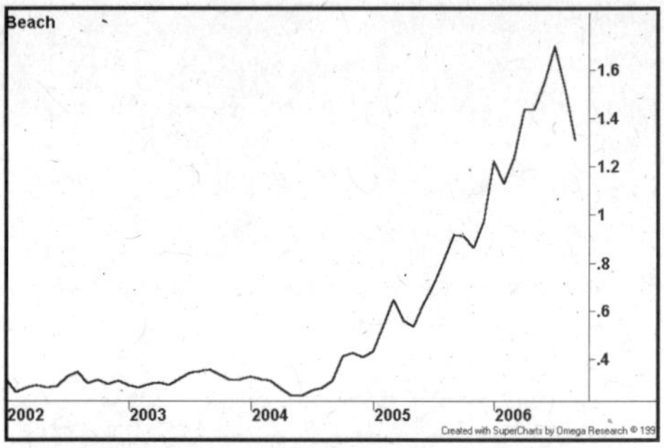

www.beachpetroleum.com.au

Adelaide-based Beach Petroleum, with a history dating back to 1962, holds interests in scores of exploration and production tenements in Australia, New Zealand and Papua New Guinea. Its main areas of operation are the Cooper/Eromanga, Surat and Gippsland basins of eastern Australia.

Latest business results (June 2006, full year)

Record production and a surging oil price combined to send Beach's profits soaring. Total production of 1.37 million barrels of oil equivalent (MMboe) was 30% up on the June 2005 year, and the average price received of $84.74 per barrel was up 39%. The company reported a 45% success rate from exploration drilling, including the discovery of three new oil fields and two new gas fields in the Cooper/Eromanga basin. Initial test production began at the Basker field in the Gippsland basin. The company's proved and probable reserves were 36.2 MMboe at June 2006, compared to just 10.8 MMboe a year earlier.

Outlook

Beach maintains an active development program, and has achieved an excellent record of strong growth. With net cash holdings of $24 million (as of June 2006), it plans much further development work. In particular, it sees great potential in the Basker and Manta oil fields in the Gippsland basin, which hold reserves of some 19.6 million barrels. Beach has raised its equity stake in these projects from 25% to 50%, and expects full production to begin late in 2006 from four wells. New discoveries in Cooper/Eromanga mean that production there is expected to rise. In September 2006 Beach acquired the Delhi Petroleum group of companies, which has given it a 21% interest in more than 200 oil and gas fields encompassing large portions of the Cooper/Eromanga basin. The acquisition is expected to raise Beach's proved and probable oil and gas reserves figure to more than 95 MMboe, as well as providing significant synergies with its existing operations in the region. It has also acquired a 40% stake in the Tipton West coal seam gas field in the Surat basin and launched development activities there, and it has acquired exploration tenements in the Canterbury basin in New Zealand.

BPT Year to 30 June	2005	2006
Revenues ($mn)	61.2	121.4
EBIT ($mn)	22.3	57.3
EBIT margin (%)	36.4	47.2
Profit before tax ($mn)	24.0	59.5
Profit after tax ($mn)	16.8	44.0
Earnings per share (¢)	5.6	9.7
Cash flow per share (¢)	9.2	14.4
Dividend (¢)	1.5	1.5
Percentage franked	0	0
Net tangible assets per share ($)	0.35	0.53
Interest cover (times)	–	–
Return on equity (%)	16.0	22.0
Debt-to-equity ratio (%)	–	–
Current ratio	4.2	0.9

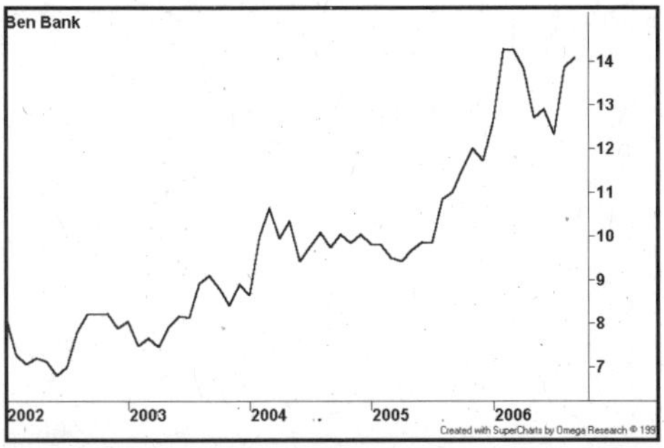

www.benbank.com.au

BENDIGO BANK LIMITED

Share price ($)	13.70
12-month high ($)	14.82
12-month low ($)	10.61
Market capitalisation ($mn)	1849.3
Price-to-NTA-per-share ratio	2.4
5-year share price return (% p.a.)	23.0

Sector: Financials	Company	Sector
Price-earnings ratio (times)	17.7	15.7
Dividend yield (%)	3.8	4.3

Established as a building society in 1858, Victoria's Bendigo Bank is today Australia's only remaining regionally based bank, and is also one of the smallest of all the listed banks. It has a growing network of branches, including 155 that are company-owned and more than 180 community-owned banks, with a steady move beyond its Victorian origins. Its businesses also include the trustee company and funds manager Sandhurst Trustees, the financial planners Bendigo Investment Services and Worley Securities, the debenture company Victorian Securities, and the mortgage originator National Mortgage Market Corporation. It has established Elders Rural Bank with Futuris Corporation, to provide banking services to rural Australia, and Tasmanian Banking Services with Tasmanian Perpetual Trustees.

Latest business results (June 2006, full year)

For the fifth straight year, Bendigo Bank achieved profit growth of more than 10%. Despite the housing slowdown, total loans under management grew 9.5% to $14 billion, while retail deposits rose 13% to $11.3 billion. Managed funds grew 10% to $3 billion. Non-interest income was up 12% to $184.5 million. Customer numbers grew 7.9% to 1.07 million. During the year the bank opened five new company branches and 28 community bank branches. Elders Rural Bank reported a 10% rise in profit.

Outlook

Bendigo Bank continues to expand, with more than half its branches now interstate, although nearly two-thirds of its business still derives from within Victoria. It expects to open around 30 new branches during the June 2007 year. Reflecting its growth, it has undertaken a major restructuring, with more decisions now being taken at the regional manager level, rather than by head office, in order to deliver a sharper focus to its activities. It is working to boost both its business banking and its financial planning arms, spreading them across its entire network, in order to reduce its dependence on housing and retail deposits. It is targeting further 10% profit growth in the June 2007 year. However, despite its impressive growth, costs remain high. In addition, Bendigo Bank is more vulnerable than most of its larger rivals to any sharp rise in interest rates and deterioration in the housing market.

BEN Year to 30 June	2005	2006
Operating income ($mn)	430.3	477.4
Net interest income ($mn)	286.1	315.1
Operating expenses ($mn)	305.0	338.1
Profit before tax ($mn)	132.0	154.5
Profit after tax ($mn)	91.7	108.3
Earnings per share (¢)	65.3	77.3
Dividend (¢)	45	52
Percentage franked	100	100
Non-interest income to total income (%)	33.5	34.0
Net tangible assets per share ($)	4.53	5.75
Cost-to-income ratio (%)	70.9	70.8
Return on equity (%)	13.1	13.4
Return on assets (%)	0.7	0.7

BHP BILLITON LIMITED

Share price ($)	28.00
12-month high ($)	32.00
12-month low ($)	19.40
Market capitalisation ($mn)	97 006.5
Price-to-NTA-per-share ratio	5.3
5-year share price return (% p.a.)	27.7

Sector: Materials	**Company**	**Sector**
Price-earnings ratio (times)	12.1	12.3
Dividend yield (%)	1.7	2.3

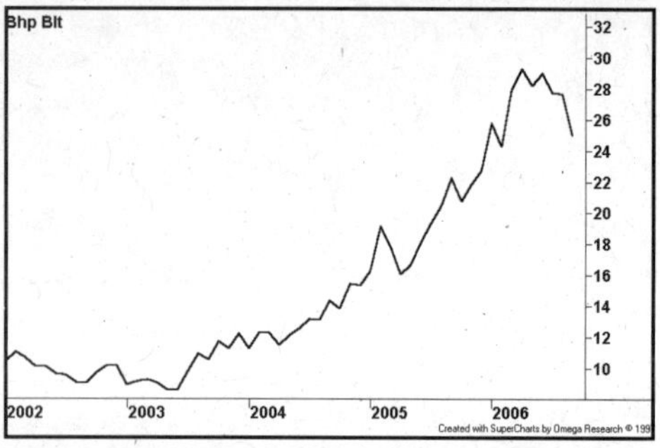

www.bhpbilliton.com

BHP Billiton, formed from the merger in 2001 of Australian resources giant BHP and British-based mining major Billiton, is the world's largest diversified resources company. It has more than 100 operations in approximately 20 countries, and occupies industry leader or near industry leader positions in major commodity businesses, including aluminium, energy coal and metallurgical coal, copper, ferro-alloys, iron ore and titanium minerals, along with substantial interests in oil, gas, liquefied natural gas, nickel, diamonds and silver.

Latest business results (June 2006, full year)

BHP reported another stunning profit, by far the largest ever achieved by an Australian company, thanks to the continuing resources boom. The star was the company's base metals business, with sales doubling and profits surging 184%, thanks to substantially higher copper prices, higher silver, zinc and lead prices, and record production at many of the company's mines. The carbon steel materials division enjoyed another strong year, with a 28% increase in sales revenues leading to a 79% jump in profits. Higher prices for aluminium and alumina offset rising costs, and the aluminium division also reported good gains, as did the petroleum division. The inclusion of a full year of results from the Nickel West operations (Australia) and the profit on the sale of BHP Billiton's interest in the Wonderkop joint venture boosted stainless steel materials. But both the energy coal and diamond divisions suffered profit declines, hit by rising costs and lower yields. (Note that BHP Billiton reports its financial results in US dollars. For the purposes of this book, these have been converted into Australian dollars at the rate of A$1 = US$0.75. Thus, BHP figures in this book should be used for general guidance only.)

BHP Year to 30 June	**2005**	**2006**
Revenues ($mn)	35 629.3	42 870.7
Carbon steel materials (%)	24	28
Petroleum (%)	19	18
Aluminium (%)	17	15
Base metals (%)	16	15
Energy coal (%)	11	9
Stainless steel materials (%)	7	9
Diamonds & specialty products (%)	5	3
EBIT ($mn)	12 361.3	19 561.3
EBIT margin (%)	34.7	45.6
Profit before tax ($mn)	11 920.0	18 888.0
Profit after tax ($mn)	8 528.0	13 933.3
Earnings per share (¢)	139.3	230.9
Cash flow per share (¢)	178.5	280.9
Dividend (¢)	36.36	47.96
Percentage franked	100	100
Net tangible assets per share ($)	3.70	5.24
Interest cover (times)	28.0	29.1
Return on equity (%)	40.2	50.0
Debt-to-equity ratio (%)	48.7	33.7
Current ratio	0.9	1.0

Outlook

BHP Billiton is one of the great beneficiaries of the global boom in resources that has in part been ignited by the spectacular growth of the Chinese economy. The company itself believes that high resources prices will continue for the short to medium term, but that cost pressures will also continue to rise. It has 13 major projects under development, with a total budgeted investment of US$9.5 billion. It plans a series of share buybacks.

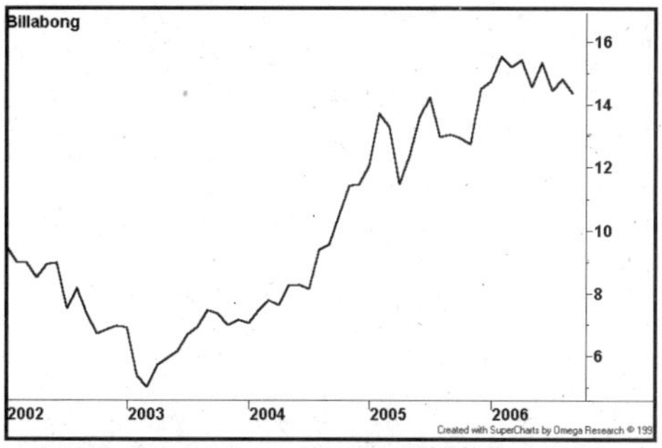

www.billabongcorporate.com

BILLABONG INTERNATIONAL LIMITED

Share price ($)	14.57
12-month high ($)	16.49
12-month low ($)	12.37
Market capitalisation ($mn)	3003.6
Price-to-NTA-per-share ratio	53.7
5-year share price return (% p.a.)	20.3

Sector: Consumer discretionary	**Company**	**Sector**
Price-earnings ratio (times)	20.6	18.8
Dividend yield (%)	3.0	4.0

Surfwear apparel company Billabong International, based on the Gold Coast, was established in 1973. It is today the leading surfwear apparel brand in Australia, and a global presence, with production facilities in a dozen countries and sales in more than 100 countries. Its major brands are Billabong, Element, Von Zipper, Honolua Surf Company, Kustom, Palmers Surf and Nixon, and its products include board shorts, t-shirts, swimwear, fleece tops, jumpers, walk shorts, pants, jeans, bags and accessories. It also operates its own retail chain of 110 company-owned stores, with a further 43 licensed stores.

Latest business results (June 2006, full year)

It was another good year for Billabong, with strong overseas sales and margin improvement in Europe providing a particular boost. American sales soared 32.8% in Australian currency to $521.9 million, with profits up 37.3%. A new management team and a strong second half lifted European sales 17% to $201.1 million, with profits surging 32.7%. Spain, France, Italy and Germany each contributed strong double-digit sales growth. Asia-Pacific sales – Australia, Japan, New Zealand and the South Pacific – were more subdued, up 7.1% to $295.2 million, with profits edging 1.1% higher, though Japan and New Zealand were strong, with double-digit sales growth. The company enjoyed particularly strong demand for Element and Von Zipper products, with global sales up 40% and 35% respectively.

Outlook

Billabong has established itself as one of the world's leading surfwear brands, and it continues to expand. The company itself is forecasting further 15% EPS growth in the June 2007 year, based on continuing strong demand in Europe and America. It has acquired a controlling interest in the Australia-based Beachculture airport retail business, and expects to expand this internationally. It has also acquired the US-based Nixon watch and accessory brand. Billabong plans to place a particular emphasis on the British market – where sales have lagged other major European markets – with the roll-out of new Billabong retail stores and the first Beachworks store outside the US. The company is also undertaking initiatives in Asia, including a new agreement with a leading apparel company to distribute its products in Hong Kong, Macau, South Korea and Thailand.

BBG Year to 30 June	**2005**	**2006**
Revenues ($mn)	844.9	1023.5
EBIT ($mn)	187.9	219.6
EBIT margin (%)	22.2	21.5
Gross margin (%)	51.7	53.2
Profit before tax ($mn)	183.7	212.9
Profit after tax ($mn)	125.2	145.9
Earnings per share (¢)	60.9	70.8
Cash flow per share (¢)	65.8	78.4
Dividend (¢)	38	44
Percentage franked	100	100
Net tangible assets per share ($)	0.48	0.27
Interest cover (times)	44.0	33.1
Return on equity (%)	20.6	21.6
Debt-to-equity ratio (%)	10.2	27.5
Current ratio	2.5	2.6

BLACKMORES LIMITED

Share price ($)	14.60
12-month high ($)	14.88
12-month low ($)	12.52
Market capitalisation ($mn)	232.4
Price-to-NTA-per-share ratio	6.7
5-year share price return (% p.a.)	26.0

Sector: Health care	Company	Sector
Price-earnings ratio (times)	16.1	31.1
Dividend yield (%)	4.7	1.8

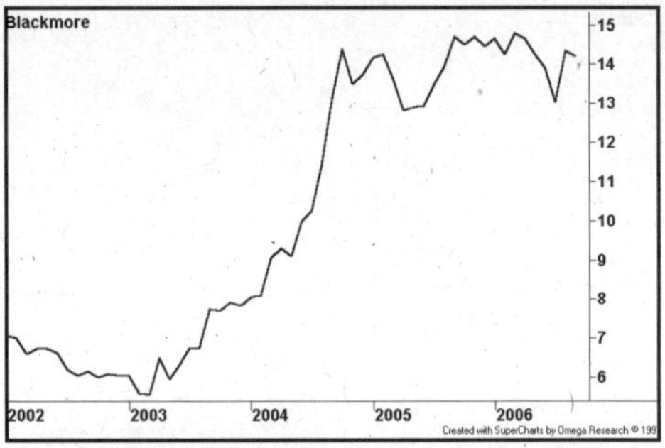

www.blackmores.com.au

Founded in the 1930s, Sydney-based Blackmores is a leading manufacturer and distributor of a wide range of natural healthcare products, nutritional supplements and cosmetics. Its brands include Vitaglow and BioACE. It exports to South East Asia and New Zealand.

Latest business results (June 2006, full year)

Strong domestic consumer spending and fast-growing sales in Asia combined to deliver Blackmores another good gain in revenues and profits. The result included an after-tax profit of $835 000 on the sale of the company's premises at Balgowlah. Excluding this, the group after-tax profit of $13.6 million was up 20% from the previous year. Sales in Australia were up 9%, and pre-tax profit rose 25%, with notably good demand for new arthritis and weight-management products. Asian sales jumped 23% – based on 20% growth in Malaysia and 29% growth in Thailand, both in local currencies – with profits up 25%. Asian business now represents about 15% of total company turnover. The small New Zealand operation saw sales and profits edge down, although profit margins in New Zealand remained very high.

Outlook

Blackmores is a beneficiary of several trends, including an ageing population that requires more health products, and a move towards natural medications. It has also benefited from its reputation for quality, which in some cases enables it to charge higher prices than competitors. It is achieving great success with its arthritis products, including two new formulations, Blackmores Glucosamine and Blackmores Glucosamine and Fish Oil. Arthritis is the largest and fastest-growing segment of the Australian natural healthcare market, and Blackmores claims to have achieved a big increase in its market share through a series of product, packaging, advertising and pricing initiatives. It sees strong potential in the weight-management market, and has realised strong market positions with two newly launched products, Metabolism Advantage and Sugar Balance. It is working to enhance its position in Asia, where business continues to exceed expectations, and it plans to enter Taiwan by the end of 2006. Blackmores has been lobbying – so far without success – to have the GST removed from complementary medicines. The company provides a shareholder card that gives a 25% discount on its products.

BKL Year to 30 June	2005	2006
Revenues ($mn)	134.4	148.0
EBIT ($mn)	17.3	21.0
EBIT margin (%)	12.9	14.2
Gross margin (%)	60.4	61.6
Profit before tax ($mn)	16.5	20.4
Profit after tax ($mn)	11.3	14.5
Earnings per share (¢)	71.4	91.0
Cash flow per share (¢)	83.3	102.6
Dividend (¢)	58	69
Percentage franked	100	100
Net tangible assets per share ($)	1.81	2.18
Interest cover (times)	21.3	35.3
Return on equity (%)	39.0	42.9
Debt-to-equity ratio (%)	16.8	9.5
Current ratio	1.5	2.4

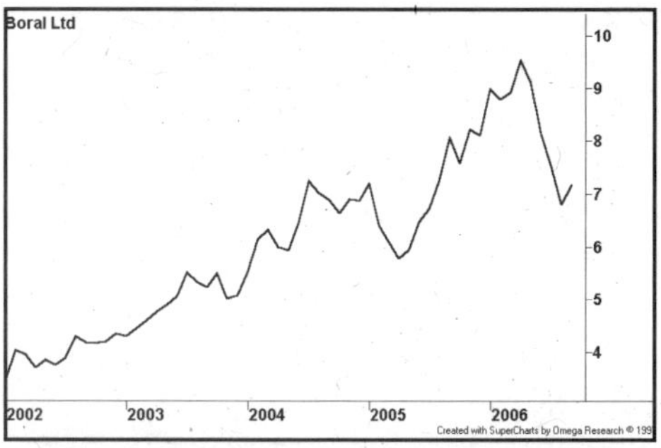

www.boral.com.au

BORAL LIMITED

Share price ($)	7.16	
12-month high ($)	10.15	
12-month low ($)	6.60	
Market capitalisation ($mn)	4213.3	
Price-to-NTA-per-share ratio	1.8	
5-year share price return (% p.a.)	24.3	
Sector: Materials	**Company**	**Sector**
Price-earnings ratio (times)	11.6	12.3
Dividend yield (%)	4.7	2.3

Sydney-based Boral – incorporated in 1946 as Bitumen and Oil Refineries (Australia) Limited – is one of Australia's largest producers of building and construction materials, and it has operations in several countries. Domestically it divides its activities into two major businesses: building products (bricks, plasterboard, roof tiles and timber, aluminium and concrete products) and construction materials (quarries, road surfacing, concrete and cement). In the US it is a major supplier of bricks, roof tiles, quarry materials, masonry and concrete. It owns half of a large plasterboard joint venture in Asia. A quarter of total sales revenues comes from abroad.

Latest business results (June 2006, full year)

Sales were up but profits fell, as the company was hit by the deterioration of the local housing market. Boral derives around 30% of its revenues from the New South Wales housing sector, and has been especially badly hurt by the downturn there. Domestically, building products EBIT tumbled 22%, with construction materials down 6%. In contrast, a buoyant US housing sector boosted profits there 27%.

Outlook

The outlook for Boral remains unclear, with uncertainty about trends in the domestic housing sector, while higher costs are also having an impact on margins. This has forced the company to close temporarily some of its plants in order to manage inventory levels more efficiently. Though the non-residential market remains strong, this is not sufficient to offset housing weakness. In America, too, the company is starting to see signs of a softening in the booming housing market, with cost escalation and possible rate rises a concern. However, non-residential construction remains solid. In Asia, the plasterboard market is competitive, and in the short term the company worries that cement and fuel cost increases could largely offset the benefits of higher sales. For the longer term, Boral has a vigorous capital spending program aimed at cutting costs and boosting growth. At June 2006 some $700 million worth of new projects had yet to benefit the company's earnings, including a $106 million plasterboard plant in Queensland, a US$55 million brick plant in Indiana and nearly US$100 million for roof tile plants in California, Florida and Nevada.

BLD Year to 30 June	2005	2006
Revenues ($mn)	4296.7	4756.1
EBIT ($mn)	619.2	614.0
EBIT margin (%)	14.4	12.9
Gross margin (%)	38.1	36.2
Profit before tax ($mn)	548.1	515.8
Profit after tax ($mn)	388.6	362.4
Earnings per share (¢)	66.7	61.7
Cash flow per share (¢)	99.5	97.3
Dividend (¢)	34	34
Percentage franked	100	100
Net tangible assets per share ($)	3.57	4.07
Interest cover (times)	8.7	6.3
Return on equity (%)	16.3	14.1
Debt-to-equity ratio (%)	57.9	57.3
Current ratio	1.4	1.6

BRAMBLES INDUSTRIES LIMITED

Share price ($)	11.90	
12-month high ($)	11.97	
12-month low ($)	8.02	
Market capitalisation ($mn)	11410.1	
Price-to-NTA-per-share ratio	6.5	
5-year share price return (% p.a.)	6.6	
Sector: Industrials	**Company**	**Sector**
Price-earnings ratio (times)	35.0	13.6
Dividend yield (%)	2.1	4.3

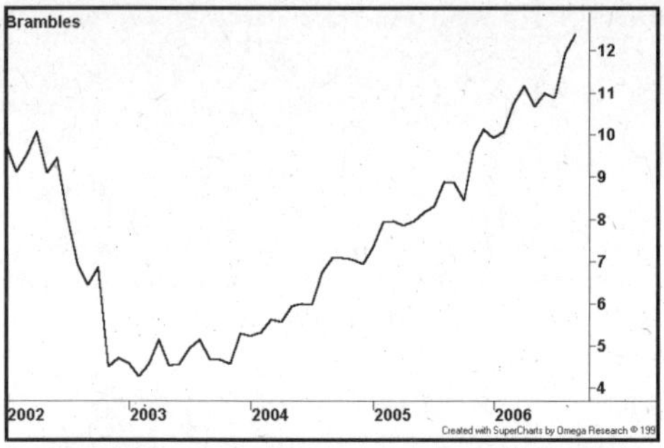

www.brambles.com.au

Sydney-based Brambles has a history that dates back to the 19th century, although it was formally established as a company in 1925. Today it is a global leader in two businesses, with operations in 45 countries. The first business is the CHEP pallet and container pooling service, which serves many of the world's largest companies, and involves collecting, repairing, washing and reissuing more than 265 million pallets and containers at some 500 service centres. The other business is the Recall document and information management service, which operates in more than 200 locations, and involves the management of physical and digital documents. Brambles operates in a dual-listing structure on the Australian and London stock exchanges.

Latest business results (June 2006, full year)

Sales and profits rose strongly, as Brambles restructured its businesses. CHEP represents about 85% of company turnover, and profits surged 32% on just a 7% sales increase. The best growth came from America, where profits were up 59%, with Europe up 17% and the rest of the world 8%. Good business in the second half helped the Recall operation to report sales growth of 10%, with profits up 16%. However, part of the gain came from the November 2005 acquisition of Ausdoc. In addition to the figures in the table, Brambles reported a June 2006 after-tax profit of approximately $289 million from discontinued operations, and approximately $1088 million from significant items. (Note that Brambles reports its financial results in US dollars. For the purposes of this book, these have been converted into Australian dollars at the rate of A$1 = US$0.75. Thus, figures in this book should be used for general guidance only.)

BIL Year to 30 June	2005	2006
Revenues ($mn)	4367.7	4696.1
EBIT ($mn)	799.7	1028.4
EBIT margin (%)	18.3	21.9
Profit before tax ($mn)	626.3	879.3
Profit after tax ($mn)	412.4	573.5
Earnings per share (¢)	24.4	34.0
Cash flow per share (¢)	55.3	66.5
Dividend (¢)	21.5	25
Percentage franked	100	100
Net tangible assets per share ($)	1.03	1.83
Interest cover (times)	4.6	6.9
Return on equity (%)	12.9	16.1
Debt-to-equity ratio (%)	92.5	57.2
Current ratio	1.1	1.9

Outlook

Brambles has successively sold a string of businesses, notably its Cleanaway waste management service, and it has the funding to expand CHEP and Recall. It has launched a best-practice initiative for CHEP which it believes will deliver annual cost savings of US$100 million within three to five years. It has established a small presence in China, and sees enormous scope there. It expects the $260 million Ausdoc acquisition to bring significant operational benefits to its Recall business. Brambles wishes to end its dual-listing structure, so that it is listed on the ASX only.

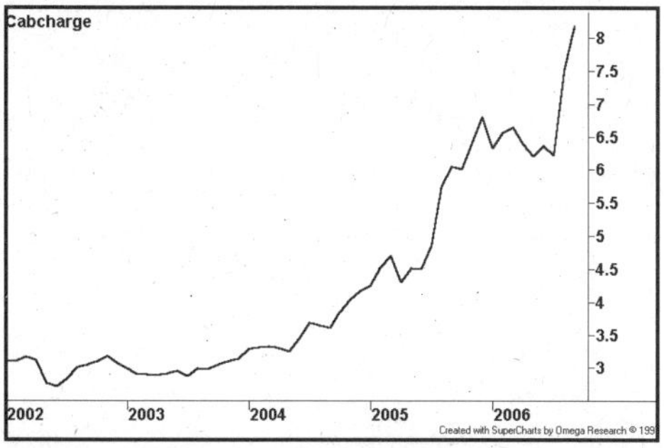

www.cabcharge.com.au

CABCHARGE AUSTRALIA LIMITED

Share price ($)	7.60
12-month high ($)	7.75
12-month low ($)	5.61
Market capitalisation ($mn)	853.0
Price-to-NTA-per-share ratio	6.8
5-year share price return (% p.a.)	23.6

Sector: Industrials	**Company**	**Sector**
Price-earnings ratio (times)	22.4	13.6
Dividend yield (%)	3.0	4.3

Sydney-based Cabcharge, founded in 1976, manages a charge-card system that allows taxi users to pay fares without requiring cash. The system is used by more than 95% of Australian taxis, and also by other companies, such as limousine services. Cabcharge has more than 44 000 account customers, ranging from large corporations and government departments to small businesses and individuals. Cabcharge also owns Australia's largest taxi company, Sydney-based Combined Communications Network, as well as Melbourne-based Black Cabs Combined and ABC Radio Taxi Cooperative in Sydney. It has established a small presence in the UK, with a joint venture operation in several cities, and is working to expand globally. In a joint venture with Singapore's ComfortDelGro Corporation it has entered the private bus industry.

Latest business results (June 2006, full year)

Cabcharge reported another excellent result, as its technological advances continued to drive down costs and boost margins. Thanks to its General Packet Radio Service (GPRS) system of EFTPOS terminals it is seeing a steady move to electronic transactions – 61% of the total, up from 57% in the June 2005 year – with reduced transaction and communication costs. In addition, the company's service fee margin rose from 8.4% in June 2005 to 9.1%, further enhancing profits. The new bus joint venture contributed $1 million to after-tax profit.

Outlook

Cabcharge continues to enhance its technology, with new systems that are aimed at reducing transaction and communication costs. In mid-2005 it completed the roll-out of 17 000 GPRS taxi terminals, and expects this to help bring further benefits in the June 2007 year. In August 2006 it launched the eTicket electronic ticketing system, which is designed to replace Cabcharge blue dockets, with further long-term cost benefits. It is engaged in a pilot eTag scheme in Melbourne to make it easier for taxis to pay tolls. It sees great potential in its bus joint venture with ComfortDelGro, which is one of the world's largest land transportation companies. Cabcharge owns 49% of the equity of the new company, which operates a fleet of more than 640 buses in metropolitan Sydney and the Hunter Valley region, and which in July 2006 acquired further bus line assets.

CAB Year to 30 June	**2005**	**2006**
Revenues ($mn)	766.5	870.4
EBIT ($mn)	36.8	53.0
EBIT margin (%)	4.8	6.1
Profit before tax ($mn)	38.9	52.7
Profit after tax ($mn)	27.8	38.0
Earnings per share (¢)	24.3	33.9
Cash flow per share (¢)	33.8	42.2
Dividend (¢)	17	23
Percentage franked	100	100
Net tangible assets per share ($)	1.00	1.12
Interest cover (times)	–	213.5
Return on equity (%)	20.8	25.6
Debt-to-equity ratio (%)	–	8.1
Current ratio	3.5	2.4

CAMPBELL BROTHERS LIMITED

Share price ($)	18.94	
12-month high ($)	19.00	
12-month low ($)	9.30	
Market capitalisation ($mn)	964.7	
Price-to-NTA-per-share ratio	8.1	
5-year share price return (% p.a.)	38.0	
Sector: Industrials	**Company**	**Sector**
Price-earnings ratio (times)	25.0	13.6
Dividend yield (%)	2.6	4.3

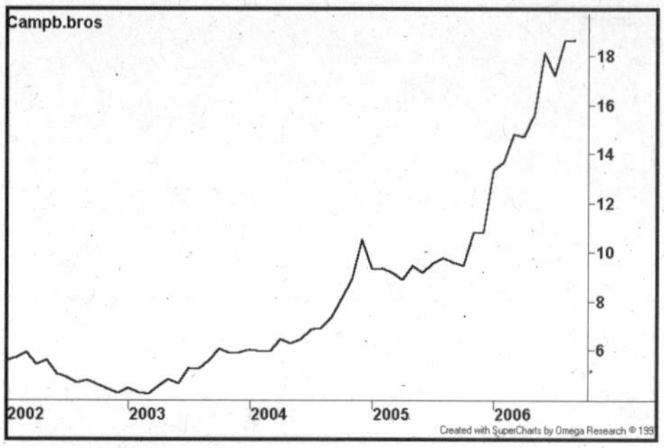

www.campbell.com.au

Brisbane-based Campbell Brothers, established in 1863, has become one of the world's largest providers of laboratory analysis services to the minerals industry. Its ALS Laboratory Group operates 51 laboratories in 22 countries. The company's second main business, Campbell Chemicals, manufactures a wide range of industrial and consumer chemical and cleaning products. A third division, Reward Distribution, is a supplier to the hospitality industry, while the small Campbell Brothers Services unit is involved in pest control, home security and cleaning services.

Latest business results (March 2006, full year)

Campbell's high-flying laboratory business powered the company to another excellent result. Though responsible for just 40% of total turnover, the ALS Laboratory Group provides more than 70% of Campbell's profit. Revenue from the Campbell Chemicals division fell, following the disposal of the consumer products business, though a rationalisation of product lines boosted profits. The Reward Distribution division enjoyed double-digit increases in sales and profits, due to significant acquisition activity in Australia and New Zealand over the previous two years. The Campbell Brothers Services division grew strongly from a small base due to acquisitions, along with greater market penetration and geographic coverage.

Outlook

Campbell believes it can achieve a further profit increase of at least 20% in the March 2007 year, thanks to organic growth from existing businesses and a series of planned acquisitions. In particular, it sees continuing strong expansion for its laboratory business, where it claims to enjoy a competitive advantage over rivals. This division has a 50% reliance on the minerals business, and to offset any downturn in the commodities market, the company is working to diversify into new analytical services markets. Recent acquisitions include two environmental laboratory groups: Enviro-Test Laboratories in Canada, and Ecochem in the Czech Republic. The company has also opened new laboratories in several countries. Campbell has launched a contested $41 million takeover bid for CCI Holdings, which provides a range of services to the coal industry. Its small Campbell Brothers Services division is showing particular promise, thanks to the company's moves into the provision of services, rather than just products.

CPB Year to 31 March	2005	2006
Revenues ($mn)	435.6	522.7
ALS Laboratory Group (%)	36	40
Campbell Chemicals (%)	40	31
Reward Distribution (%)	18	21
Campbell Brothers Services (%)	5	7
EBIT ($mn)	43.3	56.7
EBIT margin (%)	16.9	20.5
Profit before tax ($mn)	37.9	51.1
Profit after tax ($mn)	25.4	34.3
Earnings per share (¢)	62.3	75.7
Cash flow per share (¢)	96.5	112.1
Dividend (¢)	42	50
Percentage franked	100	100
Net tangible assets per share ($)	1.99	2.33
Interest cover (times)	7.9	10.2
Return on equity (%)	17.9	17.0
Debt-to-equity ratio (%)	48.4	33.4
Current ratio	2.1	2.2

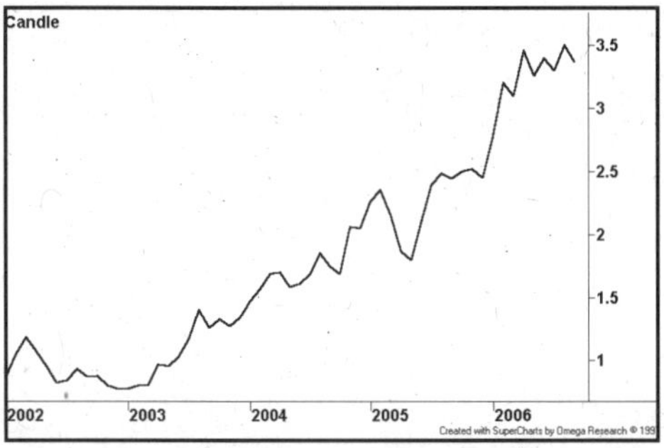

www.candle.com.au

CANDLE AUSTRALIA LIMITED

Share price ($)	3.35
12-month high ($)	3.65
12-month low ($)	2.31
Market capitalisation ($mn)	169.6
Price-to-NTA-per-share ratio	11.1
5-year share price return (% p.a.)	38.3

Sector: Industrials	**Company**	**Sector**
Price-earnings ratio (times)	13.7	13.6
Dividend yield (%)	5.1	4.3

Sydney-based Candle Australia, founded in 1984, has grown through a series of mergers and acquisitions to become a leading nationwide specialist provider of recruitment services in Australia and New Zealand, to the information communications technology (ICT), banking, finance, insurance and government sectors. It operates through six divisions: the information, communications and technology division represented by Candle ICT and Technology Co-Sourcing Solutions; the banking and finance division represented by Freeman Adams; the commercial accounting division represented by Parker Bridge Australia; the business support division represented by Alliance Recruitment; the library and records management division represented by The One Umbrella; and the executive division represented by Lloyd Morgan.

Latest business results (June 2006, full year)

A strong domestic economy and a tight labour market combined to deliver Candle another excellent result. All divisions were strong, with an excellent performance from the core Candle ICT business and strong growth from Alliance Recruitment, with several new offices established. Three acquisitions made during the year – Parker Bridge Australia, Choice IT and Lloyd Morgan – all contributed to the result, with each performing above expectations.

Outlook

Candle is a market leader in the technology recruitment field at a time when concerns are mounting of a skills shortage in Australia, and it is seeing growing demand for its services. The company itself believes that if current levels of demand for recruitment services continue it can achieve further strong profit growth in the June 2007 year. With no debt, and more than $4 million in cash holdings, it also expects to grow further through acquisition, and it is actively seeking new companies to buy, to enable it to expand both geographically and into new lines of business. Though it is working to diversify away from its strong dependence on ICT recruitment, it also views Candle ICT as offering the best growth potential of its various businesses. It sees continuing good growth prospects for its Alliance Recruitment business support division, with at least five new offices planned during 2006–07. It is working to boost its contract and temporary assignment services, which provide an element of future revenues.

CND Year to 30 June	2005	2006
Revenues ($mn)	231.8	270.0
EBIT ($mn)	11.1	17.0
EBIT margin (%)	4.8	6.3
Profit before tax ($mn)	11.0	17.2
Profit after tax ($mn)	7.6	11.8
Earnings per share (¢)	17.7	24.4
Cash flow per share (¢)	21.0	28.1
Dividend (¢)	11.5	17
Percentage franked	100	100
Net tangible assets per share ($)	0.45	0.30
Interest cover (times)	82.5	–
Return on equity (%)	14.3	18.0
Debt-to-equity ratio (%)	–	–
Current ratio	1.7	1.3

CMI LIMITED

Share price ($)	1.20	
12-month high ($)	1.69	
12-month low ($)	0.98	
Market capitalisation ($mn)	43.5	
Price-to-NTA-per-share ratio	0.8	
5-year share price return (% p.a.)	8.5	
Sector: Industrials	**Company**	**Sector**
Price-earnings ratio (times)	3.9	13.6
Dividend yield (%)	10.0	4.3

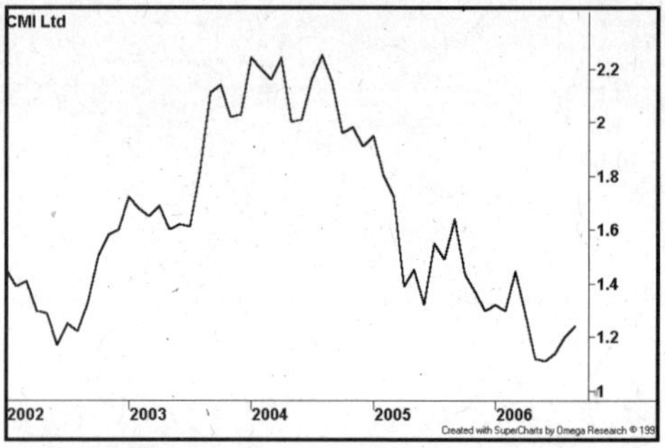

www.cmilimited.com.au

Brisbane-based CMI, established in 1991, is a manufacturer and distributor of a range of specialist industrial components, with most sales to Australian and international automotive companies. It also supplies electrical components to the mining, construction and petrochemical industries. It has 14 manufacturing and/or distribution centres in Australia, New Zealand and the US. It also operates a financial services subsidiary, Capitalcorp Finance & Leasing, with more than 30 offices throughout Australia.

Latest business results (June 2006, full year)

Revenues and profits fell, as problems in the car parts industry hit business. The company's engineered components division, representing 78% of total turnover, and largely supplying the auto industry, saw pre-tax profit plunge 47% to $5 million, on a 7% decline in sales. By contrast, the electrical components division, accounting for just 11% of turnover, was hugely profitable, with the pre-tax profit jumping 53% to $9 million, and with sales up 35%. The financial services division – the provision of consumer finance from Capitalcorp – saw revenues up 9%, but profits fell 19% to $1.9 million. It was the second straight year for revenues to rise and profits fall in this division.

Outlook

CMI is suffering from many of the same problems that have been afflicting other Australian automobile components companies, and which have sent several into bankruptcy. Rising costs are exerting particular pressure on the industry, with steel and copper prices near their record highs, and it is often difficult for the companies to pass this on to customers. The continuing relative strength of the Australian dollar increases the competition from imports and hurts CMI's own exports. At the same time, the rising petrol price is leading many car buyers to switch to smaller, imported cars, away from large Australian-made models. Financial difficulties of some of CMI's customers have been another problem. As a result, CMI has warned that it may need to rationalise – at great expense – its production facilities over the coming three years. It says this could affect its ability to continue the current level of dividend payments, and it is proposing a buyback of a substantial number of its shares.

CMI Year to 30 June	2005	2006
Revenues ($mn)	280.7	275.7
EBIT ($mn)	21.1	19.7
EBIT margin (%)	7.5	7.2
Gross margin (%)	17.6	18.1
Profit before tax ($mn)	17.7	16.0
Profit after tax ($mn)	12.2	11.2
Earnings per share (¢)	36.4	31.0
Cash flow per share (¢)	58.5	52.5
Dividend (¢)	12	12
Percentage franked	100	100
Net tangible assets per share ($)	1.45	1.57
Interest cover (times)	6.2	5.2
Return on equity (%)	15.7	13.0
Debt-to-equity ratio (%)	66.2	56.2
Current ratio	1.8	1.9

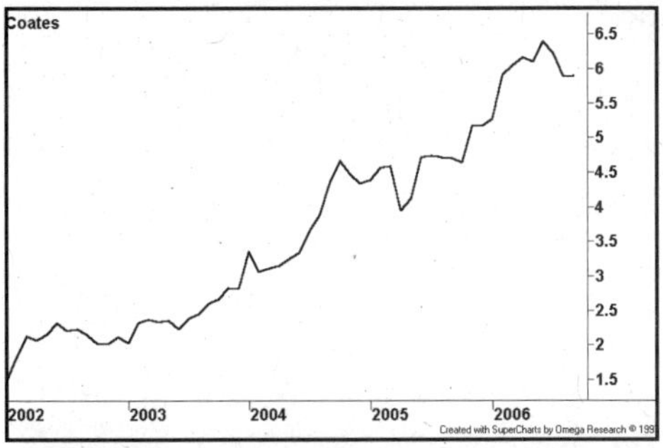

www.coates.com.au

COATES HIRE LIMITED

Share price ($)	5.92
12-month high ($)	6.61
12-month low ($)	4.33
Market capitalisation ($mn)	1470.6
Price-to-NTA-per-share ratio	2.7
5-year share price return (% p.a.)	54.0

Sector: Industrials	Company	Sector
Price-earnings ratio (times)	14.9	13.6
Dividend yield (%)	3.2	4.3

Sydney-based Coates Hire Limited is Australia's largest hire equipment company with more than 190 branches and locations nationwide. Following the sale of its Coates Conrent operation, it divides its domestic activities into three businesses: Coates Hire provides a large range of compaction, access, generator, compressor, welding and general equipment; Coates Shorco is a specialist supplier of pumps, shoring, dewatering systems, traffic management, confined space and laser equipment; and Coates Prestige provides portable buildings, commercial buildings, portable toilets, temporary fencing and containers. The company also has a small operation, Coates Offshore, in Aberdeen in the UK, providing specialised equipment to the offshore oil and gas industry, and seven offices in Indonesia supporting the mining, resources and offshore sectors.

Latest business results (June 2006, full year)

Coates enjoyed another excellent year, with sales and profits up strongly, thanks to continuing strength in the domestic non-residential construction sector and a buoyant resources sector. All regions contributed, with the company's sponsorship of the 2006 Commonwealth Games helping drive business in Victoria, and a booming Western Australian economy helping performance grow strongly in that state. Coates Prestige and Coates Shorco performed well, with the latter seeing especially strong demand for traffic management equipment. Coates Offshore was a beneficiary of a strong oil and gas market, and the small Indonesian operation also saw excellent growth.

Outlook

Coates is a major beneficiary of the strong domestic construction and resources markets, including a steady stream of major infrastructure projects. The company expects current trends to continue, and through investment and acquisition is working to strengthen its position in the most attractive areas of business. The mid-2005 acquisition of Allied Equipment has boosted the company's penetration of the mining sector, and Coates is investing heavily to expand this business. It is also working to boost its Coates Offshore business, which it believes offers global potential. It is seeking further acquisitions, as consolidation continues within the highly fragmented hire equipment industry. It is also prepared to sell non-core businesses where it believes growth potential is modest, and in July 2006 it disposed of its Coates Conrent specialist hoist business.

COA Year to 30 June	2005	2006
Revenues ($mn)	527.6	715.0
EBIT ($mn)	104.0	158.4
EBIT margin (%)	19.7	22.2
Profit before tax ($mn)	92.4	136.1
Profit after tax ($mn)	63.5	93.6
Earnings per share (¢)	30.7	39.6
Cash flow per share (¢)	66.7	89.5
Dividend (¢)	15	19
Percentage franked	100	100
Net tangible assets per share ($)	1.73	2.19
Interest cover (times)	8.9	7.1
Return on equity (%)	17.3	18.5
Debt-to-equity ratio (%)	61.3	58.1
Current ratio	1.3	1.8

COCHLEAR LIMITED

Share price ($)	52.00	
12-month high ($)	56.00	
12-month low ($)	35.51	
Market capitalisation ($mn)	2853.3	
Price-to-NTA-per-share ratio	1235.8	
5-year share price return (% p.a.)	5.3	
Sector: Health care	**Company**	**Sector**
Price-earnings ratio (times)	36.2	31.1
Dividend yield (%)	1.9	1.8

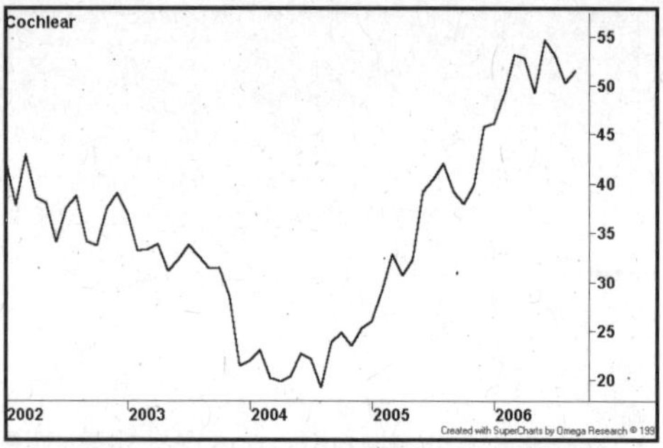

www.cochlear.com.au

Sydney-based Cochlear, founded in 1981, has more than two-thirds of the world market for cochlear bionic-ear implants, which are intended to assist the communication ability of people suffering from severe hearing impediments. It has sold more than 70 000 of its Nucleus 22 and Nucleus 24 implant systems in around 80 countries. Following the 2005 acquisition of Sweden's Entific Medical Systems, Cochlear now also sells the Baha bone-anchored hearing implant. Overseas business accounts for over 95% of sales and profits.

Latest business results (June 2006, full year)

Cochlear confirmed that it is back on a high-growth trajectory, with another excellent result. Cochlear implant sales of a record 12 901 units represented a 19% jump over the previous year, with revenues up 24% to $380 million. Baha implant products recorded sales of $51.7 million, compared to $14.8 million in the four months of the previous year that Cochlear owned the business. Based on static currency rates, American sales rose 50%, with profits more than doubling. Europe saw profits up 21% on a 35% sales rise, while Asia Pacific lagged, with a 7% rise in sales delivering just a 3% profit increase.

Outlook

Cochlear expects strong growth to continue, and its early forecast is for a June 2007 after-tax profit of $100 million. It is seeing an impressive response to the introduction in American and European markets of its new Nucleus Freedom implant, which delivers significantly better hearing performance to recipients than earlier models. This device is still awaiting regulatory approval from the important markets of China and Japan. It has successfully integrated most of its own customer support activities with those of Baha – creating significant economies of scale – and is substantially increasing research and development for Baha products. It has also introduced a 30-month program to upgrade its manufacturing capability to reduce costs and underpin future growth. The company sees particularly strong potential in Asia Pacific – currently only 14% of total sales – and has received a major order for 15 000 implants for delivery over six years from mid-2006, as a gift to the people of China from a Taiwanese philanthropist.

COH Year to 30 June	2005	2006
Revenues ($mn)	349.0	452.3
EBIT ($mn)	82.5	111.5
EBIT margin (%)	23.7	24.7
Gross margin (%)	71.3	70.8
Profit before tax ($mn)	82.3	108.8
Profit after tax ($mn)	58.5	78.2
Earnings per share (¢)	108.0	143.5
Cash flow per share (¢)	129.5	172.9
Dividend (¢)	80	100
Percentage franked	100	100
Net tangible assets per share ($)	–	0.04
Interest cover (times)	362.0	41.2
Return on equity (%)	40.5	43.8
Debt-to-equity ratio (%)	62.7	51.9
Current ratio	1.3	1.4

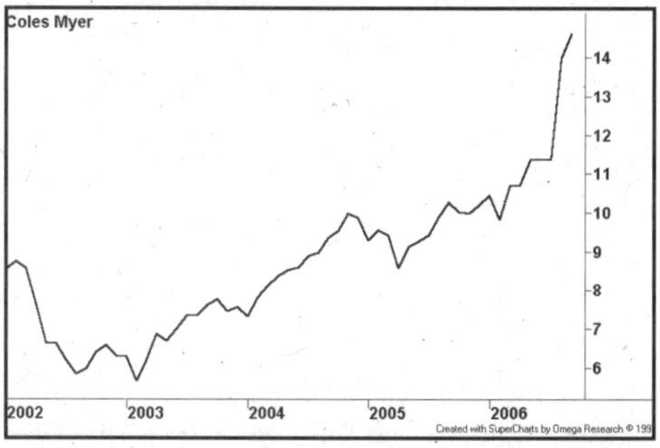

www.colesmyer.com.au

COLES MYER LIMITED

Share price ($)	13.84
12-month high ($)	13.99
12-month low ($)	9.49
Market capitalisation ($mn)	16337.1
Price-to-NTA-per-share ratio	7.5
5-year share price return (% p.a.)	19.7

Sector: Consumer staples	Company	Sector
Price-earnings ratio (times)	21.9	15.5
Dividend yield (%)	3.0	3.2

Melbourne-based Coles Myer is Australia's largest retailer and one of the biggest in the world. It operates more than 2100 stores, including Coles, Kmart, Target, Bi-Lo, Coles Express, Liquorland, Vintage Cellars, Theo's Liquor, Harris Technology and Officeworks. It has sold its Myer and Megamart stores.

Latest business results (July 2006, full year)

Profits rose, in a sound result. The core food and liquor business drove the result, with sales up 4.3% and underlying EBIT up 8.5%. The new house-brand strategy was deemed a success, with approximately 1450 products on offer. During the year, 31 new supermarkets were opened, along with 17 1st Choice liquor superstores. Among the non-food businesses, Kmart had a bad year, with flat sales and a decline in profits, despite a stronger second half. By contrast, Target stores realised a 16.2% EBIT gain on a 4.3% rise in sales, thanks to cost efficiencies, new products and some highly successful promotions. Officeworks continued its successful expansion, with EBIT up 14.4%. In addition to the figures in the table on this page, the company also reported a $583.7 million after-tax profit on the sale of its Myer stores and $207.4 million in restructuring expenses.

Outlook

As this book was going to press, Coles Myer was fending off a hostile takeover bid from one set of corporate raiders, and there were rumours that other bidders were also interested in the company. If they succeed, it could lead to the break-up of the company. Partially in response, Coles Myer management has announced an ambitious growth program, with an EPS target of 80¢ (before significant items) in July 2007 and $1.00 in July 2008. To achieve this goal, the company plans to overhaul its entire corporate structure, with the elimination of 2500 support staff jobs. It will simplify its buying procedures – including the direct sourcing of some products for supermarkets – and end Kmart, Bi-Lo and Liquorland as separate brands. It also plans a new chain of stores it calls SuperCentres, incorporating a Coles supermarket with a Kmart store. It expects the first of these to open in late 2007, building eventually to a national network of 80 stores.

CML Year to 30 July*	2005	2006
Revenues ($mn)	33018.2	34212.0
Food, liquor & fuel (%)	75	75
Kmart (%)	12	12
Target (%)	9	9
Officeworks (%)	4	4
EBIT ($mn)	958.4	1496.8
EBIT margin (%)	2.9	4.4
Gross margin (%)	23.4	23.5
Profit before tax ($mn)	903.2	1397.9
Profit after tax ($mn)	691.5	787.3
Earnings per share (¢)	56.4	63.2
Cash flow per share (¢)	94.3	102.5
Dividend (¢)	33.25	42
Percentage franked	100	100
Net tangible assets per share ($)	2.11	1.84
Interest cover (times)	17.4	15.1
Return on equity (%)	18.4	22.5
Debt-to-equity ratio (%)	28.9	14.4
Current ratio	1.1	1.0

* 25 July 2005

COLORADO GROUP LIMITED

Share price ($)	4.69	
12-month high ($)	4.95	
12-month low ($)	3.16	
Market capitalisation ($mn)	445.9	
Price-to-NTA-per-share ratio	5.0	
5-year share price return (% p.a.)	26.6	
Sector: Consumer discretionary	**Company**	**Sector**
Price-earnings ratio (times)	12.2	18.8
Dividend yield (%)	5.1	4.0

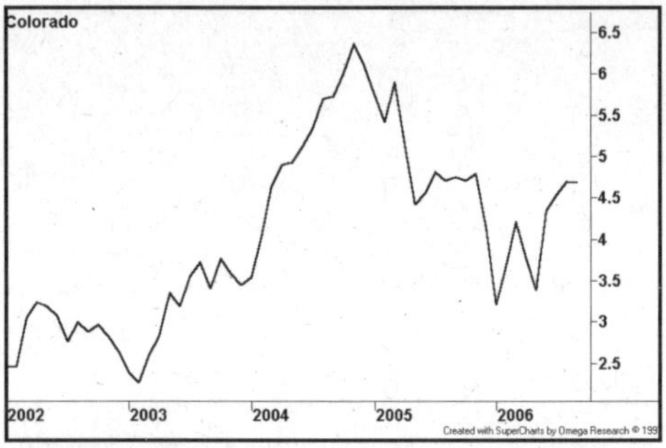

www.coloradogroup.com.au

Brisbane-based Colorado, with roots dating back to the establishment of the first Williams shoe store in Ballarat in 1864, is a prominent footwear and apparel retailer and wholesaler. It comprises some 430 stores in Australia and New Zealand, across six divisions: Colorado (a full range of clothing, footwear and accessories), Mathers (family footwear stores), Williams the Shoemen (footwear and accessories), Diana Ferrari (women's shoes), Jag (fashion clothing and accessories) and Pairs (footwear clearance stores). As this book was going to press it appeared likely that Colorado would be acquired by the private equity firm ARH Investments (Australia).

Latest business results (July 2006, half year)

Sales edged up, thanks mainly to new store openings, while profits marked time, due to the impact of higher rental and wage costs. On a like-for-like basis, retail sales actually fell by around 4% to 6%. However, the company's small wholesale business – centred around the Jag and Diana Ferrari operations – achieved an excellent result, with sales up 4% and pre-tax profit jumping 21%, thanks to stronger product offerings and successful cost control measures. Colorado's wholesale business is responsible for only about 16% of company turnover, but contributes around 60% of profit.

CDO Year to 28 January*	2005	2006
Revenues ($mn)	468.9	466.0
EBIT ($mn)	62.1	48.4
EBIT margin (%)	13.2	10.4
Gross margin (%)	55.5	54.0
Profit before tax ($mn)	62.6	49.8
Profit after tax ($mn)	44.0	35.6
Earnings per share (¢)	48.6	38.4
Cash flow per share (¢)	59.7	51.3
Dividend (¢)	24	24
Percentage franked	100	100
Interest cover (times)	–	–
Return on equity (%)	35.5	27.3

* 29 January 2005

Half year to 29 July**	2005	2006
Revenues ($mn)	210.2	212.6
Profit before tax ($mn)	11.1	10.8
Profit after tax ($mn)	7.6	7.6
Earnings per share (¢)	8.2	8.0
Dividend (¢)	6	0
Percentage franked	100	–
Net tangible assets per share ($)	1.11	0.93
Debt-to-equity ratio (%)	–	0.1
Current ratio	3.2	2.2

** 30 July 2005

Outlook

Colorado has been a prominent beneficiary of surging consumer spending in Australia, but is now being affected by a slowdown in this spending. Company management have recommended that shareholders accept a $450 million takeover bid from ARH Investments, and late in September ARH said it had acquired more than 50% of the shares. ARH Investments is part of Affinity Equity Partners, a leading private equity firm with operations throughout the Asia Pacific region, including considerable experience in managing retail businesses. It is possible that the company will be split up, and Just Group has said it is interested in acquiring one or more of Colorado's brands. Former Coles Myer chairman Solomon Lew is also believed to be interested, and late in September 2006 it was revealed that he had acquired a 10.2% equity stake in Colorado.

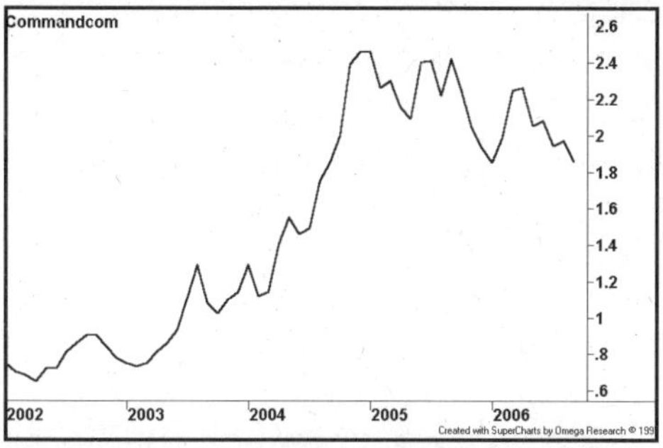

www.commander.com.au

COMMANDER COMMUNICATIONS LTD

Share price ($)	1.95
12-month high ($)	2.50
12-month low ($)	1.77
Market capitalisation ($mn)	428.4
Price-to-NTA-per-share ratio	na
5-year share price return (% p.a.)	22.8

Sector: Information technology	Company	Sector
Price-earnings ratio (times)	15.7	22.8
Dividend yield (%)	2.1	2.2

Melbourne telecommunications company Commander Communications was founded in 1998 as a joint venture between Plessey and Telstra, and was originally called PlesTel. It has grown rapidly from its origins as a simple seller of business telephone systems thanks to some major acquisitions, most recently the Volante Group, a specialist in managed services which was acquired in April 2006. Now it is a leader in the provision of a wide range of telecommunications services, spanning voice, data, internet, mobile and network products and services. Its customer base includes more than 60 000 businesses with an estimated one million individual users of its business telephone systems.

Latest business results (June 2006, full year)

Revenues soared, thanks to the impact of the Volante acquisition. However, expenses associated with the acquisition – including $2.7 million in redundancy costs, $1.2 million in integration costs and a $0.6 million finance facility fee – helped lead to a decline in profit. All divisions saw sales growth, and there was good profit growth from the company's fixed wire network services. But profits fell for the other divisions.

Outlook

Commander was one of the noteworthy survivors of the 'tech wreck' of 2000, and it has continued to thrive. It works with some of the world's leading technology companies – including NEC, Nortel Networks, Siemens, Lake Communications, Hewlett-Packard, Microsoft, Cisco Systems and Toshiba – as its partners in providing communications products to Australian businesses. It has been transformed by its hostile takeover of Volante. The company reports that synergy benefits are already flowing from the acquisition, and it is forecasting June 2007 revenues of $1.1 billion to $1.2 billion, with earnings (before interest, tax, depreciation and amortisation) of $95 million to $101 million (compared to $60.1 million in June 2006). It has begun the roll-out of a chain of franchised Commander Centre businesses in regional centres, aimed at boosting market share through the provision of local sales and service. There has been market speculation that Commander could become an acquisition target of a major telecommunications company like Telstra or Optus.

CDR Year to 30 June	2005	2006
Revenues ($mn)	599.9	764.0
Fixed wire network (%)	42	35
Data services (%)	36	33
Voice services (%)	22	19
Volante (%)	0	13
EBIT ($mn)	35.8	38.3
EBIT margin (%)	6.0	5.0
Gross margin (%)	27.2	26.6
Profit before tax ($mn)	31.8	31.2
Profit after tax ($mn)	28.1	26.0
Earnings per share (¢)	17.3	12.5
Cash flow per share (¢)	23.7	21.0
Dividend (¢)	6	4
Percentage franked	100	100
Net tangible assets per share ($)	0.20	–
Interest cover (times)	8.9	5.4
Return on equity (%)	17.4	11.0
Debt-to-equity ratio (%)	11.0	59.4
Current ratio	1.0	1.2

COMMONWEALTH BANK OF AUSTRALIA

Share price ($)	46.10
12-month high ($)	47.41
12-month low ($)	36.81
Market capitalisation ($mn)	58785.9
Price-to-NTA-per-share ratio	4.5
5-year share price return (% p.a.)	17.4

Sector: Financials	Company	Sector
Price-earnings ratio (times)	15.0	15.7
Dividend yield (%)	4.9	4.3

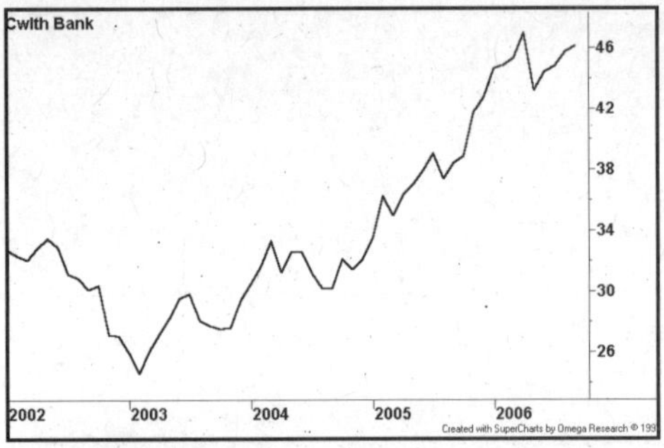

www.commbank.com.au

Australia's second-largest bank, with over seven million retail customers, the CBA is the country's top provider of home loans, personal loans and credit cards, and the largest holder of deposits. It is also Australia's largest fund manager, through Commonwealth Financial Services and Colonial First State, and the third-largest life insurer. Commonwealth Securities has become Australia's largest online stockbroker. It has significant interests in New Zealand through ASB Bank.

Latest business results (June 2006, full year)

Profits continued to rise, powered by a strong increase in business lending, and with most other areas of business also strong. Domestically, business loans surged 24% to $85 billion, with home lending up 11% to $145 billion. Strong competition led to a decline of seven basis points in the net interest margin, but tight control of expenses meant that the cost-to-income ratio also fell. Sturdy equity markets and good demand for the bank's First Choice product helped boost funds under management to $152 billion, a 23% rise, and the insurance business also enjoyed an excellent year, with strong profit growth. In New Zealand, the ASB overcame strong competition to record 16% profit growth, including the fifteenth straight year of market share growth in home loans. There was a one-off $145 million profit from the sale of the bank's Hong Kong–based insurance subsidiary.

Outlook

The Commonwealth holds an estimated 19% of the home loans market, and business continues to grow, despite a slowdown in the housing sector. However, it could be hurt – along with the other banks – in the event of any significant deterioration in the sector. Its other businesses are also vulnerable to rising interest rates, and its New Zealand operations could be affected by a slowdown in that country's economy. The bank is continuing to target business lending – where its domestic market share is only around 13% – as an area for future growth. It is also moving more firmly into selected Asian markets. In China it has taken a 19.9% interest in Hangzhou City Commercial Bank, in addition to its existing stake in Jinan City Commercial Bank, giving it an interest in two of the top 10 city commercial banks in China.

CBA Year to 30 June	2005	2006
Operating income ($mn)	11278.0	12286.0
Net interest income ($mn)	6026.0	6514.0
Operating expenses ($mn)	5869.0	5994.0
Profit before tax ($mn)	5012.0	5859.0
Profit after tax ($mn)	3400.0	3928.0
Earnings per share (¢)	269.8	308.1
Dividend (¢)	197	224
Percentage franked	100	100
Non-interest income to total income (%)	46.6	47.0
Net tangible assets per share ($)	9.29	10.15
Cost-to-income ratio (%)	52.0	48.8
Return on equity (%)	16.2	18.8
Return on assets (%)	1.1	1.1

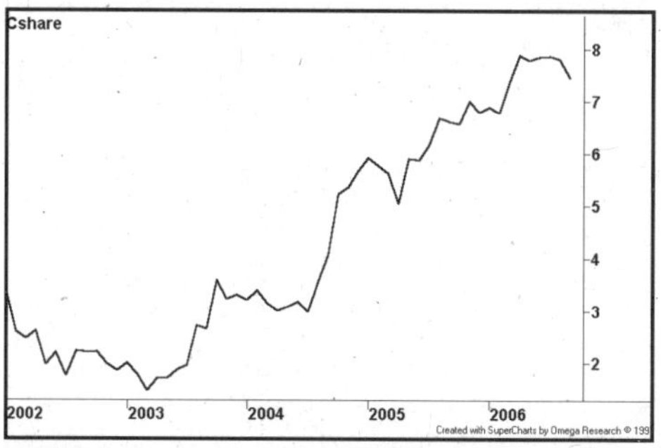

www.computershare.com.au

COMPUTERSHARE LIMITED

Share price ($)	7.75
12-month high ($)	8.38
12-month low ($)	6.10
Market capitalisation ($mn)	4590.6
Price-to-NTA-per-share ratio	na
5-year share price return (% p.a.)	13.1

Sector: Information technology	Company	Sector
Price-earnings ratio (times)	25.3	22.8
Dividend yield (%)	1.7	2.2

Melbourne-based Computershare, established in 1978, is one of the world's leading financial services and technology providers for the global securities industry, offering services to listed companies, investors, employees, exchanges and other financial institutions. It is the world's only global share registry/transfer agent, managing more than 90 million shareholder accounts for over 14 000 corporations in 17 countries. In Australia it arranges registry services for more than half of all companies, as well as 80% of those in New Zealand, 60% in Canada, 50% in Germany, and significant proportions in Britain, Ireland, South Africa, the United States and Hong Kong.

Latest business results (June 2006, full year)

Its strength in the United States delivered Computershare a big surge in revenues and profits. This followed the acquisition of the prominent American share registry and employee share plan administrator EquiServe. North American revenues more than doubled and the pre-tax profit rocketed from $15 million to $112 million. The North American region now represents roughly 60% of Computershare's business. By contrast, a weak performance by the Australian registry business offset a strong earnings contribution from Hong Kong and India, and Asia Pacific revenues dipped 5%, with profits down 12%. In the Europe, Middle East and Africa region revenues rose 16% and profits jumped 52%.

Outlook

Computershare is steadily restructuring and integrating its stream of acquisitions into its global business, and continues to derive significant synergies and cost efficiencies. Consequently it forecasts that, providing financial markets remain relatively stable, it can continue to reach its long-term target of annual EPS growth of around 20%. There is considerable speculation that the company is eyeing leading share registry businesses in the US and Britain as acquisition targets. This would enable it to introduce even more economies of scale, while the reduced competition would allow it to boost its prices. It is seeing a recovery in its lagging British operations, and it is working on ways to enter the share registry business in Japan and China, where the growth potential is huge. Computershare holds a considerable amount of clients' funds in various forms, and is a major beneficiary of rising interest rates.

CPU Year to 30 June	2005	2006
Revenues ($mn)	1063.5	1604.2
EBIT ($mn)	155.3	271.8
EBIT margin (%)	14.6	16.9
Profit before tax ($mn)	145.6	242.5
Profit after tax ($mn)	125.4	182.6
Earnings per share (¢)	22.4	30.6
Cash flow per share (¢)	28.8	37.7
Dividend (¢)	11	13
Percentage franked	5	0
Net tangible assets per share ($)	–	–
Interest cover (times)	16.0	9.3
Return on equity (%)	18.1	21.2
Debt-to-equity ratio (%)	66.5	57.7
Current ratio	1.0	1.3

CORPORATE EXPRESS AUSTRALIA LIMITED

Share price ($)	4.99
12-month high ($)	6.47
12-month low ($)	4.75
Market capitalisation ($mn)	905.2
Price-to-NTA-per-share ratio	9.4
5-year share price return (% p.a.)	6.3

Sector: Industrials	Company	Sector
Price-earnings ratio (times)	14.1	13.6
Dividend yield (%)	3.6	4.3

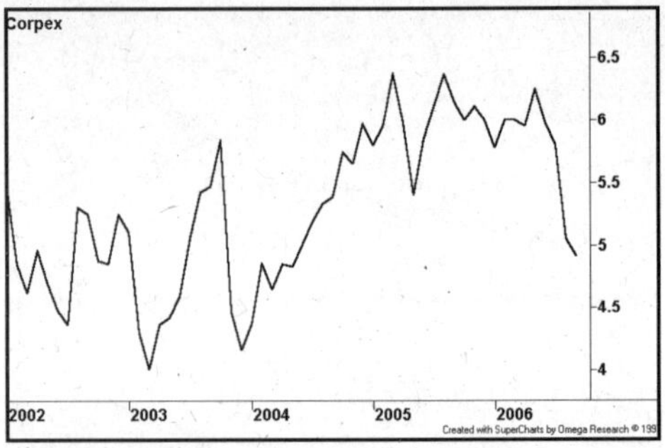

www.ce.com.au

Sydney-based Corporate Express, a 53%-owned subsidiary of the Dutch-based office provisions giant Buhrmann, has become Australia's largest distributor of office supplies to business. As well as basic office provisions, its products and services include IT equipment and supplies, business furniture, janitorial supplies, print services, promotional marketing, and liquor, coffee and kitchen supplies. It services some 38 000 corporate customers from a string of 49 regional offices throughout Australia and New Zealand.

Latest business results (June 2006, half year)

Sales and profits rose modestly, held back by a slide in demand for the company's IT hardware and software products, which had been especially buoyant in the June 2005 half. There was particularly good growth in the furniture, promotional, canteen and facilities sectors. Strong growth was also recorded among mid-size customers for office products. Part of the gain came from the acquisition during the period of three new businesses, which together have annual revenues of about $28 million.

Outlook

Corporate Express has achieved strong growth over an extended period through an aggressive policy of corporate acquisition. Many of the more than 49 businesses it has acquired – up from 45 in mid-2005 – have been small, niche office supply distributors, lacking the capital to expand, but with solid customer bases. The company has said that it will continue this acquisition policy, though some concerns have been expressed that quality takeover targets are now becoming scarce. The latest acquisitions expand the company's coverage in the Sunshine Coast and Geraldton regions. Corporate Express also continues to boost the range of products and services it is able to offer its customers. In July 2006 it launched a new education supplies business, targeting schools and tertiary institutions. It has completed a major cost-cutting project, with annual savings of $1.8 million expected from 2007.

CXP Year to 31 December	2004	2005
Revenues ($mn)	982.6	1115.2
EBIT ($mn)	88.7	95.4
EBIT margin (%)	9.0	8.6
Gross margin (%)	26.4	25.3
Profit before tax ($mn)	88.7	94.8
Profit after tax ($mn)	61.7	66.0
Earnings per share (¢)	32.2	35.3
Cash flow per share (¢)	37.6	42.5
Dividend (¢)	15	18
Percentage franked	100	100
Interest cover (times)	–	167.7
Return on equity (%)	33.0	32.5
Half year to 30 June	**2005**	**2006**
Revenues ($mn)	537.2	574.2
Profit before tax ($mn)	46.0	46.3
Profit after tax ($mn)	32.0	32.5
Earnings per share (¢)	17.2	17.7
Dividend (¢)	8.5	9
Percentage franked	100	100
Net tangible assets per share ($)	0.44	0.53
Debt-to-equity ratio (%)	7.9	14.7
Current ratio	1.2	1.3

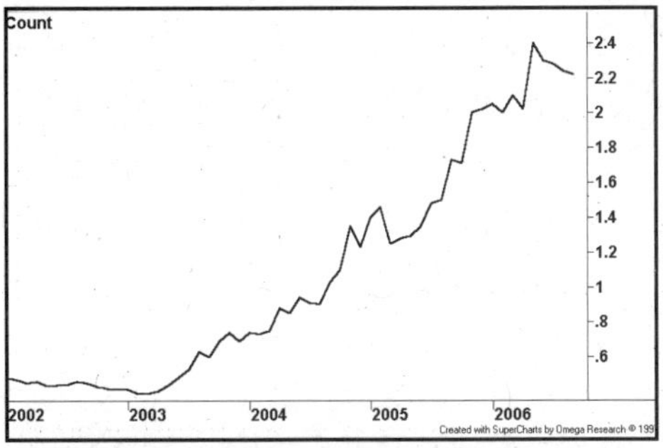

www.count.com.au

COUNT FINANCIAL LIMITED

Share price ($)	2.18
12-month high ($)	2.50
12-month low ($)	1.50
Market capitalisation ($mn)	516.3
Price-to-NTA-per-share ratio	21.8
5-year share price return (% p.a.)	45.0

Sector: Financials	Company	Sector
Price-earnings ratio (times)	28.7	15.7
Dividend yield (%)	2.8	4.3

Sydney-based financial services specialist Count Financial was established in 1980, and has since grown into Australia's largest independently owned network of financial planning accountants and advisers. It consists of a franchise network of around 460 mainly accountancy practices, employing some 890 licensed representatives. It provides accounting and financial planning services and holds investment funds under management.

Latest business results (June 2006, full year)

The company reported another excellent result, boosted by strong investment markets. Fees and commission income rose 15% to $14.1 million, reflecting growth in insurance and lending activity. Asset-based income jumped 46% to $19.9 million (reduced to a 36% rise after the figures are normalised to reflect changes in allocation). Despite fast-rising revenues, expenses actually fell 2%, further bolstering profits. At year-end, loans outstanding totalled $2.21 billion, which was a rise of 33%, and other retail investments were up 24% to $5.75 billion. Altogether, funds and loans under advice totalled more than $13 billion.

Outlook

With growing numbers of baby boomers worried about their retirement and superannuation, the Australian financial planning industry continues to flourish, and Count is a leading beneficiary. It also benefits from continuing modifications to the country's complex superannuation legislation. Its three-pronged strategy for maintaining growth involves boosting the number of franchisees, boosting their productivity – particularly through the introduction of new computer systems – and adding new services, and its initial expectations are for a strong June 2007 result, although it has conceded it may struggle to achieve its target of 25% EPS growth. Count plans a major new initiative with the launch of countplus, a company that will buy and consolidate the businesses of existing franchisees and other accountants who are seeking to retire and sell their practices. Payment to buy the businesses will be a mixture of cash and equity, and Count plans to list countplus on the ASX, which could deliver it a substantial profit. However, there are risks involved, as evidenced by the failure of some earlier efforts at accountancy practice consolidation, and there will be competition from WHK, which has been the most successful consolidator.

COU Year to 30 June	2005	2006
Revenues ($mn)	83.5	104.8
EBIT ($mn)	16.2	24.6
EBIT margin (%)	19.4	23.5
Profit before tax ($mn)	16.6	25.6
Profit after tax ($mn)	11.5	17.6
Earnings per share (¢)	5.1	7.6
Cash flow per share (¢)	5.4	7.9
Dividend (¢)	4.5	6
Percentage franked	100	100
Net tangible assets per share ($)	0.07	0.10
Interest cover (times)	–	–
Return on equity (%)	80.0	86.2
Debt-to-equity ratio (%)	–	–
Current ratio	1.7	2.0

CRANE GROUP LIMITED

Share price ($)	11.08	
12-month high ($)	13.83	
12-month low ($)	9.45	
Market capitalisation ($mn)	659.6	
Price-to-NTA-per-share ratio	2.9	
5-year share price return (% p.a.)	18.7	
Sector: Industrials	**Company**	**Sector**
Price-earnings ratio (times)	15.4	13.6
Dividend yield (%)	5.4	4.3

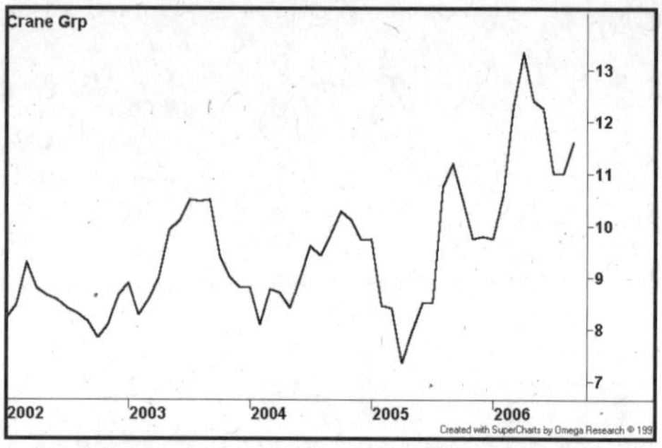

www.crane.com.au

Sydney-based Crane, founded in 1867, is a top manufacturer and distributor of non-ferrous metal products and plumbing supplies. Its Tradelink division is one of Australia's largest distributors of plumbing supplies, with 192 outlets, and its CDNZ division is a prominent New Zealand plumbing and electrical supplies distribution business. It also operates Iplex Pipelines, a leading manufacturer of plastic pipeline systems, while its Austral Wright Metals business imports and distributes a range of specialty metals. Crane exports non-ferrous metal products to over 50 countries.

Latest business results (June 2006, full year)

Profits rose modestly as Crane continued restructuring its operations. Sales from continuing businesses rose just 2%, dented by a slowdown in residential construction, by metal price increases, and by a weakening of the New Zealand dollar. The company also reported an after-tax-profit of $26.8 million – treated as a significant item – that included the sale of its aluminium business. The Tradelink division was hurt by a significant construction slowdown in New South Wales, and EBIT fell 9%. Iplex too saw profits down, due to a change in the customer mix. CDNZ enjoyed a good year, with profits up 4% in New Zealand dollars, though down slightly in Australian currency. A new range of copper and brass products helped lift the metals division profit by 3%.

Outlook

Crane's big corporate restructuring is aimed at boosting long-term profitability. The company has sold underperforming businesses, decommissioned obsolete technology and rehabilitated several sites. It sees great potential in the supply of infrastructure for water conservation projects in rural Australia, and has increased its shareholding in Iplex from 75% to 100%. Profit margins for this division are substantially higher than for most of Crane's other businesses. It plans to open 10 new Tradelink stores in the June 2007 year, and to upgrade and relocate others. Nevertheless, some 75% of Crane's sales are building sector–related, and the company's immediate outlook is quite dependent on trends in this market, as well as on movements in the price of raw materials. In addition, it could be hurt by a looming slowdown in the New Zealand economy.

CRG Year to 30 June	2005	2006
Revenues ($mn)	1902.7	1941.5
Tradelink (%)	31	33
Iplex (%)	24	26
Metals (%)	25	21
CDNZ (%)	20	20
EBIT ($mn)	95.4	91.7
EBIT margin (%)	5.0	4.7
Gross margin (%)	18.2	25.0
Profit before tax ($mn)	67.9	73.5
Profit after tax ($mn)	37.4	41.8
Earnings per share (¢)	66.8	71.9
Cash flow per share (¢)	138.8	137.7
Dividend (¢)	60	60
Percentage franked	100	100
Net tangible assets per share ($)	3.87	3.82
Interest cover (times)	3.5	5.0
Return on equity (%)	9.4	10.0
Debt-to-equity ratio (%)	51.2	41.2
Current ratio	1.9	1.6

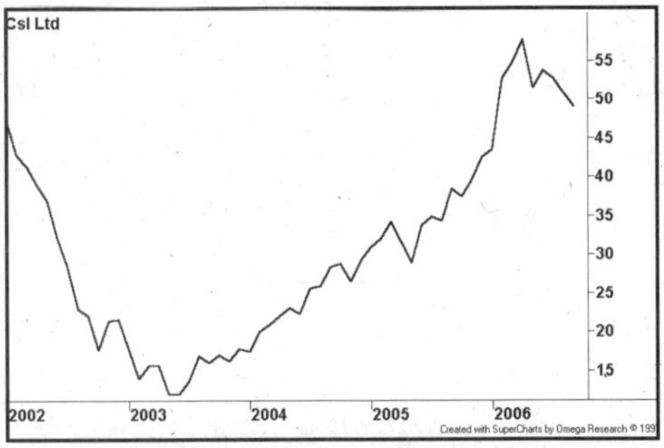

www.csl.com.au

CSL LIMITED

Share price ($)	51.34
12-month high ($)	59.39
12-month low ($)	34.35
Market capitalisation ($mn)	9284.3
Price-to-NTA-per-share ratio	8.0
5-year share price return (% p.a.)	4.2

Sector: Health care	Company	Sector
Price-earnings ratio (times)	26.6	31.1
Dividend yield (%)	1.3	1.8

Melbourne-based CSL, formerly the state-owned Commonwealth Serum Laboratories, was founded in 1916. It has grown through acquisition to become a global concern, with more than 80% of revenues deriving from outside Australia. Its principal business now is the provision of a range of plasma therapies and services through its CSL Behring division, which was formed from the acquisition of ZLB of Switzerland and the plasma assets of Aventis Behring of the US. Its CSL Biotherapies division (formerly called CSL Pharmaceuticals) is prominent in the development of a wide variety of vaccines. The CSL Bioplasma division works domestically in the plasma therapeutics business. CSL operates from major facilities in Australia, Europe and America. It has high market shares for many of its products, and exports to numerous countries.

Latest business results (June 2006, full year)

CSL reported excellent results, driven by CSL Behring, responsible for more than 85% of total company turnover. The division benefited from strength across its product portfolio, and in particular from growing demand in the US for intravenous immunoglobulin. The division also benefited significantly from synergies that resulted from the restructuring of its operations undertaken by CSL after the merger of the ZLB and the Aventis Behring businesses. The much smaller CSL Biotherapies division saw modest sales growth, thanks to growing demand for flu vaccine. But policy changes by the Australian government led to a decline in sales for CSL Bioplasma. In addition to the reported results, there was a significant item of a US$250 million performance-based payment related to the Aventis Behring acquisition.

Outlook

CSL has strategies in place for continuing growth, and it is forecasting that revenues will be up about 6% in the June 2007 year, with EPS growth of 15% to 20%. Of particular interest is the company's cervical cancer vaccine Gardasil, the first of its kind in the world. It received US Food and Drug Administration approval in June 2006, and some analysts have suggested it could become a multi-billion dollar drug. As a global leader in flu vaccines, the company is doubling its production capacity with the intention of entering the US market.

CSL Year to 30 June	2005	2006
Revenues ($mn)	2749.9	2848.9
EBIT ($mn)	432.2	515.0
EBIT margin (%)	15.7	18.1
Gross margin (%)	37.7	40.2
Profit before tax ($mn)	410.3	499.0
Profit after tax ($mn)	234.7	350.9
Earnings per share (¢)	119.8	192.8
Cash flow per share (¢)	183.6	256.5
Dividend (¢)	47	68
Percentage franked	100	0
Net tangible assets per share ($)	7.02	6.43
Interest cover (times)	19.8	32.1
Return on equity (%)	11.2	17.1
Debt-to-equity ratio (%)	13.6	15.3
Current ratio	4.2	2.3

CSR LIMITED

Share price ($)	3.23
12-month high ($)	4.58
12-month low ($)	2.66
Market capitalisation ($mn)	2951.0
Price-to-NTA-per-share ratio	3.2
5-year share price return (% p.a.)	20.0

Sector: Industrials	Company	Sector
Price-earnings ratio (times)	11.8	13.6
Dividend yield (%)	4.6	4.3

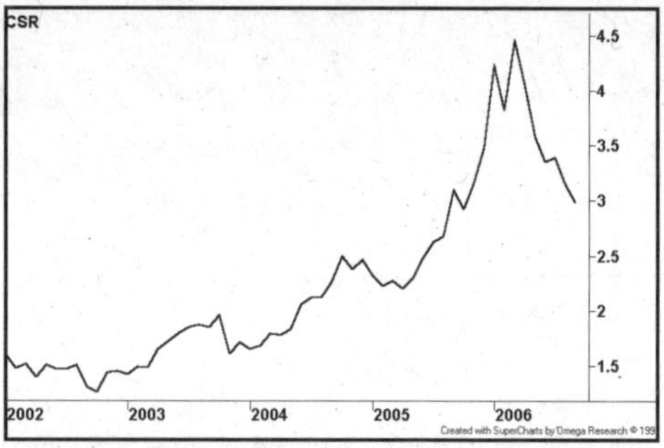

www.csr.com.au

CSR, founded in 1855 as a sugar refiner, now operates principally in three industries: it is one of the world's leading sugar producers; it makes building products, such as bricks, pavers, plasterboard and roofing tiles; and it owns 70% of Gove Aluminium Finance, which holds more than a third of the equity of NSW's Tomago Aluminium Smelter, responsible for the production of about a quarter of Australia's aluminium output. It is also building a property development business.

Latest business results (March 2006, full year)

The continuing recovery in world sugar prices offset a building products slowdown to boost total sales and profits. The company received an average of $316 a tonne for its sugar, up from $255 in the previous year, and sugar revenues jumped 42%, with profits up 27%. Productivity improvements helped boost the sugarcane crop by nearly 3% to a record 15.4 million tonnes. Higher world prices and increased volumes boosted aluminium revenues and profits by 10%. Building product revenues rose by nearly 5%, thanks especially to new product introductions, but a sharp downturn in residential construction in NSW and Queensland hurt profits, which were down 9%. The company took a further one-off $21 million hit from the closure of two manufacturing plants. Property EBIT leapt nearly three times to $76 million, largely due to the sale of industrial land at Erskine Park in Sydney.

CSR Year to 31 March	2005	2006
Revenues ($mn)	2398.2	2946.1
Building products (%)	38	32
Sugar – milling (%)	26	25
Sugar – ethanol & refining (%)	13	20
Aluminium (%)	19	17
EBIT ($mn)	358.6	416.8
EBIT margin (%)	15.0	14.1
Gross margin (%)	28.1	27.4
Profit before tax ($mn)	320.3	366.0
Profit after tax ($mn)	214.0	249.8
Earnings per share (¢)	23.4	27.4
Cash flow per share (¢)	34.7	40.2
Dividend (¢)	12	15
Percentage franked	100	100
Net tangible assets per share ($)	1.19	1.01
Interest cover (times)	9.4	8.2
Return on equity (%)	19.4	23.7
Debt-to-equity ratio (%)	21.5	51.9
Current ratio	1.6	1.4

Outlook

CSR is concerned that sugar prices have fallen by around 25% since July 2006, which will have an impact on year-end profits. However, much also depends on the size of the crop, with heavy rains and disease both posing a threat. The company has said that aluminium profits could be down by around 15%, even if world prices remain strong, because of hedging at lower levels carried out in previous years. CSR also believes that building product profits could fall again, with a recovery in the residential construction sector unlikely before 2007. Sales of residential lots from the company's development at Ferntree Gully in Melbourne are beginning during 2006, but property returns are likely to fall below the high levels of March 2006.

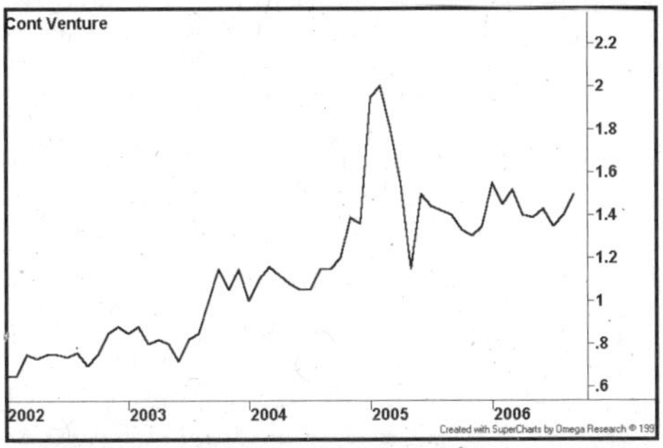

www.cvc.com.au

CVC LIMITED

Share price ($)	1.47	
12-month high ($)	1.65	
12-month low ($)	1.25	
Market capitalisation ($mn)	176.0	
Price-to-NTA-per-share ratio	1.1	
5-year share price return (% p.a.)	20.5	
Sector: Financials	**Company**	**Sector**
Price-earnings ratio (times)	7.9	15.7
Dividend yield (%)	4.1	4.3

Sydney finance company CVC was founded in 1984 as Continental Venture Capital. It provides venture capital to new businesses. It also seeks investment opportunities in profitable, high-growth companies, and typically invests between $1 million and $5 million, then works with company managers in developing the business. Through its investment company CVC Sustainable Investments and its CVC Renewable Energy Equity Fund it has a particular interest in environmentally friendly ventures. In addition, it assists management buyouts of companies, and it is also involved in property development.

Latest business results (June 2006, full year)

CVC's profits are heavily influenced by the timing of asset sales, and fell in the June 2006 year, after a big increase in the previous year. The main contribution was a $16.5 million profit from the sale of shares in Stargames Limited. A further $4.5 million came from dividends provided by listed companies in which CVC held an equity stake. The other main source of profit was CVC's property business, principally the Fern Bay residential property development north of Newcastle, NSW. The funds management business recorded a strong increase in profit, thanks to the increase in the net asset value of CVC's portfolios, and private equity profits also rose.

Outlook

Because of timing issues it is difficult to forecast whether profits will rise or fall in any particular financial year. Nevertheless, CVC has been steadily building its recurrent earnings base and the long-term outlook appears favourable. Its Fern Bay development, in which it holds a 50% stake, has the scope to provide a significant revenue stream over many years, with strong sales already evident. In August 2006 permission was obtained to develop 950 lots at Fern Bay, compared to the original plan of just 200 lots. CVC has a 45% interest in another project, to develop a bulky goods retail centre in Belrose, NSW, by December 2007. It expects a public listing late in 2006 of one of its investments, the functional food and natural health supplement maker Probiotec, which should realise a good profit. It plans to launch new managed funds, with the first of these expected to be a listed property fund.

CVC Year to 30 June	2005	2006
Revenues ($mn)	57.6	35.1
EBIT ($mn)	30.7	25.3
EBIT margin (%)	53.3	72.0
Profit before tax ($mn)	33.5	30.3
Profit after tax ($mn)	24.0	23.3
Earnings per share (¢)	21.0	18.7
Cash flow per share (¢)	21.3	18.8
Dividend (¢)	5	6
Percentage franked	100	100
Net tangible assets per share ($)	1.15	1.35
Interest cover (times)	–	–
Return on equity (%)	20.3	14.4
Debt-to-equity ratio (%)	–	–
Current ratio	36.6	5.7

DAVID JONES LIMITED

Share price ($)	3.59	
12-month high ($)	3.62	
12-month low ($)	2.15	
Market capitalisation ($mn)	1541.6	
Price-to-NTA-per-share ratio	4.6	
5-year share price return (% p.a.)	31.4	
Sector: Consumer discretionary	**Company**	**Sector**
Price-earnings ratio (times)	19.2	18.8
Dividend yield (%)	4.5	4.0

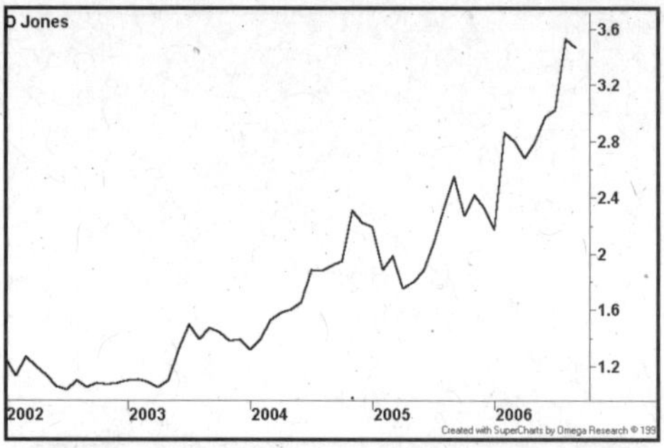

www.davidjones.com.au

Sydney-based retailer David Jones dates back to 1838 and the opening of the David Jones & Company general store in Sydney. It is Australia's oldest department store chain, and claims to be the oldest in the world still trading under its original name. It operates 37 stores, with representation in every state and in the ACT.

Latest business results (July 2006, full year)

David Jones reported an excellent result, with restructuring and cost-cutting measures leading to strong growth in profits, despite just a modest increase in sales. There was particularly strong expansion in the second half, with 4.4% sales growth translating into a 50% boost to profits. The company experienced a strong performance in apparel, footwear, accessories, cosmetics, homewares and home entertainment, with growth across all regions, including a particularly strong result from Western Australia. The company's high-margin credit card business continued to grow, with EBIT up 6.4%.

Outlook

The reorganisation efforts of David Jones over several years are yielding impressive results, and the company forecasts further profit growth, of 5% to 10%, for both its July 2007 and July 2008 years. The restructuring has involved store upgrades, the abandonment of some ancillary businesses and a tight focus on a portfolio of successful brands, along with a major IT centralisation project, enhanced inventory control systems and new promotional campaigns. There will be an additional benefit as the company re-acquires – as of 29 September 2006 – its flagship Sydney and Melbourne CBD stores, meaning the end of expensive rental payments. It continues to expand, and has entered into an agreement with Westfield Management to open new David Jones stores in the Burwood, Chermside and Doncaster shopping centres. It is also adding a number of exclusive brands, including Tigerlily, Simone Perele, Sara, Luxaflex and Mambo, and Country Road is to launch retail outlets at all David Jones stores, after an absence of three years. Nevertheless, the company remains vulnerable to rising interest rates, higher petrol prices and the possibility of a downturn in consumer spending. Coles Myer's mid-2006 sale of its Myer department store chain to private investors also raises the possibility of intensified competition.

DJS Year to 29 July*	2005	2006
Revenues ($mn)	1800.8	1821.6
EBIT ($mn)	119.7	146.1
EBIT margin (%)	6.6	8.0
Gross margin (%)	38.4	38.8
Profit before tax ($mn)	98.1	121.5
Profit after tax ($mn)	68.0	81.1
Earnings per share (¢)	16.2	18.7
Cash flow per share (¢)	24.0	25.4
Dividend (¢)	13	16
Percentage franked	100	100
Net tangible assets per share ($)	0.84	0.78
Interest cover (times)	5.5	5.9
Return on equity (%)	16.5	22.2
Debt-to-equity ratio (%)	58.4	60.8
Current ratio	1.3	1.2

* 30 July 2005

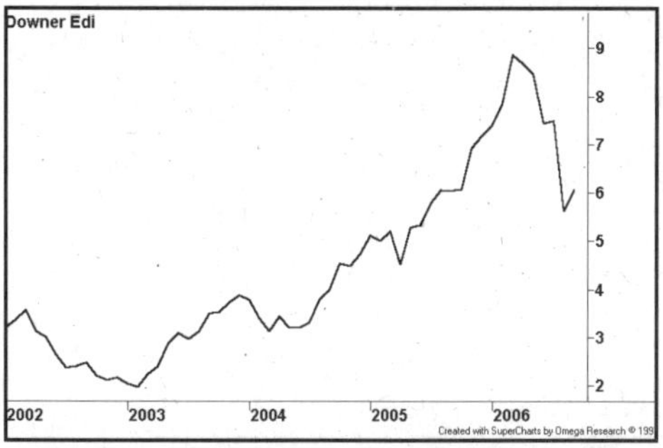

www.downeredi.com.au

DOWNER EDI LIMITED

Share price ($)	5.47
12-month high ($)	9.45
12-month low ($)	4.91
Market capitalisation ($mn)	1696.5
Price-to-NTA-per-share ratio	4.2
5-year share price return (% p.a.)	23.3

Sector: Industrials	Company	Sector
Price-earnings ratio (times)	11.8	13.6
Dividend yield (%)	3.7	4.3

Sydney-based Downer EDI – Australia's second-largest listed engineering, infrastructure and resource services company, after Leighton Holdings – has grown through a long series of mergers in Australia and New Zealand. It provides design, project and facilities management, operations and maintenance services to the public and private power, rail, road, telecommunications, mining, mineral processing, resources, capital works and process engineering sectors in Australia, New Zealand, Asia and the Pacific. It operates through five broad divisions: Works Infrastructure, Downer Engineering, Roche Mining, Century Resources and EDI Rail.

Latest business results (June 2006, full year)

Downer EDI reported another good year for its regular operating activities. However, the result was overshadowed by a $199 million one-off after-tax loss, mainly from its Douglas Mineral Sands project, treated in this book as a significant item. One of the best results came from the rail division, where EBIT grew 39% despite a dip in revenues, reflecting a change in the business mix to more service and maintenance work and less manufacturing. Though a relatively small part of the company's business, its rail division provides the highest margins. The infrastructure division was also strong, with revenues up 24% and EBIT ahead 24%, thanks to acquisitions and firm organic growth. Engineering saw revenues up 25%, but EBIT grew by only 18%, due to a growing percentage of lower margin electrical business. Mining and resources recorded growth, excluding the big Douglas Mineral Sands loss, but it was held back by the impact of construction contract disputes.

Outlook

Downer EDI is a major beneficiary of a wave of infrastructure spending in Australia and in some other countries. However, it has not been able to take full advantage of the resources boom, due to contractual disputes, and it is moving to introduce a greater proportion of alliance-style contracts, which allow for the recovery of rising costs. Downer EDI believes the dispute concerning design and plant installation for the Douglas Mineral Sands project could take well over a year to resolve. However, with an order book of approximately $7 billion, the company is forecasting June 2007 revenues of $5.2 billion and an after-tax profit of $155 million.

DOW Year to 30 June	2005	2006
Revenues ($mn)	3724.9	4619.2
Mining & resources (%)	34	35
Engineering (%)	33	35
Infrastructure services (%)	23	23
Rail (%)	10	7
EBIT ($mn)	187.7	233.9
EBIT margin (%)	5.0	5.1
Profit before tax ($mn)	148.8	182.8
Profit after tax ($mn)	129.3	137.8
Earnings per share (¢)	43.0	46.3
Cash flow per share (¢)	76.6	82.7
Dividend (¢)	18	20
Percentage franked	63	42
Net tangible assets per share ($)	1.83	1.30
Interest cover (times)	4.8	4.6
Return on equity (%)	15.0	14.9
Debt-to-equity ratio (%)	37.8	49.7
Current ratio	1.5	1.2

FAIRFAX (JOHN) HOLDINGS LIMITED

Share price ($)	4.00	
12-month high ($)	4.69	
12-month low ($)	3.55	
Market capitalisation ($mn)	3990.6	
Price-to-NTA-per-share ratio	na	
5-year share price return (% p.a.)	10.3	
Sector: Consumer discretionary	**Company**	**Sector**
Price-earnings ratio (times)	15.9	18.8
Dividend yield (%)	4.9	4.0

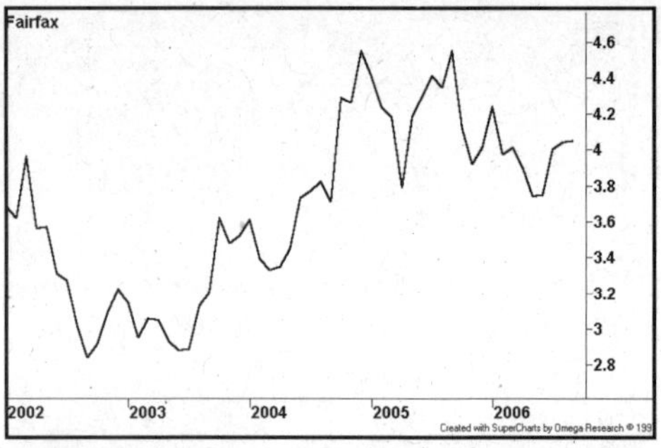

www.fxj.com.au

John Fairfax Holdings is one of Australia's leading media companies. It publishes *The Sydney Morning Herald*, Melbourne's *The Age*, *The Australian Financial Review* and *BRW* magazine, as well as local and specialist newspapers and magazines. It also provides a range of online services through its Fairfax Digital and Trade Me subsidiaries. It operates New Zealand's largest publishing business, including a string of metropolitan and regional newspapers and many magazine titles. Fairfax also owns 43% of AAP Information Services.

Latest business results (June 2006, full year)

Revenues were up but profits fell as the company's Australian publications were hit by weaker advertising markets, particularly in NSW and Victoria, and despite a rise in newspaper subscription levels. However, the company's Australian regional newspapers and its business publications were strong. The Fairfax Digital operation achieved excellent growth, with revenues up 76% to $96.4 million and profits at the EBITDA level surging from $6.6 million in the June 2005 year to $24.3 million. New Zealand business – 28% of company turnover, but around 40% of total earnings – saw small gains in revenues and profit.

Outlook

The publishing business has high fixed costs, and profits are greatly affected by economic conditions. Small increases in advertising and circulation can translate into a big rise in profits, and the reverse is also true. With economic growth slowing in New Zealand and possibly also in Australia the company is vulnerable. It has been achieving some good circulation growth for many of its titles, but the long-term outlook for newspapers is not rosy. Its business publications remain strong, with good profitability. It is seeing excellent growth for its digital businesses, but they remain a relatively tiny part of company business. In April 2006 Fairfax acquired the leading New Zealand online classifieds site Trade Me for NZ$700 million, and it believes this has huge potential. Fairfax shares have been supported by speculation that the company could become a takeover target as media regulations are changed in Australia. There has also been speculation that the company could be acquired by a private equity group and broken up.

FXJ Year to 30 June	2005	2006
Revenues ($mn)	1872.3	1906.8
EBIT ($mn)	427.3	425.5
EBIT margin (%)	22.8	22.3
Profit before tax ($mn)	350.7	328.3
Profit after tax ($mn)	256.2	234.3
Earnings per share (¢)	27.9	25.2
Cash flow per share (¢)	36.6	33.7
Dividend (¢)	18.5	19.5
Percentage franked	100	100
Net tangible assets per share ($)	–	–
Interest cover (times)	5.6	4.4
Return on equity (%)	12.1	10.9
Debt-to-equity ratio (%)	42.2	68.1
Current ratio	1.0	0.4

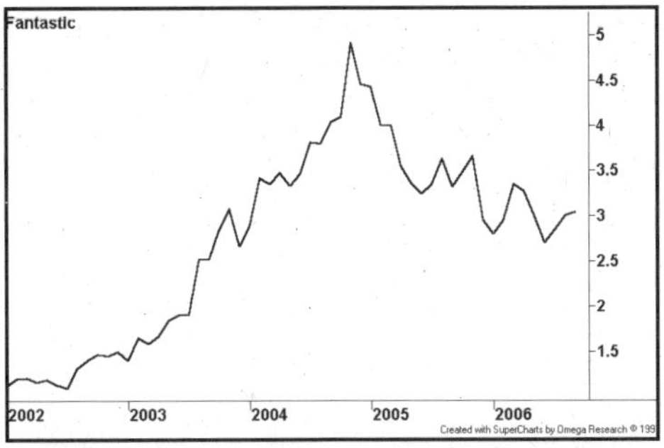

www.fantasticfurniture.com.au

FANTASTIC HOLDINGS LIMITED

Share price ($)	3.03
12-month high ($)	3.70
12-month low ($)	2.60
Market capitalisation ($mn)	286.3
Price-to-NTA-per-share ratio	6.7
5-year share price return (% p.a.)	26.1

Sector: Consumer discretionary	Company	Sector
Price-earnings ratio (times)	19.2	18.8
Dividend yield (%)	3.6	4.0

Sydney-based furniture manufacturer and retailer Fantastic Holdings evolved from a struggling furniture chain that was acquired in 1996 by a group of partners, including managing director Julian Tertini, who earlier had helped launch Freedom Furniture. Today, Fantastic is one of Australia's leading budget furniture chains, operating nationwide apart from Western Australia and the Northern Territory. It has a total of 52 company-owned and franchised Fantastic Furniture stores and 19 Plush leather goods stores. In July 2006 it launched its first Original Mattress Factory store.

Latest business results (June 2006, full year)

Sales rose, thanks to the opening of 11 new stores during the year, but profits fell for the first time since the company's listing on the ASX in 1999. Comparable store sales declined by 2%, with rising interest rates, the housing downturn and higher petrol prices cited as negative factors. Business generally held up well for the budget-level Fantastic Furniture stores. However, the Plush stores, which are aimed at a more upmarket clientele, did not perform well.

Outlook

Fantastic has achieved great success in the budget furniture sector through a policy of careful planning and strict cost containment. It sees the current downturn in its business as part of a cycle, and is continuing to invest for future growth. It has constructed a new purpose-built factory/warehouse in Sydney aimed at enhancing logistics and boosting productivity, and it relocates there in October 2006. It is also moving its support office to new and improved premises and has introduced a new computer system for its Plush business. It plans to open six new Fantastic Furniture stores during the June 2007 year. Looking to the longer term, its target is to be operating in all states and territories, with 92 Fantastic Furniture stores and 40 Plush stores. It is also considering expansion to New Zealand. In July 2006 it acquired a medium-sized mattress manufacturer and has opened a trial mattress store in Sydney, billed as a factory-direct store. It is smaller than typical bedding stores, and if successful the company believes it can quickly launch similar stores faster and at lower cost than Fantastic or Plush stores.

FAN Year to 30 June	2005	2006
Revenues ($mn)	221.0	233.8
EBIT ($mn)	25.0	20.3
EBIT margin (%)	11.3	8.7
Gross margin (%)	41.6	41.2
Profit before tax ($mn)	25.0	20.7
Profit after tax ($mn)	17.4	14.4
Earnings per share (¢)	20.9	15.8
Cash flow per share (¢)	22.8	17.8
Dividend (¢)	11	11.02
Percentage franked	100	100
Net tangible assets per share ($)	0.44	0.45
Interest cover (times)	–	–
Return on equity (%)	48.1	33.9
Debt-to-equity ratio (%)	–	–
Current ratio	2.2	2.2

FLEETWOOD CORPORATION LIMITED

Share price ($)	6.85	
12-month high ($)	7.82	
12-month low ($)	6.04	
Market capitalisation ($mn)	334.8	
Price-to-NTA-per-share ratio	4.2	
5-year share price return (% p.a.)	44.2	
Sector: Consumer discretionary	**Company**	**Sector**
Price-earnings ratio (times)	15.6	18.8
Dividend yield (%)	3.0	4.0

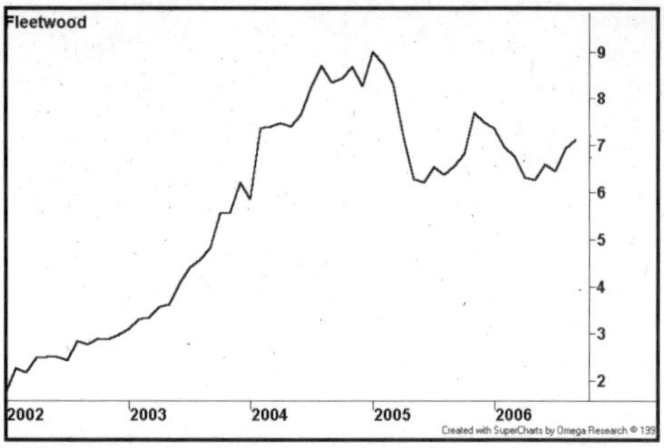

www.fleetwood.com.au

West Australian company Fleetwood, established in 1964, is a leader in the caravan, recreational vehicle and portable accommodation businesses. Its Perth-based Coromal Caravans division is the second-largest caravan manufacturer in Australia and its Melbourne-based Windsor Caravans business is the fourth-largest. Its Camec Group is Australia's largest caravan spare parts and accessories manufacturer and retailer, and Flexiglass Challenge is Australia's largest manufacturer of canopies for utility vehicles. Fleetwood is also a prominent manufacturer of park homes and portable accommodation, for recreational and commercial use, with operations in Western Australia and Victoria.

Latest business results (June 2006, full year)

Revenues edged down, but profits rose, as Fleetwood started to realise the benefits of a big restructuring of its operations. The recreational vehicle business saw sales up 1%, with EBIT rising 2%, affected by tight labour conditions. Both the Camec and the Flexiglass Challenge operations achieved record results. The manufactured accommodation division was influenced by relocations to new premises in both Perth and Melbourne, and sales fell 11%. However, strong demand and enhanced productivity meant that EBIT for the division jumped 24%.

Outlook

With its restructuring program now completed, Fleetwood has the capacity for considerable growth over an extended period, and the long-term outlook remains positive. Most caravan purchasers are aged over 55, and Fleetwood is a big beneficiary of this growing demographic. However, a tight labour market, particularly in Western Australia, remains a negative, leading to high staff turnover and staff shortages, although Fleetwood reported in September 2006 that conditions seemed to be improving. Both the Coromal and Windsor caravan businesses have expanded their manufacturing facilities, and orders have been running at record levels. The Camec business has relocated its Sydney operations to a new warehouse-style facility. The manufactured accommodation division has the potential for strong growth, following its relocation to larger, purpose-built facilities in Perth and Melbourne. Demand from both the resources and the retirement sectors remains high, and production has reached record levels.

FWD Year to 30 June	2005	2006
Revenues ($mn)	261.8	252.4
Recreational vehicles (%)	64	66
Manufactured accommodation (%)	36	33
EBIT ($mn)	27.3	31.0
EBIT margin (%)	10.4	12.3
Gross margin (%)	20.9	24.9
Profit before tax ($mn)	26.4	29.4
Profit after tax ($mn)	18.7	20.7
Earnings per share (¢)	40.5	43.9
Cash flow per share (¢)	53.4	60.1
Dividend (¢)	20	20.5
Percentage franked	100	100
Net tangible assets per share ($)	1.67	1.64
Interest cover (times)	30.5	19.4
Return on equity (%)	18.4	19.1
Debt-to-equity ratio (%)	17.4	20.3
Current ratio	1.2	1.2

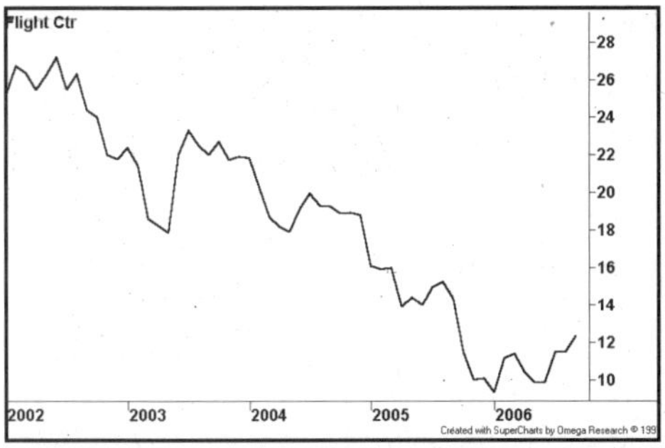

www.flightcentre.com.au

FLIGHT CENTRE LIMITED

Share price ($)	12.50
12-month high ($)	15.60
12-month low ($)	9.06
Market capitalisation ($mn)	1136.5
Price-to-NTA-per-share ratio	5.5
5-year share price return (% p.a.)	–4.6

Sector: Consumer discretionary	Company	Sector
Price-earnings ratio (times)	14.8	18.8
Dividend yield (%)	4.2	4.0

Brisbane-based Flight Centre is the largest independent retail travel agency in Australia and New Zealand, and has an estimated 20% market share. It operates under various brands, including Escape Travel, Student Flights, Travel Associates, Overseas Working Holidays, FCm Travel Solutions and Infinity Holidays, as well as some online brands. It has expanded to South Africa, Britain, Canada and the US, with a total of some 1600 sales outlets, and it is building a presence in Asia.

Latest business results (June 2006, full year)

Profits bounced back after the decline – Flight Centre's first ever – of the previous year, but only modestly, with a strong second half offsetting first-half weakness. The Australian leisure sector, the company's biggest profit generator, was hurt by the decision of some airlines to levy fuel surcharges from which the retailer does not receive a margin. There was significant growth from the FCm Travel Solutions corporate travel business, in just its second year of operations. The company's small South African unit enjoyed particularly strong growth and North American operations delivered a good result on the corporate travel side. However, New Zealand and Britain were disappointing.

Outlook

Flight Centre's stellar growth of its early years has come to a halt, as the airlines increasingly move to undertake direct ticket sales on the internet, rather than selling through agents. This has heavily dented the agents' sales, and reduced the margins on those sales that remain. In response, Flight Centre is striving to cut costs, to boost its corporate travel business and to expand overseas. Its new FCm Travel Solutions network is achieving excellent growth, and is now represented in 50 countries. Flight Centre predicts that within five years it will be contributing at least half the company's profit. The company also believes much future growth will come from Asia. Its small Indian operation saw business double in the June 2006 year, and the even smaller China/Hong Kong unit achieved double-digit sales growth. Flight Centre is boosting its already-strong internet presence, including the introduction of internet terminals in its stores to allow store customers to do their own research and make bookings.

FLT Year to 30 June	2005	2006
Revenues ($mn)	871.1	973.7
EBIT ($mn)	106.3	111.1
EBIT margin (%)	12.2	11.4
Profit before tax ($mn)	115.6	120.0
Profit after tax ($mn)	76.9	79.9
Earnings per share (¢)	81.4	84.6
Cash flow per share (¢)	115.5	123.2
Dividend (¢)	50.5	52
Percentage franked	100	100
Net tangible assets per share ($)	2.19	2.27
Interest cover (times)	–	–
Return on equity (%)	19.3	20.4
Debt-to-equity ratio (%)	–	–
Current ratio	1.3	1.4

GAZAL CORPORATION LIMITED

Share price ($)	2.55	
12-month high ($)	3.14	
12-month low ($)	1.99	
Market capitalisation ($mn)	157.3	
Price-to-NTA-per-share ratio	4.3	
5-year share price return (% p.a.)	11.4	
Sector: Consumer discretionary	**Company**	**Sector**
Price-earnings ratio (times)	13.6	18.8
Dividend yield (%)	5.5	4.0

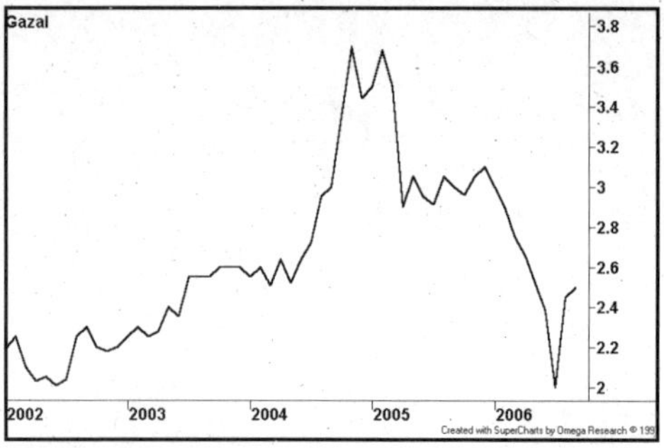

www.gazal.com.au

Sydney-based Gazal, founded in 1958, is one of Australia's largest publicly listed clothing companies, specialising mainly in business shirts, men's casual wear and surfwear, ladies' intimate apparel and school wear. It owns the Mambo label, and in Australia it is a licence holder for such brands as Calvin Klein, Trent Nathan, Nautica, Kenneth Cole, Van Heusen, Playboy, Lovable, Crystelle, Maui and Sons, Bisley, Midford, Oroton, Morrissey, Davenport and Kookai. It also makes house-brand merchandise for major retailers, operates some retail outlets and has some sales in Europe. The controlling Gazal family hold more than 60% of the shares.

Latest business results (June 2006, full year)

Booming domestic business helped the company post a strong increase in profits. Sales in Australia rose 12% with EBIT surging 47%. There were strong performances from the Van Heusen, Calvin Klein and Lovable brands, and the Bisley brand continued to achieve excellent growth in the workwear market segment. The company's Trade Secret and Brands United factory outlets recorded good business. However, the company also reported a $4 million loss from its Mambo business in Europe. As Mambo is moving from a company-owned operation to a licensing model, it is treated in the accounts as a discontinued business, and is separated from the results for continuing businesses.

Outlook

Gazal has been suffering from difficulties in promoting the iconic Mambo brand in Australia and Europe. Strong competition in the surfwear market has hurt domestic demand, and in Europe it has recorded a large trading loss. As a result, in August 2006 Gazal announced a five-year licensing agreement for the Mambo brand in Europe with Blacks Leisure Group, a prominent British outdoor and boardwear retailer. Among the company's other brands, Bisley workwear continues to grow strongly, recently winning one of the largest government uniform contracts in Australia, to supply New South Wales Health. It has also secured the uniform contract for St George Bank. Gazal is working to expand this business with the acquisition in November 2005 of the uniforms contracts division of Australian Defence Apparel and in March 2006 of Coronet Corporate, a uniform business serving mainly the hospitality industry.

GZL Year to 30 June	2005	2006
Revenues ($mn)	193.3	215.8
EBIT ($mn)	13.3	19.6
EBIT margin (%)	6.9	9.1
Gross margin (%)	49.9	50.7
Profit before tax ($mn)	11.1	16.8
Profit after tax ($mn)	7.3	11.5
Earnings per share (¢)	12.2	18.8
Cash flow per share (¢)	18.1	25.1
Dividend (¢)	16	14
Percentage franked	100	100
Net tangible assets per share ($)	0.68	0.59
Interest cover (times)	6.1	6.9
Return on equity (%)	9.1	16.7
Debt-to-equity ratio (%)	51.4	69.0
Current ratio	2.0	1.3

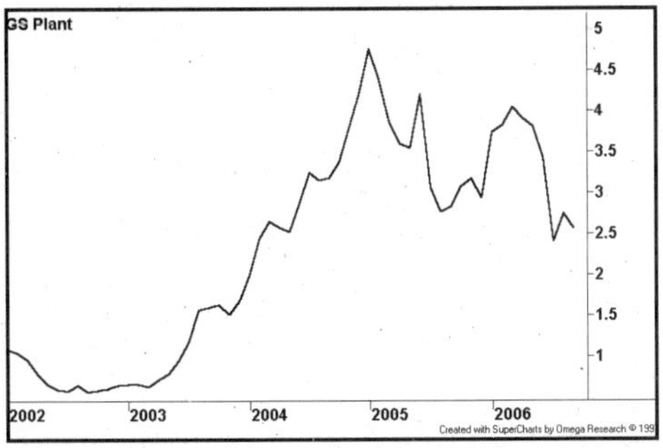

www.great-southern.com.au

GREAT SOUTHERN PLANTATIONS LIMITED

Share price ($)	2.74
12-month high ($)	4.20
12-month low ($)	2.24
Market capitalisation ($mn)	821.4
Price-to-NTA-per-share ratio	1.2
5-year share price return (% p.a.)	50.1

Sector: Materials	**Company**	**Sector**
Price-earnings ratio (times)	6.3	12.3
Dividend yield (%)	5.5	2.3

Perth-based Great Southern Plantations, founded in 1987, is an agribusiness investment manager providing investors with tax-effective investment products. It manages eucalypt plantations, mainly in Western Australia, Victoria and Queensland. It also manages a viticulture project in the Frankland River wine region of Western Australia, an organic olives project in the Preston Valley region of Western Australia, and a beef cattle project on King Island. Altogether, it manages funds of more than $1 billion for some 35 000 investors.

Latest business results (June 2006, full year)

Strong investor interest in most of Great Southern's new managed investment schemes led to a big increase in sales revenues. However, sharply rising operating costs meant the increase in profits was more subdued. The company had five projects on offer during the year – its two new forestry plantation projects generated sales of $314.3 million, its first beef cattle project raised $75.2 million, the organic olive project accounted for $48 million, and the wine grape project was below target at $19.4 million. (Not all sales were included in the June 2006 accounts.) Rising costs reflected the increased sales as well as heavy investments in new staff and infrastructure to support future growth. Great Southern has announced that it is changing its financial year end from 30 June to 30 September.

Outlook

Great Southern is a big beneficiary of investor interest in managed schemes targeting agriculture, and it continues to expand. Having achieved critical mass with the scale of its forestry projects, it is now working to develop a growing stream of non-forestry investment, and is realising strong investor interest in most of these. Non-forestry projects now represent more than 30% of company sales. In 2004 it announced its first hardwood woodchip contract, to export more than 500 000 tonnes of woodchip over three years to Nichimen in Japan, and in mid-2006 it announced a contract to supply up to 200 000 tonnes per year of blue gum logs for an innovative new timber plant being built in Western Australia by Lignor. Some concerns have been expressed that the government might cut back on the tax benefits of agribusiness investments.

GTP Year to 30 June	2005	2006
Revenues ($mn)	297.4	485.1
EBIT ($mn)	178.3	206.8
EBIT margin (%)	60.0	42.6
Profit before tax ($mn)	178.9	193.0
Profit after tax ($mn)	126.8	132.9
Earnings per share (¢)	48.0	43.8
Cash flow per share (¢)	48.5	45.7
Dividend (¢)	14	15
Percentage franked	100	100
Net tangible assets per share ($)	2.34	2.20
Interest cover (times)	–	15.0
Return on equity (%)	21.5	17.8
Debt-to-equity ratio (%)	2.2	16.0
Current ratio	1.0	1.0

GUD HOLDINGS LIMITED

Share price ($)	7.08	
12-month high ($)	8.70	
12-month low ($)	6.68	
Market capitalisation ($mn)	418.2	
Price-to-NTA-per-share ratio	3.7	
5-year share price return (% p.a.)	42.5	
Sector: Consumer discretionary	**Company**	**Sector**
Price-earnings ratio (times)	10.6	18.8
Dividend yield (%)	8.5	4.0

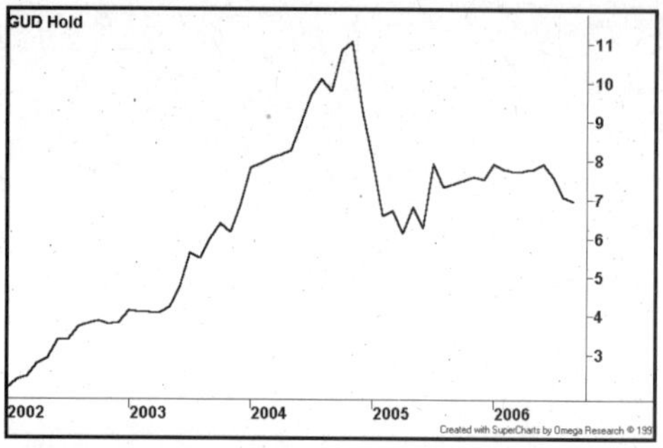

www.gud.com.au

GUD, based in Melbourne and founded in 1940, is a diversified manufacturer and distributor with six broad product lines: Sunbeam small electrical appliances; Victa lawnmowers; Oates cleaning products; Ryco, Wesfil and Goss automotive filtration and associated products; Davey water pumps, pump sets and water pressure systems; and Lock Focus security products and associated hardware. It exports to more than 50 countries.

Latest business results (June 2006, full year)

GUD achieved good sales growth, but the increase in profits was more modest, held back by increased competition and higher freight and raw material costs. The company was also hurt by a lower-than-expected contribution from its new Oates cleaning products business. The Victa lawnmower operation showed a good recovery, after the previous year's weakness, thanks to a strong market and moves to offshore sourcing. Sunbeam appliances remained strong, and a series of acquisitions helped the water products business deliver a 26% profit increase. The automotive division overcame rising raw material costs to record a slight rise in profits, but the security products business was hurt by a slowdown in construction activity and by sharp increases in zinc and brass prices, and profits tumbled 26%.

Outlook

GUD has warned that continuing raw material cost pressures and higher freight charges could lead to a profit decline in the 2007 financial year. It is also affected by a weak New Zealand dollar. In response, it is working to cut costs, introduce new products and make new bolt-on acquisitions. The offshore sourcing program for Victa lawnmowers has delivered higher margins, and the company expects further improvements during 2007. The Sunbeam brand remains strong in a competitive market, and GUD expects a positive contribution from new categories such as gas barbecues. The $30 million acquisition in mid-2006 of Monarch Pool Systems – a prominent swimming pool product manufacturer – should lead to strong growth for the company's water businesses, and GUD is seeking further expansion opportunities. The automotive products business is struggling to achieve growth, although the company has achieved success in lowering costs, and margins remain high.

GUD Year to 30 June	2005	2006
Revenues ($mn)	394.4	462.4
Consumer products (%)	55	61
Water products (%)	22	21
Automotive products (%)	20	15
EBIT ($mn)	60.2	63.6
EBIT margin (%)	15.3	13.8
Gross margin (%)	39.1	37.2
Profit before tax ($mn)	56.4	56.9
Profit after tax ($mn)	39.3	40.2
Earnings per share (¢)	64.9	67.1
Cash flow per share (¢)	78.5	86.5
Dividend (¢)	50	60
Percentage franked	100	100
Net tangible assets per share ($)	1.86	1.94
Interest cover (times)	15.6	9.5
Return on equity (%)	28.4	29.2
Debt-to-equity ratio (%)	28.0	38.2
Current ratio	1.9	1.7

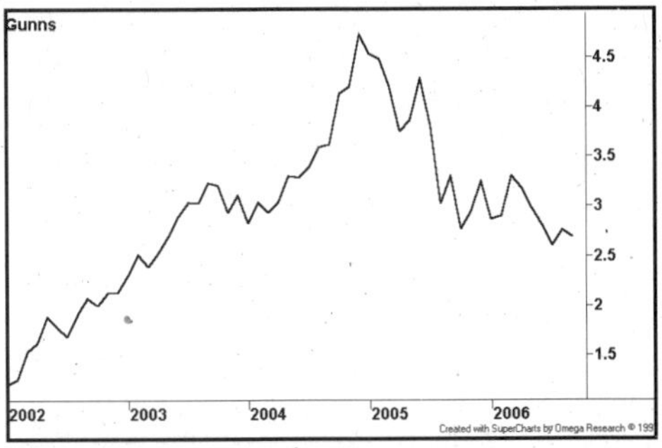

www.gunns.com.au

GUNNS LIMITED

Share price ($)	2.85
12-month high ($)	3.45
12-month low ($)	2.42
Market capitalisation ($mn)	949.5
Price-to-NTA-per-share ratio	1.3
5-year share price return (% p.a.)	28.4

Sector: Materials	Company	Sector
Price-earnings ratio (times)	11.1	12.3
Dividend yield (%)	5.6	2.3

Launceston timber company Gunns was founded in 1875, and claims to be one of Australia's oldest companies. It owns 175 000 hectares of land, manages over 90 000 hectares of plantations, and is Australia's largest hardwood producer, with five sawmills around Tasmania. It also maintains two veneer factories in Tasmania and one in New Zealand. It operates four woodchip export ports in Tasmania, and woodchip sales to Asian pulp mills are a major activity. Other businesses include six Gunns Mitre 10 hardware stores in Northern Tasmania, the building contracting company Hinman Wright and Manser, and Tamar Ridge Wines. The Gunns Plantations subsidiary offers managed investment products in timber plantations to the public.

Latest business results (June 2006, full year)

Revenues edged down and profits fell by double-digit amounts – the company's second straight profit decline – as forest product demand dropped. Forest product revenues were down 20% to $414 million, with EBIT tumbling 41%. The continuing relative strength of the Australian dollar hurt export business, while domestic timber markets, particularly in the eastern states, were highly competitive. The company was also hit by high fuel prices. By contrast, the managed investment business enjoyed an excellent year, with revenues surging 92% to $124 million and earnings more than doubling, thanks to a big expansion of activity under the company's woodlot program. Though only 20% of company turnover, this business contributed more than 40% of profit.

Outlook

Gunns continues to be hurt by a combination of weak Australian demand for forest products, a strong dollar and rising costs. Its own forecast is that domestic demand will remain subdued in early 2007, and though overseas demand is strong, export trends are much influenced by the currency. Gunns continues to assess opportunities for expansion in forestry-based operations outside Tasmania. However, its long-term future is heavily dependent on its planned $1.1 billion Bell Bay Pulp Mill, which it hopes could be operational in 2008, and which it believes could add more than $650 million to annual company revenues, with over $300 million in annual EBITDA (earnings before interest, tax, depreciation and amortisation). The company is also working to expand its managed investments portfolio.

GNS Year to 30 June	2005	2006
Revenues ($mn)	638.5	637.5
EBIT ($mn)	172.8	154.2
EBIT margin (%)	27.1	24.2
Gross margin (%)	15.8	6.1
Profit before tax ($mn)	143.4	123.6
Profit after tax ($mn)	100.3	87.2
Earnings per share (¢)	29.6	25.7
Cash flow per share (¢)	34.8	30.9
Dividend (¢)	12.5	16
Percentage franked	100	100
Net tangible assets per share ($)	1.69	2.15
Interest cover (times)	5.9	5.0
Return on equity (%)	19.7	13.3
Debt-to-equity ratio (%)	66.3	58.8
Current ratio	1.0	1.2

GWA INTERNATIONAL LIMITED

Share price ($)	3.09
12-month high ($)	3.50
12-month low ($)	2.73
Market capitalisation ($mn)	860.0
Price-to-NTA-per-share ratio	12.6
5-year share price return (% p.a.)	13.5

Sector: Industrials	Company	Sector
Price-earnings ratio (times)	14.3	13.6
Dividend yield (%)	5.8	4.3

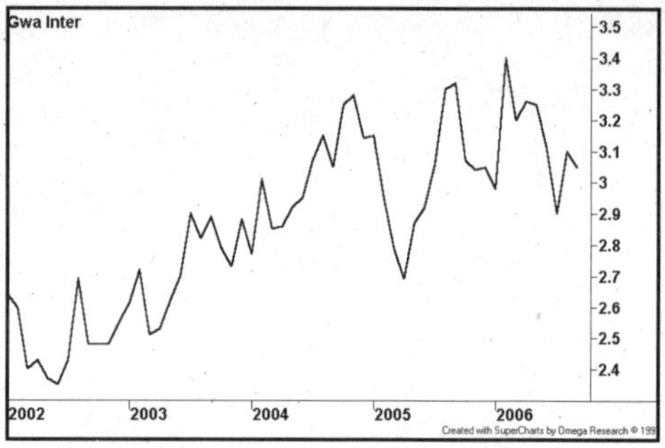

www.gwail.com.au

Brisbane-based GWA is a manufacturer of a wide range of household products, including 90% of Australia's toilets. Its Caroma division is a leading supplier of bathroom fittings, and has operations in Asia, Europe and America. The Sebel contract furniture business provides a wide range of commercial seating, and also operates in several countries. In addition, the company makes Rover lawnmowers, Dorf Clark tapware, Dux hot water systems and Gainsborough door fittings, and it owns the Wisa Beheer cistern producer in the Netherlands.

Latest business results (June 2006, full year)

The slowdown in home building and renovation, particularly in NSW, hit the company, and sales and profits were down, though with a modest recovery in the second half, following a poor first half. Another factor behind the decline in revenues was weak demand for Sebel furniture, particularly from the NSW education sector, and sluggish exports. Sales of most other products were roughly flat on the previous year. The door fittings business saw profits up, and sanitaryware and hot water systems both performed reasonably well. However, tapware profits were dented by the necessity to clear stocks in advance of new water efficiency labelling requirements, while cheap lawnmower imports hurt the Rover business. The company also reported one-off restructuring costs of $22 million, including the closure of its Penrith tapware and Coburg sanitaryware factories, largely offset by a $16 million gain from property sales.

GWT Year to 30 June	2005	2006
Revenues ($mn)	626.9	620.0
Building fixtures & fittings (%)	84	84
Commercial furniture (%)	10	9
EBIT ($mn)	103.4	95.2
EBIT margin (%)	16.5	15.4
Gross margin (%)	47.3	47.4
Profit before tax ($mn)	92.2	83.7
Profit after tax ($mn)	63.9	60.1
Earnings per share (¢)	23.0	21.6
Cash flow per share (¢)	32.6	29.6
Dividend (¢)	18	18
Percentage franked	100	100
Net tangible assets per share ($)	0.24	0.24
Interest cover (times)	9.3	8.3
Return on equity (%)	15.2	14.6
Debt-to-equity ratio (%)	39.5	34.2
Current ratio	3.5	3.8

Outlook

Over 80% of GWA's sales are geared to the residential and commercial construction and renovation markets, and the company continues to experience the impact of a slowdown. It forecasts little growth in the June 2007 year. It continues to restructure its operations, and believes that it will be in a position to reap the rewards when the housing cycle turns. It has merged the Caroma and Dorf Clark businesses and closed some of its domestic production facilities. The establishment of GWA Trading (Shanghai) is enabling it to source much product from Asia, helping reduce costs further. It has announced plans to seek buyers for its Sebel furniture and Rover lawnmower businesses.

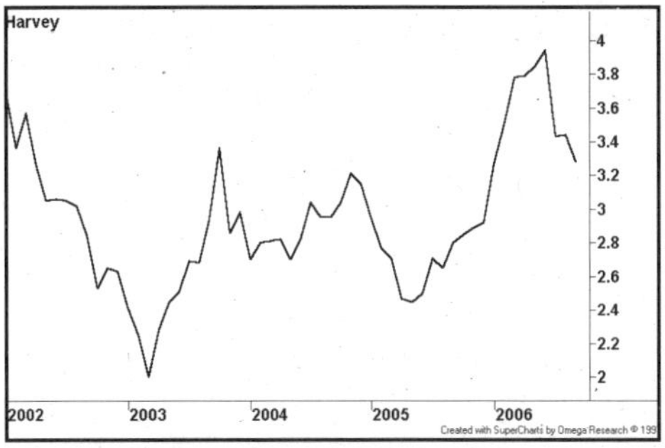

www.harveynorman.com.au

HARVEY NORMAN HOLDINGS LIMITED

Share price ($)	3.51
12-month high ($)	4.09
12-month low ($)	2.66
Market capitalisation ($mn)	3670.5
Price-to-NTA-per-share ratio	2.8
5-year share price return (% p.a.)	2.9

Sector: Consumer discretionary	Company	Sector
Price-earnings ratio (times)	16.2	18.8
Dividend yield (%)	2.3	4.0

Sydney-based Harvey Norman, established in 1982, operates a chain of more than 215 retail stores specialising in electrical and electronic goods, home appliances, furniture, flooring, carpets and manchester, throughout Australia, New Zealand, Ireland, Singapore, Malaysia and Slovenia, under the Harvey Norman, Domayne and Joyce Mayne banners. Many of the stores are independently held as part of a franchise operation, from which Harvey Norman receives income for advisory and advertising services. It also receives rental income from property investments, from its own stores, and from the provision of finance to franchisees and customers. It owns a controlling stake in Rebel Sport.

Latest business results (June 2006, full year)

Profits recovered, after their fall of the previous year, although much of this was due to a revaluation of the company's property portfolio. New Zealand again recorded an excellent performance, with the 20 stores there reporting a sales increase of 19.7% in local currency, or 15.6% in Australian dollars, with the pre-tax profit leaping 27% to $44.6 million. Singapore profits were up 9% and the tiny Slovenia operation moved from loss to profit. Rebel Sport profits jumped 38%, buoyed by the Commonwealth Games and the FIFA World Cup, but other domestic business was weak. Total group sales, including franchised stores but excluding Rebel Sport, rose 12.7% to $4.6 billion, or a 7% gain on a like-for-like basis. A total of 12 new stores were opened in Australia during the year, one in New Zealand and six in Ireland.

Outlook

Harvey Norman is a major beneficiary of the continuing Australian appetite for new furnishings and the latest high-tech gadgets. It plans to open nine new stores in Australia during the June 2007 year, along with the relocation of three others to larger premises, and four in New Zealand. There will also be new stores in Singapore, Malaysia, Ireland and Slovenia. It is investigating moves elsewhere in Europe, as well as expansion into China and India. Nevertheless, around three-quarters of company profit derives from its various Australian operations, and it could be hurt by rising interest rates or by any big economic slowdown or loss of consumer confidence.

HVN Year to 30 June	2005	2006
Revenues ($mn)	1902.5	2172.4
Franchising operations (%)	29	30
Retail - New Zealand (%)	22	22
Retail - Rebel Sport (%)	16	16
Retail - Asia (%)	16	15
Non-franchised retail (%)	10	10
EBIT ($mn)	335.2	391.9
EBIT margin (%)	17.6	18.0
Gross margin (%)	29.7	29.8
Profit before tax ($mn)	298.3	351.7
Profit after tax ($mn)	191.6	229.6
Earnings per share (¢)	18.1	21.7
Cash flow per share (¢)	25.3	30.3
Dividend (¢)	6.5	8
Percentage franked	100	100
Net tangible assets per share ($)	1.09	1.25
Interest cover (times)	9.1	9.7
Return on equity (%)	16.3	18.0
Debt-to-equity ratio (%)	49.4	50.6
Current ratio	1.8	2.0

HGL LIMITED

Share price ($)	1.91	
12-month high ($)	2.14	
12-month low ($)	1.69	
Market capitalisation ($mn)	98.5	
Price-to-NTA-per-share ratio	1.8	
5-year share price return (% p.a.)	21.2	
Sector: Industrials	**Company**	**Sector**
Price-earnings ratio (times)	10.5	13.6
Dividend yield (%)	5.3	4.3

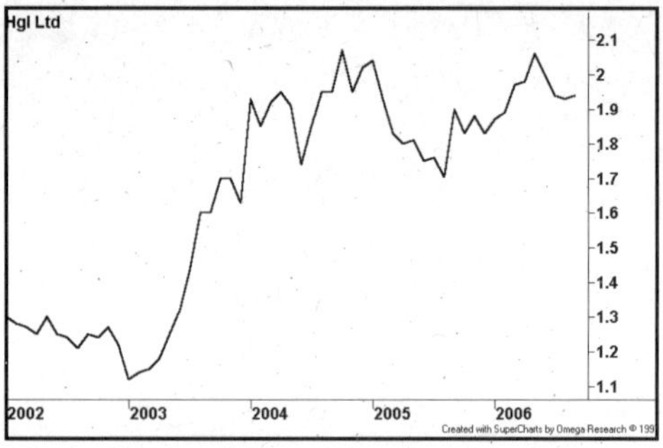

www.hgl.com.au

Sydney-based HGL is a small diversified investment group that specialises in acquiring and rejuvenating underperforming niche companies in the import and distribution business, and it is now part-owner of 11 of these, including firms that specialise in cosmetics, fabrics, spectacle frames, headwear and imaging equipment. Generally, the companies are partially owned by their management or other industry experts, who work in partnership with HGL executives. HGL also participates in public company investing and the funds management sector, including a 39% interest in the boutique fund manager MMC Asset Management and a 6% stake in the listed investment company Hunter Hall International.

Latest business results (March 2006, half year)

The company's import operations realised an EBIT of $7.8 million, up from $5.7 million, thanks to acquisitions and to improved business conditions. At March 2006 the company had $57.8 million invested in import and distribution businesses, up from $43.3 million in 2005. EBIT from funds management interests remained steady at $1.2 million. Dividend income from investments declined to $0.4 million from $0.6 million. The sale of listed securities realised a profit of $0.7 million, up from $0.1 million a year earlier. At March 2006 the company's share portfolio was valued at $28.7 million.

HNG Year to 30 September	2004	2005
Revenues ($mn)	108.5	116.6
EBIT ($mn)	18.3	13.9
EBIT margin (%)	16.9	11.9
Gross margin (%)	48.0	48.2
Profit before tax ($mn)	18.7	14.1
Profit after tax ($mn)	10.5	9.2
Earnings per share (¢)	21.3	18.2
Cash flow per share (¢)	25.6	22.9
Dividend (¢)	9	10.2
Percentage franked	100	100
Interest cover (times)	–	–
Return on equity (%)	17.2	13.2
Half year to 31 March	**2005**	**2006**
Revenues ($mn)	57.8	65.5
Profit before tax ($mn)	5.4	8.6
Profit after tax ($mn)	2.6	4.6
Earnings per share (¢)	5.5	9.6
Dividend (¢)	4.4	5.4
Percentage franked	100	100
Net tangible assets per share ($)	1.18	1.03
Debt-to-equity ratio (%)	–	1.9
Current ratio	2.8	2.0

Outlook

HGL's growth prospects depend to a large degree on management's success in identifying high-potential, underperforming niche businesses that require fresh capital and business know-how. HGL management must also then negotiate a satisfactory partnership deal with the entity's owners. The company's target is businesses where the return on capital employed is likely to exceed 20% in a reasonably short period of time. In October 2005 it acquired JSB Lighting for an initial payment of $4 million, with additional payments to be made over three years based on profits, and it continues to seek out new acquisitions.

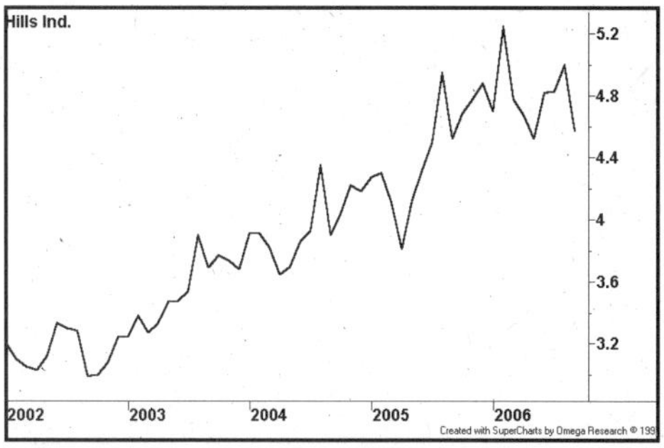

www.hills.com.au

HILLS INDUSTRIES LIMITED

Share price ($)	4.80
12-month high ($)	5.25
12-month low ($)	4.31
Market capitalisation ($mn)	794.1
Price-to-NTA-per-share ratio	4.0
5-year share price return (% p.a.)	20.4

Sector: Industrials	**Company**	**Sector**
Price-earnings ratio (times)	16.6	13.6
Dividend yield (%)	5.4	4.3

Adelaide-based Hills, founded in 1946, is famous for its clothes hoists. However, it also manufactures a diverse range of other products, including garden equipment, structural tubing, a wide range of commercial and industrial steel products, closed circuit TV systems, satellite dishes, electronic security systems and television antennas. It owns 47% of the listed metal products manufacturer Korvest.

Latest business results (June 2006, full year)

A sharp rise in profits for both the electronic security and entertainment division and the home and hardware division overcame a disappointing performance from building and industrial to deliver Hills a good result. EBIT was up 44.5% for electronic security and entertainment, thanks especially to some large contracts for closed circuit video security systems and a better-than-expected performance from the newly acquired Audio Telex and Crestron Control Solutions businesses. This division contributed 47% of total company profit, despite accounting for just 28% of revenues. The home and hardware business saw a 28.9% jump in EBIT, from just a small rise in sales, largely reflecting its recovery from a slump in the previous year. The building and industrial business recorded a solid gain in sales, but sharp competition from imported piping forced the company to cut its prices, at the same time as it was facing higher raw material costs, and profits for the division fell 13.7%.

Outlook

Hills believes it is on track for a satisfactory result in the June 2007 year, but much will depend on consumer spending trends, the continuing strength of the non-residential construction sector, and raw material prices, especially steel. The high-margin electronics business continues to power ahead. Demand for closed circuit security systems remains high, and Hills is also experiencing good sales of television reception equipment to Foxtel and Austar. The April 2006 acquisition of the Australian Audio Supplies business is intended to boost the division further. The home and hardware division continues to benefit from a major restructuring, which included sourcing more products from China. However, trends in the building and industrial sector remain a concern, with further steel price rises and stronger competition both looming.

HIL Year to 30 June	2005	2006
Revenues ($mn)	786.8	931.8
Building & industrial (%)	53	53
Electronic security & entertainment (%)	25	28
Home & hardware (%)	20	18
EBIT ($mn)	63.7	73.3
EBIT margin (%)	8.1	7.9
Gross margin (%)	34.2	32.8
Profit before tax ($mn)	60.4	67.4
Profit after tax ($mn)	41.7	48.2
Earnings per share (¢)	27.2	28.9
Cash flow per share (¢)	40.6	39.4
Dividend (¢)	24	26
Percentage franked	100	100
Net tangible assets per share ($)	1.22	1.19
Interest cover (times)	19.3	12.5
Return on equity (%)	17.0	16.0
Debt-to-equity ratio (%)	27.4	36.7
Current ratio	1.9	1.9

HOUSEWARES INTERNATIONAL LIMITED

Share price ($)	1.60	
12-month high ($)	1.96	
12-month low ($)	1.23	
Market capitalisation ($mn)	203.7	
Price-to-NTA-per-share ratio	2.6	
5-year share price return (% p.a.)	26.6	
Sector: Consumer discretionary	**Company**	**Sector**
Price-earnings ratio (times)	12.0	18.8
Dividend yield (%)	8.1	4.0

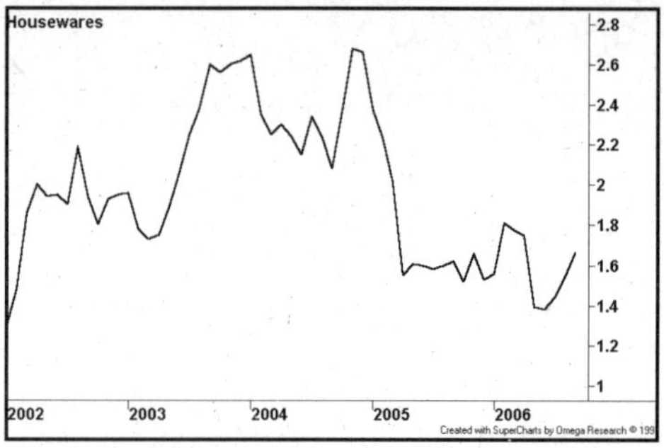

www.housewares.com.au

Melbourne-based Housewares International has evolved from its 1957 beginnings as a small local importer into a large distributor of household products in several countries. Its wholly-owned brands include Breville, Kambrook, Ronson and Goldair for home appliances, and Arcosteel, alex liddy, Baccarat, Forum, Mayfair & Jackson and Pronto for kitchenware. It also owns the Sabco household cleaning goods company. Its distribution companies include Metro Marketing in the US and a 50% stake in Anglo Canadian in Canada.

Latest business results (June 2006, full year)

Sales rose, but profits declined for the second straight year, as the company continued to struggle to restructure its domestic activities. Australian sales revenues – about 64% of the total – were down 8%, with homeware products declining 19% and electrical goods down 4%. Australian EBIT plummeted 58%. By contrast, conditions in the company's overseas markets – principally the US, Canada, Hong Kong and New Zealand – were excellent, with homeware sales up 17% and electrical sales surging 45%. Overseas EBIT jumped 70%. The company reported as a significant item a loss of $2.7 million involving mainly restructuring costs.

Outlook

Housewares has been hit by a highly competitive domestic sales environment for its products, and it is working to cut costs and build a new base for long-term profitability. In particular, it is striving to boost its brands, in order to differentiate them from the flood of cheap Chinese imports in local stores, and it has built a product development centre in Sydney to devise innovative new goods. It is also slimming down its distribution channels, allowing Australian retailers in some cases to buy directly from its Chinese office. It expects its restructuring efforts to provide a boost to domestic profits in the June 2007 year, even though it believes local trading conditions will remain difficult. Housewares is seeing strong growth continue in its overseas markets, with North America especially buoyant. It has achieved good brand recognition for Breville products, several of which have been very well received in the market. It is expanding its US sales force and is boosting its product development capability. It is also seeking to develop markets in Europe.

HWI Year to 30 June	2005	2006
Revenues ($mn)	408.4	424.2
EBIT ($mn)	32.2	28.0
EBIT margin (%)	7.9	6.6
Gross margin (%)	27.7	25.8
Profit before tax ($mn)	26.4	21.4
Profit after tax ($mn)	18.8	16.1
Earnings per share (¢)	15.8	13.3
Cash flow per share (¢)	19.0	16.6
Dividend (¢)	13	13
Percentage franked	100	100
Net tangible assets per share ($)	0.65	0.61
Interest cover (times)	5.6	4.3
Return on equity (%)	12.0	10.3
Debt-to-equity ratio (%)	48.1	40.5
Current ratio	3.3	3.0

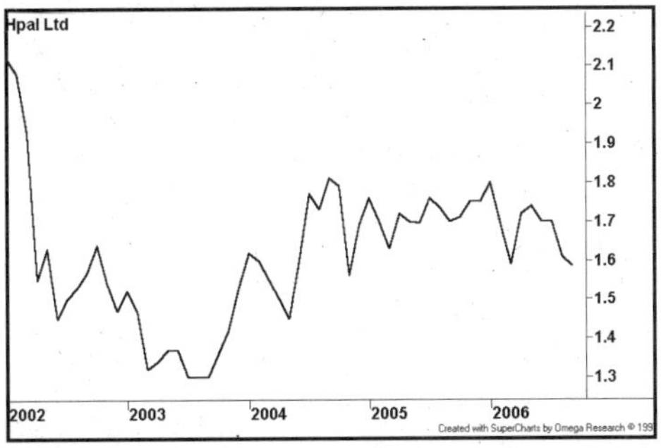

www.hpa.com.au

HPAL LIMITED

Share price ($)	1.57	
12-month high ($)	1.86	
12-month low ($)	1.56	
Market capitalisation ($mn)	183.0	
Price-to-NTA-per-share ratio	6.5	
5-year share price return (% p.a.)	–0.5	
Sector: Information technology	**Company**	**Sector**
Price-earnings ratio (times)	10.6	22.8
Dividend yield (%)	7.3	2.2

Sydney-based HPAL – established as Hermes Precisa in 1989 through the merger of Endata, Datamail and Bell & Howell Australia – is now a 51% subsidiary of Kodak (Australasia). It specialises in the provision of outsourcing services for companies, particularly the management of 'essential mail' business communications, such as invoices, credit card statements and direct mail marketing. It also manages inbound communication such as insurance claims, and 'on demand' information such as customer transaction records or land titles, and it provides image scanning – electronic document capture, storage and retrieval – services.

Latest business results (June 2006, half year)

Sales and profits fell, due largely to a $7.5 million drop in imaging revenues. This resulted from the absence of income from the CommSee scanning project for the Commonwealth Bank, which had boosted the June 2005 result. The company's essential mail operation saw a $1.1 million rise in revenues, thanks to growing business, though competitive pressures forced HPAL to lower prices, which hurt profits. The direct mail operation saw steady growth, with several significant new contracts.

Outlook

HPAL is working to diversify its sources of income, to boost growth and minimise lumpiness in its revenue stream. A new statement processing application has led to a sharp increase in demand for electronic document distribution services, and further new applications are planned. Other recent highlights include a contract with a state government for the management of a land information system, and new essential mail work for a large federal government department. HPAL has formed an alliance with two direct marketing specialist organisations to launch a new group, The Marketing Continuum, which aims to help companies respond more effectively to customer-initiated contacts. It is also looking at possible acquisitions. It believes that new contracts will help boost the second half, and that 2006 full-year revenues and profits will be roughly in line with 2005.

HPX Year to 31 December	2004	2005
Revenues ($mn)	163.9	180.1
EBIT ($mn)	21.5	24.4
EBIT margin (%)	13.1	13.6
Profit before tax ($mn)	21.5	24.6
Profit after tax ($mn)	15.0	17.2
Earnings per share (¢)	13.0	14.8
Cash flow per share (¢)	18.5	21.0
Dividend (¢)	10.25	11.5
Percentage franked	100	100
Interest cover (times)	–	–
Return on equity (%)	26.5	27.7
Half year to 30 June	**2005**	**2006**
Revenues ($mn)	89.1	82.8
Profit before tax ($mn)	12.0	10.5
Profit after tax ($mn)	8.3	7.3
Earnings per share (¢)	7.2	6.3
Dividend (¢)	4.75	4.75
Percentage franked	100	100
Net tangible assets per share ($)	0.26	0.24
Debt-to-equity ratio (%)	–	–
Current ratio	1.8	1.6

HUNTER HALL INTERNATIONAL LIMITED

Share price ($)	8.70
12-month high ($)	8.70
12-month low ($)	5.90
Market capitalisation ($mn)	227.5
Price-to-NTA-per-share ratio	11.1
5-year share price return (% p.a.)	45.7

Sector: Financials	Company	Sector
Price-earnings ratio (times)	16.8	15.7
Dividend yield (%)	5.5	4.3

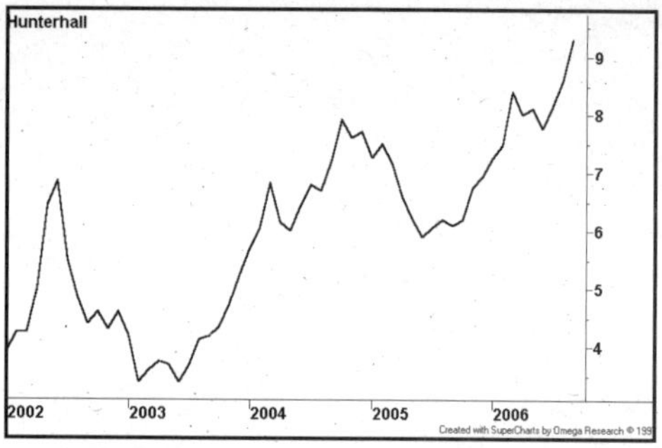

www.hunterhall.com.au

Sydney-based Hunter Hall International, founded in 1993, is a fund management company with a specialty in ethical funds. Its main funds are the Hunter Hall Value Growth Trust, the Hunter Hall Global Ethical Trust, and the Hunter Hall International Ethical Fund. It also operates the Hunter Hall Australian Value Trust, it is trustee for the Hunter Hall Ethical Superannuation Fund, and investment manager for the listed Global Value Limited. As a matter of policy, Hunter Hall gives 5% of its pre-tax profit to charities selected by shareholders. The executive chairman, Peter Hall, owns half the company's equity.

Latest business results (June 2006, full year)

The booming Australian managed fund business delivered a big boost in profits to Hunter Hall, with total funds under management jumping 30% to $1.73 billion. This growth was largely driven by investment performance, with net inflows from investors amounting to only $84 million. The pre-tax profit from the company's business as investment manager rose 23% to $14.5 million and the company received a performance fee of $3.53 million, up from $1.25 million in the previous year. The company designated $937 000 to be donated to charity, 35% higher than in the year before. The company's flagship product, the Value Growth Trust, which is Australia's largest ethical investment trust, recorded a 30.1% return, and the Global Ethical Trust was up 31.5%. Both outperformed their benchmarks. The International Ethical Fund's return of 15.1% was a modest underperformance.

Outlook

Hunter Hall has achieved great success with most of its funds, thanks to the stock-picking abilities of its investment managers. The Value Growth Trust has achieved a positive return annually for 11 years, and has outperformed its benchmark in 10 of those years. According to the Morningstar fund rating service, it is Australia's top-performing retail fund over 10 years. Most other funds have also performed strongly, although the company has expressed disappointment with recent underperformance by the small Australian Value Trust, which has led to some outflows. Concerned that its business is heavily dependent on the skills of its key staff, Hunter Hall is working to reward them more generously.

HHL Year to 30 June	2005	2006
Revenues ($mn)	26.3	36.4
EBIT ($mn)	12.0	18.2
EBIT margin (%)	45.7	50.1
Profit before tax ($mn)	12.4	18.5
Profit after tax ($mn)	8.6	12.7
Earnings per share (¢)	36.0	51.9
Cash flow per share (¢)	37.4	53.5
Dividend (¢)	36.2	47.5
Percentage franked	100	100
Net tangible assets per share ($)	0.58	0.78
Interest cover (times)	–	–
Return on equity (%)	64.0	72.8
Debt-to-equity ratio (%)	–	–
Current ratio	3.9	2.7

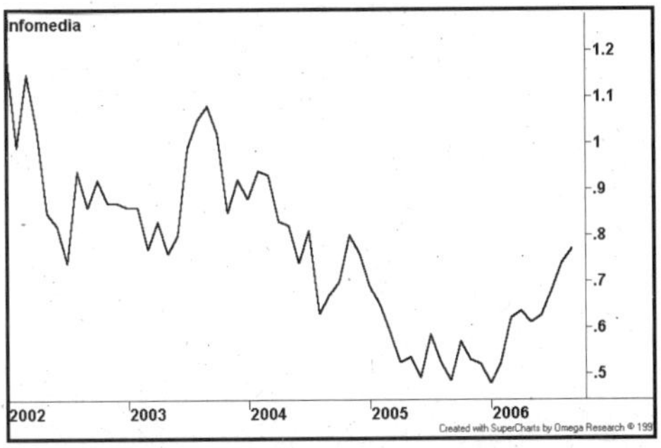

www.infomedia.com.au

INFOMEDIA LIMITED

Share price ($)	0.76
12-month high ($)	0.76
12-month low ($)	0.46
Market capitalisation ($mn)	250.6
Price-to-NTA-per-share ratio	10.1
5-year share price return (% p.a.)	–9.3

Sector: Information technology	Company	Sector
Price-earnings ratio (times)	15.0	22.8
Dividend yield (%)	5.3	2.2

Sydney software company Infomedia was formed in 1990, and has grown into a world leader in the development of specialised electronic catalogues. Its main product, Microcat, is an electronic parts catalogue (EPC) for the automotive industry – with versions for 15 leading car companies, including General Motors, Ford, Toyota, Honda, Mitsubishi and Hyundai – and it is shipped to customers in over 160 countries, in 25 languages. It operates from CD-ROM, DVD-ROM and the internet, and enables service personnel in a motor dealership to identify the correct replacement parts for a vehicle. The company is also active in the provision of data management and business systems services. It operates support centres in key locations around the world.

Latest business results (June 2006, full year)

A combination of cost control, lower depreciation and taxation benefits handed the company a modest boost in profits. However, a stronger Australian dollar forced revenues down. EPC subscription numbers grew 2.1% to 47 718. The company's Superservice Menus data management product, which provides automotive dealers with a range of service, repair, and warranty management tools, continued its powerful growth, with a 158% increase in subscriber numbers to 1671. Infomedia's non-EPC business – representing about 7% of company turnover – moved from loss to profit. The company also reported a $1.6 million after-tax profit from the sale of its Frenchs Forest corporate headquarters.

Outlook

Infomedia is bouncing back after being forced to restructure many of its operations. This followed the loss of exclusive EPC agreements with Ford Europe and General Motors in North America, causing a sharp decline in June 2005 profit. It has launched new subsidiaries in Europe and North America, and reports continuing strong acceptance for its products. It has successfully renewed data licences with Holden, Honda and Hyundai, and in mid-2006 announced a major three-year contract to provide its EPC product to 3500 Kia dealers around the world. It has also signed new contracts with Isuzu and Mazda, and sees good growth in subscriber numbers during 2006–07. The Superservice Menus product is now supplied to eight franchises in Europe and Asia. Infomedia will launch sales in America during 2006–07, and expects continuing rapid growth.

IFM Year to 30 June	2005	2006
Revenues ($mn)	59.1	55.6
EBIT ($mn)	21.7	22.3
EBIT margin (%)	36.7	40.1
Gross margin (%)	70.6	68.6
Profit before tax ($mn)	21.9	22.4
Profit after tax ($mn)	15.5	16.5
Earnings per share (¢)	4.8	5.1
Cash flow per share (¢)	6.2	6.1
Dividend (¢)	3.4	4
Percentage franked	100	100
Net tangible assets per share ($)	0.10	0.08
Interest cover (times)	–	–
Return on equity (%)	31.5	37.4
Debt-to-equity ratio (%)	–	–
Current ratio	2.3	2.9

INSTITUTE OF DRUG TECHNOLOGY AUST. LTD

Share price ($)	1.49
12-month high ($)	2.06
12-month low ($)	1.03
Market capitalisation ($mn)	62.3
Price-to-NTA-per-share ratio	2.4
5-year share price return (% p.a.)	–14.4

Sector: Health care	Company	Sector
Price-earnings ratio (times)	17.7	31.1
Dividend yield (%)	5.4	1.8

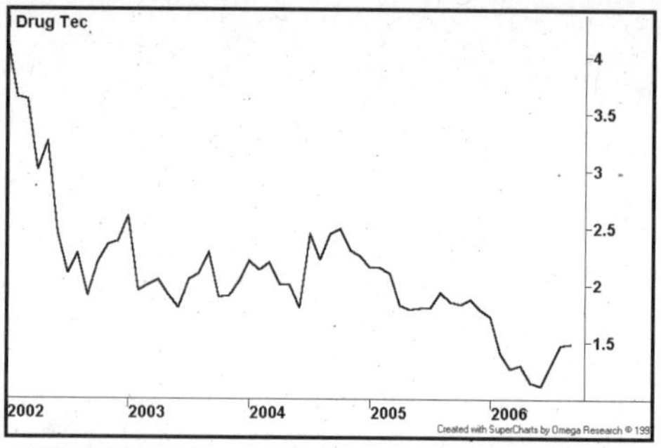

www.idtaus.com.au

The Melbourne-based Institute of Drug Technology Australia (IDT), established in 1975, is a small, well-regarded developer and manufacturer of active pharmaceutical ingredients (APIs) for local and international companies. It also provides technical consulting and clinical trial services to the pharmaceuticals, chemical and biotechnology industries. In addition, it operates a research and development business for clients. Its Melbourne manufacturing facilities and laboratories have been licensed by the Australian Therapeutic Goods Administration and the United States Food and Drug Administration for production of APIs, and the company has developed a strong reputation for its dedicated facilities for the development and production of anti-cancer drugs. Through its CMAX division, IDT offers early-stage clinical trial services.

Latest business results (June 2006, full year)

IDT overcame a weak first half to recover in the second half, although the full-year sales and pre-tax profit figures were down from the previous year. However, a lower tax payment meant that the after-tax profit and EPS rose. The company cited three areas of its business as making a particular contribution to the result: increased finished-product manufacturing, notably for Celgene Corporation in the US; increased fee-for-service drug development activity, including some significant new projects for new and long-term clients in the US; and increased clinical trial business for CMAX, mainly from clients in the US and Europe.

Outlook

IDT is steadily moving away from the production of generic APIs. Though these were once the mainstay of its operations, they are expected to represent just 10% of business in the June 2007 year. The company's strategy now is to use its expertise to develop finished products – typically capsules and tablets – and this business is starting to generate good returns, as well as offering great potential for future growth. IDT is working with Pfizer and other pharmaceuticals specialists to develop a range of products, and believes these can contribute significantly to business in coming years. The company is experiencing growing demand for its Adelaide-based CMAX clinical trial service, including a trend towards larger and more complex studies, and it has restructured this business and expanded it to Melbourne.

IDT Year to 30 June	2005	2006
Revenues ($mn)	26.7	24.9
EBIT ($mn)	5.2	5.0
EBIT margin (%)	19.4	20.2
Gross margin (%)	79.8	81.0
Profit before tax ($mn)	5.2	5.0
Profit after tax ($mn)	3.3	3.6
Earnings per share (¢)	7.8	8.4
Cash flow per share (¢)	13.1	13.3
Dividend (¢)	8	8
Percentage franked	100	100
Net tangible assets per share ($)	0.62	0.63
Interest cover (times)	–	239.8
Return on equity (%)	11.9	12.7
Debt-to-equity ratio (%)	–	4.1
Current ratio	3.4	3.9

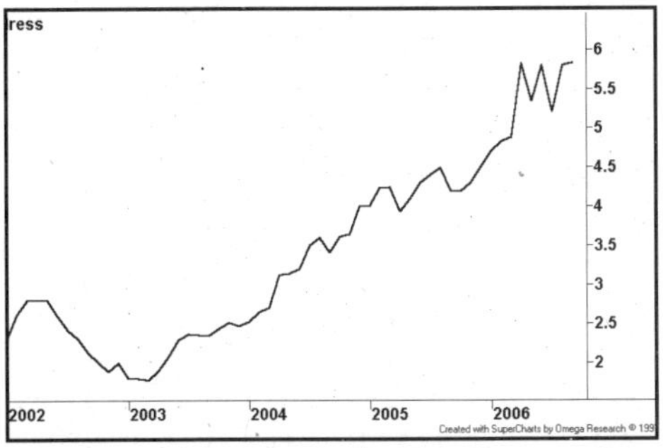

www.iress.com.au

IRESS MARKET TECHNOLOGY LIMITED

Share price ($)	6.10
12-month high ($)	6.30
12-month low ($)	3.81
Market capitalisation ($mn)	667.4
Price-to-NTA-per-share ratio	21.2
5-year share price return (% p.a.)	26.0

Sector: Information technology	**Company**	**Sector**
Price-earnings ratio (times)	33.6	22.8
Dividend yield (%)	3.0	2.2

Melbourne-based IRESS was founded in 1993, and was formerly called BridgeDFS. It produces the prominent IRESS (Integrated Real-time Equity System) sharemarket information system. Within the IRESS system it offers a range of trading products with numerous applications, for stockbrokers, fund managers and other wealth professionals. It has moved into financial planning software, with Xplan, which has enjoyed strong early success. IRESS also operates in New Zealand, and it has moved into Canada. The Australian Stock Exchange owns 14% of the equity.

Latest business results (June 2006, half year)

A buoyant stock market helped IRESS report another excellent result, with strong organic growth for the company's established market trading products. There was further excellent growth for Xplan, with revenues of $3.5 million, up 68% from the 2005 first half, and the pre-tax profit soaring more than fourfold to $1 million. Revenues in Canada jumped 87% to $3.3 million, although this business moved into the red, after recording a small profit in the June 2005 period.

Outlook

IRESS is heavily geared to levels of stock market activity, which has fuelled some strong growth. The provision of real-time stock market data and order processing systems is a very competitive business, and IRESS must continually upgrade its products to maintain a market advantage. However, it is the company of choice for a majority of large broking houses and for many others, and it reports high levels of customer loyalty. It sees enormous potential for the high-margin Xplan product, and a major contract with Genesys Wealth Advisers will provide a significant boost to business from late 2006. An agreement with an important New Zealand client is helping develop Xplan in that country. IRESS is making a strong capital investment to develop its Canadian business. Thanks to an agreement with Reuters Canada to convert part of that company's trader base to an IRESS system, it has gained some important blue-chip clients.

IRE Year to 31 December	**2004**	**2005**
Revenues ($mn)	61.1	71.6
EBIT ($mn)	20.4	28.2
EBIT margin (%)	33.3	39.3
Profit before tax ($mn)	21.5	29.7
Profit after tax ($mn)	13.0	19.6
Earnings per share (¢)	12.4	18.2
Cash flow per share (¢)	16.1	21.9
Dividend (¢)	15.5	18
Percentage franked	100	100
Interest cover (times)	–	–
Return on equity (%)	42.3	53.0
Half year to 30 June	**2005**	**2006**
Revenues ($mn)	35.0	43.3
Profit before tax ($mn)	13.4	17.8
Profit after tax ($mn)	8.8	12.2
Earnings per share (¢)	8.3	11.1
Dividend (¢)	6.5	8
Percentage franked	100	100
Net tangible assets per share ($)	0.32	0.29
Debt-to-equity ratio (%)	–	–
Current ratio	4.3	3.1

JUBILEE MINES NL

Share price ($)	9.83	
12-month high ($)	9.88	
12-month low ($)	6.07	
Market capitalisation ($mn)	1189.5	
Price-to-NTA-per-share ratio	5.6	
5-year share price return (% p.a.)	62.8	
Sector: Materials	**Company**	**Sector**
Price-earnings ratio (times)	12.2	12.3
Dividend yield (%)	4.1	2.3

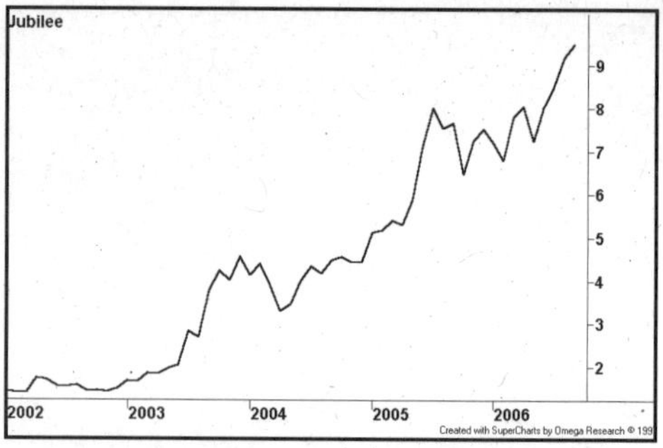

www.jubileemines.com.au

Perth-based Jubilee Mines, founded in 1987 as Jubilee Gold Mines, is now a major nickel producer. Its work is concentrated at the Cosmos Nickel Project, discovered in 1997, which is in the Kathleen Valley area, north of Leinster in the north-eastern goldfields of Western Australia. Nickel concentrate production from the project is shipped to Canada for smelting and refining by Inco, the world's second-largest nickel producer. Jubilee is also developing two other deposits, named Prospero and Tapinos, that it has discovered near Cosmos, and it maintains an active exploration program in the region.

Latest business results (June 2006, full year)

Surging global nickel prices handed Jubilee a big profit increase, despite just a modest rise in nickel-in-concentrate production, from 11 030 tonnes to 11 430 tonnes. Production costs rose from $3.02 per pound to $3.37, due to a reduction in the grade of ore produced, along with generally higher expenses prevailing in the resources industry. During the year the company made new discoveries at Tapinos and also at Sinclair, which is in Bannockburn, 100 kilometres south of Cosmos. There were also upgrades to several existing deposits and the start of work on the new Helene Decline, to provide access to the new Tapinos and Prospero deposits. The company said that despite the higher profits it was reducing the dividend payout ratio in order to boost capital spending for the continued expansion of its operations.

Outlook

With no debt and $125 million in cash holdings, Jubilee is in a strong position to fund both the development of recent discoveries and new exploration work. Its growth strategy is based on the discovery and development of additional high-grade nickel sulphide mines at Cosmos and Bannockburn. Thanks to recent high-grade discoveries, the company believes that Cosmos will continue to deliver a significant amount of new resources for many years. Based on current development work, Jubilee is forecasting production of at least 9000 tonnes of nickel-in-concentrate in 2006–07, rising to more than 12 000 tonnes in 2007–08 and to more than 16 000 tonnes annually from 2008–09. However, fast-escalating costs are a concern.

JBM Year to 30 June	2005	2006
Revenues ($mn)	237.1	293.7
EBIT ($mn)	109.9	147.1
EBIT margin (%)	46.3	50.1
Gross margin (%)	57.5	62.2
Profit before tax ($mn)	114.2	150.6
Profit after tax ($mn)	75.3	103.4
Earnings per share (¢)	59.9	80.4
Cash flow per share (¢)	76.6	102.2
Dividend (¢)	45	40
Percentage franked	100	100
Net tangible assets per share ($)	1.29	1.75
Interest cover (times)	–	–
Return on equity (%)	50.4	52.9
Debt-to-equity ratio (%)	–	–
Current ratio	4.9	12.8

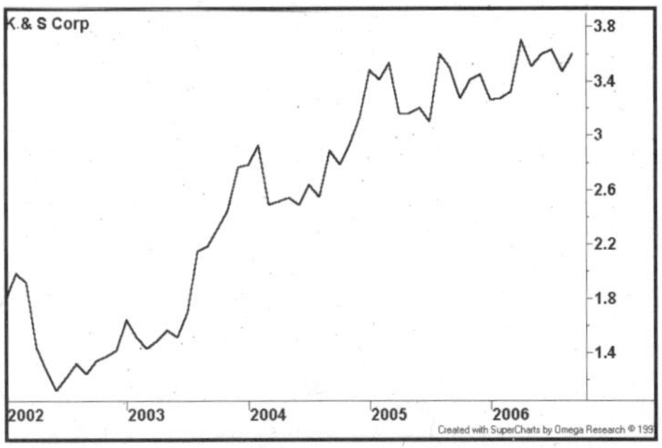

www.ksgroup.com.au

K&S CORPORATION LIMITED

Share price ($)	3.65
12-month high ($)	3.80
12-month low ($)	3.05
Market capitalisation ($mn)	240.8
Price-to-NTA-per-share ratio	2.5
5-year share price return (% p.a.)	36.0

Sector: Industrials	Company	Sector
Price-earnings ratio (times)	13.1	13.6
Dividend yield (%)	3.8	4.3

Based in Mt Gambier, and operating since 1945, K&S is one of Australia's leading transport, warehousing and logistics companies, with a strategy directed towards large national contracts. It controls one of the largest company-owned fleets in Australia, as well as owning over 160000 square metres of warehousing and a large range of rail and sea containers. It operates through four divisions: K&S Freighters is involved in road, rail and coastal sea forwarding; K&S Integrated Distribution handles warehousing, storage and local distribution; K&S Agencies manages Ampol fuel distribution throughout regions of South Australia and Victoria; and K&S (NZ) provides distribution throughout New Zealand. The company founder, Allan Scott, owns more than 60% of the equity.

Latest business results (June 2006, full year)

Revenues were up, reflecting strong organic growth from existing customers, along with the impact of a new Holden contract in Adelaide, but profits fell. However, this was largely due to a series of one-off profits that are no longer reported as significant items. In the previous year the company's profit included the reversal of a building revaluation decrement of $0.84 million and fraud-related recoveries of $4.2 million. In the latest year the accounts included an after-tax profit of $2.3 million from the sale of a Melbourne terminal. The company reported that after removing these one-off amounts the normalised after-tax profit in June 2006 of $15.6 million was a 4.3% rise from the previous year. The fuel business, about 13% of total company turnover, enjoyed a particularly good year, with revenues up 17% and EBIT jumping 38%.

Outlook

The business of K&S is strongly geared to the domestic economy, and it is a beneficiary of buoyant economic conditions. During 2005–06 it re-signed most of its major customer contracts for periods of three to five years, which will underpin 50% of its revenue base. Despite quite a degree of consolidation in recent years, the transport industry in Australia is still fragmented, and K&S continues to seek out new acquisitions. In April 2006 it started operations at its new $28 million transport and warehouse facility at Truganina in western Melbourne.

KSC Year to 30 June	2005	2006
Revenues ($mn)	340.8	367.1
EBIT ($mn)	31.7	29.5
EBIT margin (%)	9.3	8.0
Gross margin (%)	8.0	7.5
Profit before tax ($mn)	29.0	26.2
Profit after tax ($mn)	20.4	18.4
Earnings per share (¢)	34.0	27.8
Cash flow per share (¢)	57.3	51.9
Dividend (¢)	13.5	14
Percentage franked	100	100
Net tangible assets per share ($)	1.19	1.45
Interest cover (times)	11.8	8.8
Return on equity (%)	28.1	20.1
Debt-to-equity ratio (%)	40.5	34.8
Current ratio	1.1	1.0

KINGSGATE CONSOLIDATED LIMITED

Share price ($)	5.29
12-month high ($)	6.80
12-month low ($)	3.15
Market capitalisation ($mn)	473.9
Price-to-NTA-per-share ratio	3.7
5-year share price return (% p.a.)	49.0

Sector: Materials	**Company**	**Sector**
Price-earnings ratio (times)	27.4	12.3
Dividend yield (%)	1.9	2.3

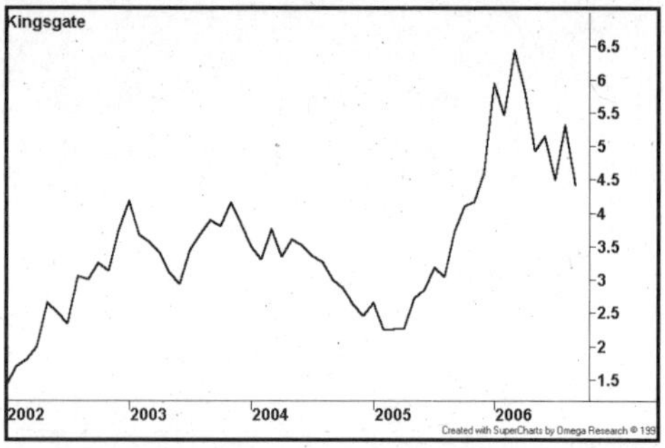

www.kingsgate.com.au

Sydney-based Kingsgate is a gold, silver and precious metals mining and exploration company. Through its wholly-owned Thai subsidiary Akara Mining it owns and operates Thailand's only modern gold mine, the Chatree Gold Mine, 280 kilometres north of Bangkok. The company is also engaged in substantial exploration activity in the Chatree region, and elsewhere in Thailand, and it has exploration projects in South America.

Latest business results (June 2006, full year)

The surging gold price handed Kingsgate a major boost to its profits. Production rose from 126 550 ounces in the June 2005 year to 140 071 ounces, thanks especially to higher plant throughput following the full commissioning of a pebble crusher. The amount would have been higher but for the early onset of the wet season. Cash costs fell from US$212 an ounce to US$206. Profits were dampened by the company's decision to deliver as much gold as possible into its hedge positions. Kingsgate also produced 459 701 ounces of silver.

Outlook

Kingsgate believes it is on target for 2006–07 production roughly in line with the June 2006 year, with similar production costs – it expects that because its mining operations are located in Thailand it will be able to avoid much of the cost escalation that is taking place in the resources industry. It claims that its costs are among the lowest 20% of gold producers globally. It is working to unwind its hedging positions as quickly as possible, in order that investors in Kingsgate might be exposed fully to spot prices. Only about one-third of gold sales in 2006–07 will be hedged, and these will be the company's final hedged sales. It maintains an active exploration program around Chatree, and in August 2006 was granted 51 new exploration licences in the region. It has announced that gold resources at Chatree total 3.8 million ounces. Kingsgate also maintains exploration projects in Peru and Chile. In addition, it has taken a 22% equity stake in Andean Resources, which is exploring in Argentina, and a 20% stake in Goldstar Resources, which is exploring potentially high-grade gold quartz veins in Victoria.

KCN Year to 30 June	**2005**	**2006**
Revenues ($mn)	64.3	72.8
EBIT ($mn)	7.3	16.7
EBIT margin (%)	11.4	23.0
Gross margin (%)	36.8	39.6
Profit before tax ($mn)	8.4	16.7
Profit after tax ($mn)	8.4	16.7
Earnings per share (¢)	9.8	19.3
Cash flow per share (¢)	19.9	28.4
Dividend (¢)	7	10
Percentage franked	0	0
Net tangible assets per share ($)	1.41	1.44
Interest cover (times)	–	298.5
Return on equity (%)	6.5	13.4
Debt-to-equity ratio (%)	–	–
Current ratio	4.8	0.6

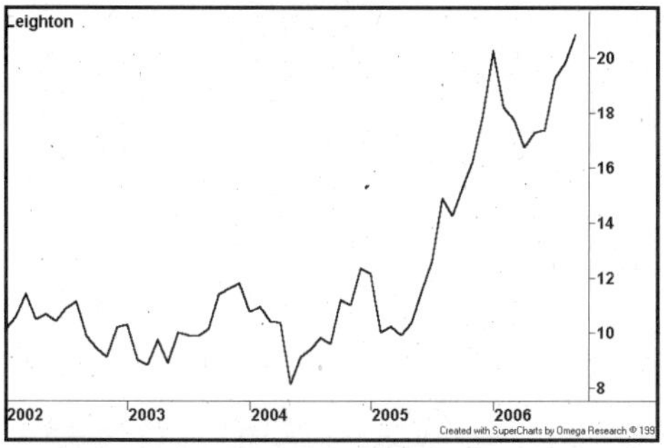

www.leighton.com.au

LEIGHTON HOLDINGS LIMITED

Share price ($)	20.10
12-month high ($)	20.40
12-month low ($)	13.51
Market capitalisation ($mn)	5613.3
Price-to-NTA-per-share ratio	5.3
5-year share price return (% p.a.)	19.4

Sector: Industrials	Company	Sector
Price-earnings ratio (times)	20.1	13.6
Dividend yield (%)	3.3	4.3

Founded in 1949, Leighton is Australia's largest project development and contracting group. It incorporates Leighton Contractors, Thiess Contractors, Leighton Asia, Leighton Properties and John Holland, and operates in Australia and Asia, with a growing presence elsewhere. The German construction company Hochtief owns 53% of Leighton's shares.

Latest business results (June 2006, full year)

Continuing strength in the construction and resources sectors in Australia and Asia delivered another excellent result. Total revenues of $10 billion – including $1.5 billion in joint venture revenues – rose 32% from the previous year. Asian operations showed particular strength, with EBIT soaring 68% to $107 million, which was 28% of the total, despite this region representing just 17% of company revenues. There was particularly strong business in Indonesia, where Thiess is active in coal mining and process engineering. Australia recorded a 10% rise in EBIT, with strong contributions from Melbourne's EastLink project – Australia's largest urban road development – and from contract coal mining operations in Queensland and NSW. In Sydney, Leighton Contractors completed the $1.6 billion WestLink M7 project eight months ahead of schedule. The February 2006 acquisition of contract mining assets of the Henry Walker Eltin Group (HWE) helped boost total work in hand at June 2006 to $16 billion, up from $15.5 billion a year earlier.

Outlook

Leighton forecasts total June 2007 revenues – including from joint ventures – of at least $11 billion, and a further strong profit increase. Transport infrastructure will be one of the keys, with the EastLink project in Melbourne and the Lane Cove Tunnel in Sydney supplemented by the North-South Bypass Tunnel in Brisbane. On the horizon are opportunities such as the Sydney–Melbourne track upgrade, the Gateway Bridge duplication in Brisbane, the AirportLink in Brisbane, and further duplication of the Pacific Highway in NSW. Contract coal and iron ore mining operations are also expected to make a solid contribution, thanks especially to the HWE acquisition. Leighton expects a further good result from Asia, with large infrastructure and building projects in Hong Kong, the construction of casinos in Macao, coal mining business in Indonesia, and new work in emerging markets in India and the Gulf region.

LEI Year to 30 June	2005	2006
Revenues ($mn)	6252.4	8502.6
EBIT ($mn)	313.6	379.6
EBIT margin (%)	5.0	4.5
Profit before tax ($mn)	299.4	371.2
Profit after tax ($mn)	215.2	276.1
Earnings per share (¢)	75.3	100.2
Cash flow per share (¢)	203.7	265.0
Dividend (¢)	50	66
Percentage franked	50	50
Net tangible assets per share ($)	3.17	3.77
Interest cover (times)	22.1	45.0
Return on equity (%)	24.8	27.7
Debt-to-equity ratio (%)	–	–

LEND LEASE CORPORATION LIMITED

Share price ($)	15.71
12-month high ($)	15.85
12-month low ($)	12.77
Market capitalisation ($mn)	6299.8
Price-to-NTA-per-share ratio	2.9
5-year share price return (% p.a.)	10.8

Sector: Financials	Company	Sector
Price-earnings ratio (times)	15.1	15.7
Dividend yield (%)	3.9	4.3

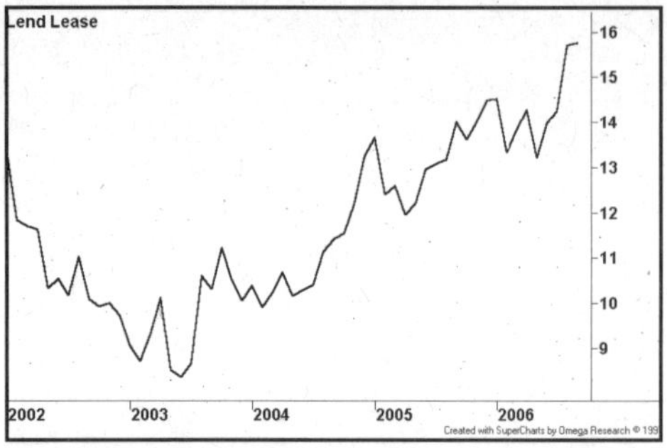

www.lendlease.com.au

Sydney-based Lend Lease, founded in 1958, is a global property developer and investment manager, with particular strength in Australia, Britain and the US. It classifies its businesses into three broad areas: it is a prominent developer and manager of retail shopping complexes and housing estates, including domestically through Delfin Lend Lease; it manages property funds; and through Bovis Lend Lease it is one of the world's leading project management and construction companies, with a presence in over 40 countries.

Latest business results (June 2006, full year)

The company's revival continued, with a big surge in profits, although much of the gain came from property revaluations. Without these, the after-tax profit was up 24% to $354.2 million. The best result came from the company's retail and communities operation (shopping centres and housing), with profits surging 78% before revaluations, including a $33 million after-tax profit from the completion of the Chapelfield, Norwich, retail complex in the UK. The investment management business saw profits up 11%, thanks to strong investment returns. But profits dipped 4% for the construction and project management business, following losses on two projects in the UK.

Outlook

After a period of stagnation, Lend Lease appears to be recovering, and the company itself is confident that growth will continue for the short to medium term. It has a steady stream of housing projects under development in Australia, and it is also moving more strongly into the development and management of retirement communities. In the UK it sees scope for the development of several major integrated residential, commercial and community projects. In the US it is involved in a big community development project in Denver, and it sees strong growth potential for its Actus business, which is extensively involved in the development of military housing. Lend Lease is also working to boost its property funds management business, through the introduction of new products, including funds offering higher risk. The company has embarked on a restructuring of its Bovis construction arm, aimed at boosting profitability. With a strong balance sheet, Lend Lease is also seeking to grow through acquisition.

LLC Year to 30 June	2005	2006
Revenues ($mn)	8971.3	11903.3
EBIT ($mn)	356.6	604.2
EBIT margin (%)	4.0	5.1
Profit before tax ($mn)	350.2	572.7
Profit after tax ($mn)	225.5	415.2
Earnings per share (¢)	56.5	104.0
Cash flow per share (¢)	61.6	110.3
Dividend (¢)	57	61
Percentage franked	51	100
Net tangible assets per share ($)	5.22	5.36
Interest cover (times)	55.7	19.2
Return on equity (%)	8.2	14.8
Debt-to-equity ratio (%)	–	9.5
Current ratio	0.8	1.1

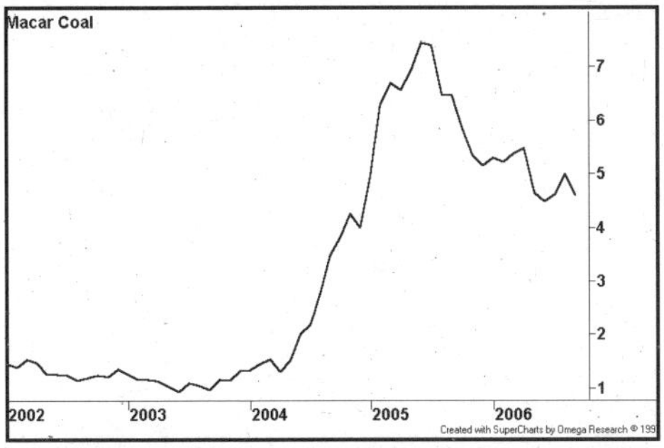

www.macarthurcoal.com.au

MACARTHUR COAL LIMITED

Share price ($)	4.97
12-month high ($)	6.57
12-month low ($)	4.20
Market capitalisation ($mn)	910.1
Price-to-NTA-per-share ratio	2.4
5-year share price return (% p.a.)	36.0

Sector: Materials	Company	Sector
Price-earnings ratio (times)	5.7	12.3
Dividend yield (%)	8.2	2.3

Brisbane-based Macarthur Coal is involved in coal exploration and development, as well as mine management. Its activities are centred on Queensland's Bowen Basin, where it holds 73.3% of the Coppabella and the Moorvale mines, which are responsible for more than 45% of Australian exports of low volatile pulverised coal injection coal (PCI coal). It also produces some thermal and coking coal. Through a series of joint ventures the company has a large number of prospective exploration tenement holdings. The managing director Ken Talbot owns 35% of Macarthur's shares.

Latest business results (June 2006, full year)

A 120% jump in the price of PCI coal for the 2006 contract year (to 31 March 2006) sent Macarthur's profits soaring. Coal sales of 4.9 million tonnes (excluding purchased coal) were slightly down on the previous year, due to production difficulties at Coppabella. PCI coal accounted for 89% of sales, thermal coal 10% and coking coal 1%. Rising fuel, labour and materials expenses added approximately $1.40 a tonne to costs, and a $5 million abnormal cost resulted from a highwall failure.

Outlook

PCI coal is used for steel production, and as a key global supplier Macarthur is set to benefit from growing demand, particularly from Asia. Nevertheless, following the surge in the price for the 2006 contract year, the company forecasts a significantly lower profit in June 2007, based on softer prices, a 20% jump in mining costs and sales of around 4.5 million tonnes. Though the company is capable of producing more, a major constraint on higher sales is inadequate infrastructure, particularly transportation and port facilities. A longer term concern is port capacity. Macarthur is worried that even when planned expansions are completed at the Dalrymple Bay Coal Terminal there may still be insufficient capacity to handle all the company's output. Another concern is Macarthur's contractual dispute with its mining contractor Roche Mining, a division of Downer EDI, which it accuses of underperformance. Macarthur and Roche have lodged claims against each other, with an arbitration hearing due for 2007. New mining technology is intended to help lower production costs at Coppabella by $5 a tonne from 2009.

MCC Year to 30 June	2005	2006
Revenues ($mn)	370.2	534.8
EBIT ($mn)	94.7	211.6
EBIT margin (%)	25.6	39.6
Gross margin (%)	37.2	46.2
Profit before tax ($mn)	89.6	214.0
Profit after tax ($mn)	64.1	149.6
Earnings per share (¢)	41.5	86.6
Cash flow per share (¢)	41.8	86.7
Dividend (¢)	18	41
Percentage franked	100	100
Net tangible assets per share ($)	1.37	2.09
Interest cover (times)	18.8	–
Return on equity (%)	30.9	47.7
Debt-to-equity ratio (%)	7.8	–
Current ratio	1.5	2.6

MACQUARIE BANK LIMITED

Share price ($)	65.47
12-month high ($)	78.23
12-month low ($)	58.02
Market capitalisation ($mn)	16204.4
Price-to-NTA-per-share ratio	5.9
5-year share price return (% p.a.)	17.9

Sector: Financials	**Company**	**Sector**
Price-earnings ratio (times)	15.9	15.7
Dividend yield (%)	3.3	4.3

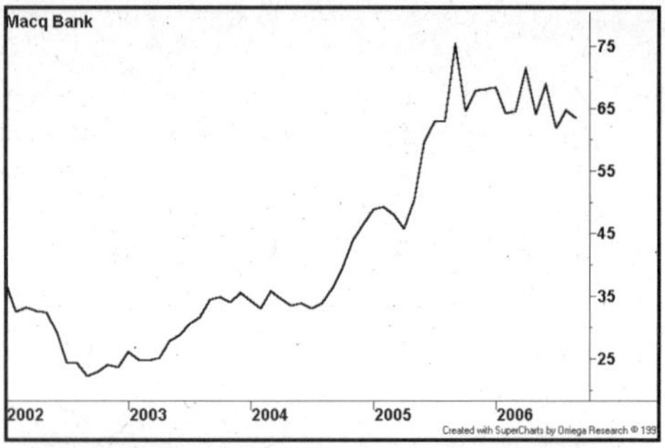

www.macquarie.com.au

Macquarie, established in 1969 as Hill Samuel Australia, a subsidiary of a British merchant bank, is Australia's leading locally-owned investment bank. Its activities are divided into six operating divisions: Investment Banking is responsible for wholesale structuring, stockbroking, underwriting and advisory businesses; Equity Markets engages in principal equity trading, market making, product origination, structuring, warrants and derivatives sales and distribution activities; Treasury and Commodities is responsible for commodity, commodity derivatives and futures trading, commodity finance, treasury and foreign exchange; Banking and Property provides a range of banking and property-related services; Funds Management manages funds across a range of asset classes for corporations, businesses and individuals; and Financial Services distributes financial services via financial advisers and directly to individuals. Macquarie's international business now accounts for more than 45% of total company income.

Latest business results (March 2006, full year)

Macquarie achieved another excellent result, its 14th consecutive year of record profit. Excluding the impact of the new accounting regulations and the previous year's one-off $91 million profit from the formation of the Macquarie Goodman Group, the after-tax profit actually rose 33%. All six operating divisions recorded double-digit rises, with the best performance from the Equity Markets group, where profits soared 50% from the previous year. Though the bank benefited from a strong domestic economy and equity market, the main driver of growth was its overseas business, with international income soaring 59% to $2 billion.

Outlook

Macquarie continues to race ahead, and its shares have been excellent performers. It continues its involvement in a wide range of global corporate activities, many with the potential for high earnings. And the roll-out of a succession of infrastructure and other specialist funds around the world is expected to provide a steady and stable source of management fee income. It is particularly active in Asia, and the 2004 acquisition of ING's Asian cash equities business is providing a platform for strong growth. The establishment of a corporate finance joint venture with Japan's Shinsei Bank is expected to provide further expansion opportunities. It has established a Middle East infrastructure investment fund with Abu Dhabi Commercial Bank.

MBL Year to 31 March	2005	2006
Operating income ($mn)	3752.0	4393.0
Net interest income ($mn)	536.0	592.0
Operating expenses ($mn)	2594.0	3106.0
Profit before tax ($mn)	1158.0	1287.0
Profit after tax ($mn)	841.0	945.0
Earnings per share (¢)	382.8	413.0
Dividend (¢)	161	215
Percentage franked	90	96
Non-interest income to total income (%)	85.7	86.5
Net tangible assets per share ($)	12.46	11.13
Cost-to-income ratio (%)	69.1	70.7
Return on equity (%)	26.4	23.5
Return on assets (%)	1.5	1.1

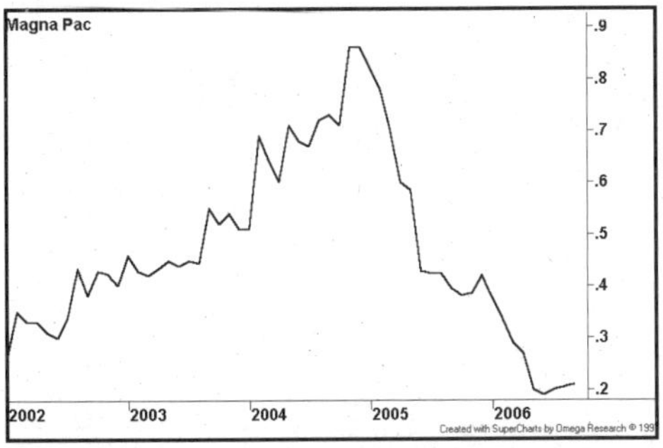

www.magnapacific.com.au

MAGNA PACIFIC (HOLDINGS) LIMITED

Share price ($)	0.21	
12-month high ($)	0.44	
12-month low ($)	0.19	
Market capitalisation ($mn)	22.7	
Price-to-NTA-per-share ratio	1.2	
5-year share price return (% p.a.)	4.1	
Sector: Consumer discretionary	**Company**	**Sector**
Price-earnings ratio (times)	6.2	18.8
Dividend yield (%)	8.1	4.0

Brisbane-based Magna Pacific is a leading wholesale distributor of DVDs and videos to retailers and rental outlets throughout Australia and New Zealand. It owns a new 6000-square-metre facility in Brisbane capable of round-the-clock manufacture and packaging of DVDs and videos. It has also moved into cinema distribution of first-release movies. Magna Pacific shares are listed on the ASX and also on German stock exchanges.

Latest business results (June 2006, full year)

Sales and profits fell sharply, as a deteriorating DVD market hit business. Back catalogue sales were down, and prices were softer. In addition, the company was hit by a scarcity of attractive new titles. The June 2005 results included a $2 million profit – not included in the figures in the table on this page – from the sale of the company's shareholding in the Becker Group.

Outlook

Magna Pacific has grown to become one of the leaders in Australia and New Zealand in the highly fragmented DVD distribution business. It is a major beneficiary of the continuing attraction of DVD products, and in particular of the growth in demand for home theatre entertainment hardware and software. Its 6000 shopfronts across Australia and New Zealand incorporate rental chains, mass merchant retailers, specialist music stores, specialist home video retailers, newsagents, bookstores, home entertainment stores and direct mail houses. It has been working to make itself one of the lowest-cost manufacturers of DVDs, and in July 2006 moved to a major new purpose-built $14 million plant in Brisbane's Eagle Farm area. This plant immediately triples the company's manufacturing capacity, and in the long term it will provide six times the capacity of the former facility. In line with its moves into cinema distribution, Magna Pacific has scheduled the release of 10 new movies over two years, including *A Prairie Home Companion* with Meryl Streep, *Lonely Hearts* with John Travolta, and *Penelope* with Reese Witherspoon. Looking further ahead, the company hopes to boost the number of cinema releases. With no debt, it is also interested in a strategic acquisition, should a suitable opportunity arise. But weak DVD prices remain a threat in the absence of popular new titles.

MPH Year to 30 June	2005	2006
Revenues ($mn)	36.7	30.0
EBIT ($mn)	10.3	4.9
EBIT margin (%)	28.1	16.4
Gross margin (%)	52.6	48.2
Profit before tax ($mn)	11.3	5.3
Profit after tax ($mn)	7.3	3.7
Earnings per share (¢)	6.3	3.4
Cash flow per share (¢)	7.7	4.3
Dividend (¢)	3	1.7
Percentage franked	100	100
Net tangible assets per share ($)	0.18	0.18
Interest cover (times)	–	–
Return on equity (%)	20.0	11.4
Debt-to-equity ratio (%)	–	–
Current ratio	3.2	2.7

MAXITRANS INDUSTRIES LIMITED

Share price ($)	0.55
12-month high ($)	0.95
12-month low ($)	0.45
Market capitalisation ($mn)	94.5
Price-to-NTA-per-share ratio	2.3
5-year share price return (% p.a.)	37.8

Sector: Industrials	Company	Sector
Price-earnings ratio (times)	8.8	13.6
Dividend yield (%)	7.7	4.3

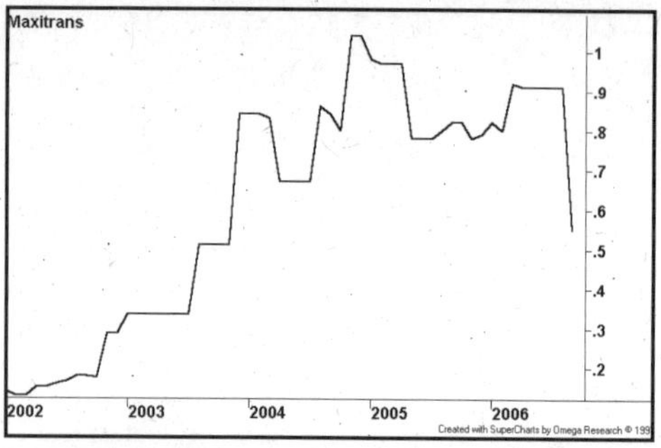

www.maxitrans.com.au

Based in Melbourne, MaxiTRANS was formed in 1998 from the merger of Freighter Industries, which had been established in 1946, and Maxi-CUBE, started in 1972. It is today a leading manufacturer of a wide range of specialised truck trailers for the road transportation industry, mainly produced in Ballarat and Auckland. It operates a Chinese joint venture operation named MTC with a major Chinese transport equipment manufacturer, to produce fibreglass wall panels, which are sold throughout China, including in the manufacture of insulated and refrigerated trailers. Through its Lusty EMS and Hamelex White subsidiaries it is Australia's largest manufacturer of tip trailers. The company also operates a significant truck and trailer parts business, through its new subsidiary Colrain. In September 2005 it entered the rigid body sector with the acquisition of assets of Peki Transport Equipment.

Latest business results (June 2006, full year)

Sales were up, but profits fell as the company was hit by problems at its Colrain parts business. These were a combination of one-off significant items of expense, computer difficulties and troubles in the integration of the business's wholesale warehousing function. As a result, the company's parts and service operation, nearly 20% of total turnover, went from profit to loss. Hamelex White also performed poorly. In contrast, the company's traditional trailer and van production businesses enjoyed record sales.

Outlook

MaxiTRANS has embarked on a major restructuring of its operations, and it views 2006–07 as a period of consolidation, although it also continues to seek out new acquisition opportunities. It has moved from 70% to 100% ownership of Colrain, closed that subsidiary's unprofitable manufacturing operation, reorganised its computer systems and appointed new management. It has also restructured operations at Hamelex White, aimed at boosting quality and cutting production costs. It is concerned that demand seems to be slowing for its trailers and vans, as high fuel prices force customers to cut orders. However, it believes improved earnings in the June 2007 year from Colrain, Hamelex White and Lusty EMS will more than offset any slowdown in trailer and van sales. It sees enormous growth potential in China, and is seeking new joint ventures there.

MXI Year to 30 June	2005	2006
Revenues ($mn)	223.2	245.0
EBIT ($mn)	18.5	16.8
EBIT margin (%)	8.3	6.9
Gross margin (%)	19.6	15.3
Profit before tax ($mn)	16.3	14.0
Profit after tax ($mn)	12.4	10.7
Earnings per share (¢)	7.3	6.2
Cash flow per share (¢)	9.9	9.4
Dividend (¢)	4	4.25
Percentage franked	100	100
Net tangible assets per share ($)	0.18	0.24
Interest cover (times)	8.4	6.1
Return on equity (%)	18.4	14.9
Debt-to-equity ratio (%)	59.5	48.0
Current ratio	1.9	1.8

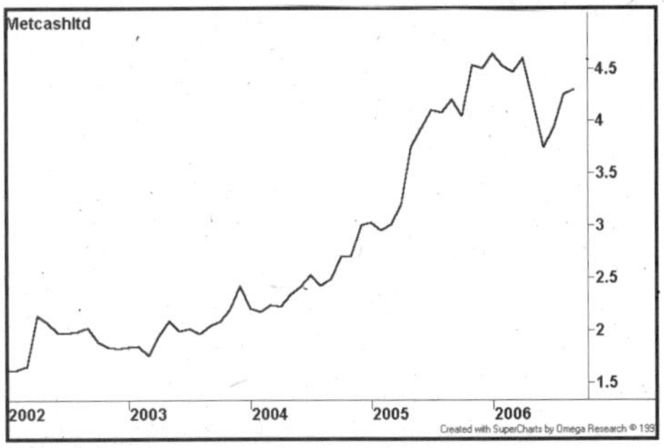

www.metcash.com

METCASH LIMITED

Share price ($)	4.35
12-month high ($)	4.90
12-month low ($)	3.66
Market capitalisation ($mn)	3231.9
Price-to-NTA-per-share ratio	na
5-year share price return (% p.a.)	31.9

Sector: Consumer staples	Company	Sector
Price-earnings ratio (times)	20.2	15.5
Dividend yield (%)	2.6	3.2

Sydney-based Metcash, a subsidiary of South Africa's Metro Cash and Carry, is one of Australia's leading grocery retail and wholesale companies. Its principal business is IGA Distribution, which operates from eight distribution centres and supplies some 4500 independent grocery stores on the eastern seaboard and in South Australia. Its Australian Liquor Marketers division supplies liquor to more than 13 000 outlets throughout Australia and New Zealand. The Campbells Cash and Carry business operates from 41 warehouses, and supplies groceries to convenience stores, petrol stations and other smaller outlets. Late in 2005, Metcash acquired most of the Australian assets of Foodland Associated.

Latest business results (April 2006, full year)

Profits were flat, despite the gain in sales from the Foodland acquisition, with the grocery environment remaining highly competitive, and the company incurring expenses as it worked to integrate the Foodland businesses with its existing operations. However, comparisons with the previous year were difficult, because the new accounting rules meant that the company restated its previous year's results, with a higher April 2005 profit and a hugely inflated debt-to-equity ratio.

Outlook

The acquisition of most of Foodland's Australian assets is transforming Metcash, with the company forecasting that it will add $80 million to $90 million to total EBIT in the April 2007 year, and its national grocery market share rising to around 20%. It is in the process of disposing of around 60 retail stores in Western Australia and Queensland that were part of the acquisition. In addition, it is transforming Foodland's fresh fruit and vegetable business into a major supplier to the national network of 1300 IGA stores, and expects this operation's annual revenues to quadruple to $300 million. Separately, it has formed a new strategic alliance with New Zealand's largest grocery distributor, Foodstuffs, with an initial focus on building the two companies' respective private label businesses through their combined buying power, while also sharing information, technology, training and other aspects of their operations. In Australia, the Campbells Cash and Carry division is achieving strong growth in the petrol and convenience store sector, and now claims a 26% market share.

MTS Year to 30 April	2005	2006
Revenues ($mn)	6991.0	8192.5
Food distribution (%)	55	57
Liquor distribution (%)	31	29
Cash & carry distribution (%)	14	14
EBIT ($mn)	186.6	220.8
EBIT margin (%)	2.7	2.7
Gross margin (%)	8.5	9.6
Profit before tax ($mn)	185.1	180.3
Profit after tax ($mn)	126.8	127.9
Earnings per share (¢)	18.9	21.6
Cash flow per share (¢)	23.7	28.6
Dividend (¢)	9.5	11.5
Percentage franked	100	100
Net tangible assets per share ($)	–	–
Interest cover (times)	128.2	5.4
Return on equity (%)	53.5	24.7
Debt-to-equity ratio (%)	3575.3	52.5
Current ratio	1.4	1.4

MONADELPHOUS GROUP LIMITED

Share price ($)	6.45	
12-month high ($)	7.00	
12-month low ($)	3.37	
Market capitalisation ($mn)	525.3	
Price-to-NTA-per-share ratio	8.8	
5-year share price return (% p.a.)	90.3	
Sector: Industrials	**Company**	**Sector**
Price-earnings ratio (times)	17.7	13.6
Dividend yield (%)	3.7	4.3

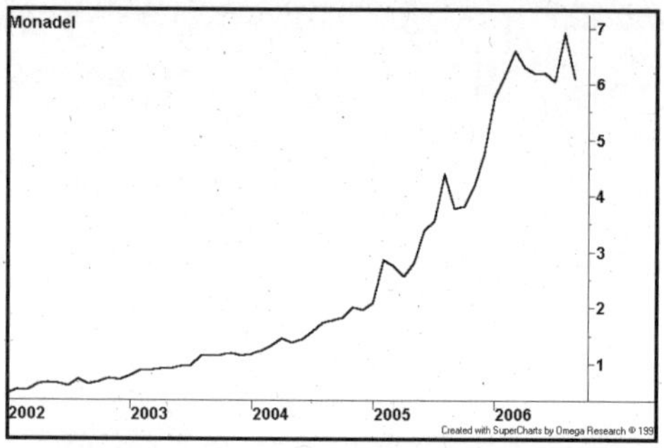

www.monadel.com.au

Perth-based Monadelphous is an engineering company that provides project management, construction, maintenance and support services to the mining, mineral processing, chemicals and associated industries. It operates from branches at key mining and mineral processing centres throughout Australia, with a client base that includes most of the country's resource majors.

Latest business results (June 2006, full year)

Monadelphous enjoyed another outstanding year, with sales and profits surging for the fifth straight year. In just five years the company's after-tax profit has appreciated more than eightfold. The star of the latest reporting period was the company's maintenance and industrial services division, with revenues soaring 61% to $243 million. There was particularly strong growth in Queensland, including the start of a two-year contract at Comalco's Boyne Smelter in Gladstone. The Queensland-based instrumentation and electrical company MIE, acquired by Monadelphous in May 2005, provided an initial full-year revenue contribution of $26 million, and subsidiary Skystar Airport Services doubled its revenues to $15 million. The engineering construction division increased revenues 21% to $289 million, with particular strength in Western Australia, including contracts for Rio Tinto Iron Ore at Dampier and Yandicoogina and for BHP Billiton iron ore and nickel projects at Port Hedland and Ravensthorpe.

Outlook

Monadelphous has become a major stock market beneficiary of the resources boom, and its spectacular growth continues, with over $500 million dollars of new contracts won by the company between December 2005 and August 2006. These include its largest ever contract, for $180 million worth of expansion works for BHP Billiton's iron ore project at Port Hedland, scheduled for completion by December 2007. A second major project win was for $120 million of work at BHP Billiton's iron ore facilities in the Pilbara region. However, the company faces capacity restraints, including skills shortages, and it is concentrating on projects offering superior earnings quality. It has conceded that organic growth rates achieved over the 2004–06 period are not sustainable. It is also striving to develop a more diversified revenues base to limit the company's dependence on resources, including moves into electrical and instrumentation services and into the power and water industry sectors.

MND Year to 30 June	2005	2006
Revenues ($mn)	390.6	532.0
EBIT ($mn)	23.8	41.4
EBIT margin (%)	6.1	7.8
Gross margin (%)	9.3	10.3
Profit before tax ($mn)	23.9	42.2
Profit after tax ($mn)	16.7	29.4
Earnings per share (¢)	21.1	36.5
Cash flow per share (¢)	27.7	45.8
Dividend (¢)	14.25	24
Percentage franked	100	100
Net tangible assets per share ($)	0.55	0.73
Interest cover (times)	–	–
Return on equity (%)	39.0	54.3
Debt-to-equity ratio (%)	–	–
Current ratio	1.4	1.2

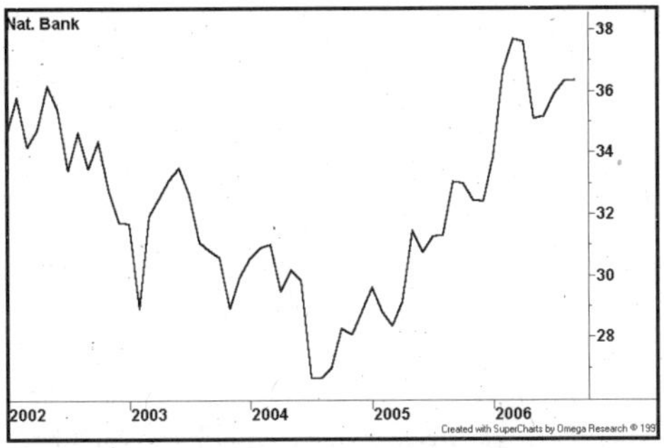

www.nabgroup.com

NATIONAL AUSTRALIA BANK LIMITED

Share price ($)	36.50
12-month high ($)	38.10
12-month low ($)	31.06
Market capitalisation ($mn)	58268.5
Price-to-NTA-per-share ratio	2.8
5-year share price return (% p.a.)	12.5

Sector: Financials	Company	Sector
Price-earnings ratio (times)	15.1	15.7
Dividend yield (%)	4.5	4.3

The National Australia Bank, based in Melbourne, has a history dating back to the establishment of the National Bank of Australasia in 1858. It is Australia's largest bank, with a wide spread of financial activities. It owns the Clydesdale Bank and Yorkshire Bank in Britain, and the Bank of New Zealand. Its Institutional Markets & Services business operates globally, focusing on debt, risk management and investment products for corporate and institutional customers. Its MLC business is one of Australia's leading funds management operations.

Latest business results (March 2006, half year)

Profits were up, in a pleasing result for the bank. The key factor was solid growth in domestic banking, following management changes and restructuring initiatives. The bank reported that it maintained its national housing loan market share of more than 14%, and its share of business lending rose to nearly 19%. The domestic wealth management operation saw profits fall, mainly due to the loss of transitional tax relief in the investments business. British profits fell – though only marginally in British currency – largely reflecting increased expenses. New Zealand business overcame a competitive banking environment to post a solid gain, with strong growth in home and business lending. Overall, total bank lending increased by 16.5% to $322 billion, and deposit volumes were up 3.9% to $216 billion. Total funds under management and administration rose from $85 billion to $96 billion.

Outlook

NAB appears to have achieved success in turning around its businesses, after a period of stagnating profits. However, much now depends on global economic conditions, with rising interest rates a concern, while stock market volatility could adversely affect the wealth management business. UK operations are seeing good growth. However, New Zealand business faces a period of uncertainty, with competition remaining strong at a time of economic slowdown. National Australia is reported to be seeking to radically change its corporate make-up, with the separation of its bank and non-bank activities and the creation of a new holding company structure.

NAB Year to 30 September	2004	2005
Operating income ($mn)	13034.0	13856.0
Net interest income ($mn)	7191.0	7082.0
Operating expenses ($mn)	6915.0	7402.0
Profit before tax ($mn)	5423.0	6255.0
Profit after tax ($mn)	3561.0	3761.0
Earnings per share (¢)	235.0	241.2
Dividend (¢)	166	166
Percentage franked	100	80
Non-interest income to total income (%)	44.8	48.9
Cost-to-income ratio (%)	53.1	53.4
Return on equity (%)	13.5	13.9
Return on assets (%)	0.9	0.9
Half year to 31 March	**2005**	**2006**
Operating income ($mn)	6933.0	7687.0
Profit before tax ($mn)	2750.0	3484.0
Profit after tax ($mn)	1747.0	1967.0
Earnings per share (¢)	106.2	118.8
Dividend (¢)	83	83
Percentage franked	80	80
Net tangible assets per share ($)	12.87	12.88

NATIONAL CAN INDUSTRIES LIMITED

Share price ($)	1.75	
12-month high ($)	1.89	
12-month low ($)	1.26	
Market capitalisation ($mn)	118.9	
Price-to-NTA-per-share ratio	1.0	
5-year share price return (% p.a.)	23.6	
Sector: Materials	**Company**	**Sector**
Price-earnings ratio (times)	8.4	12.3
Dividend yield (%)	5.7	2.3

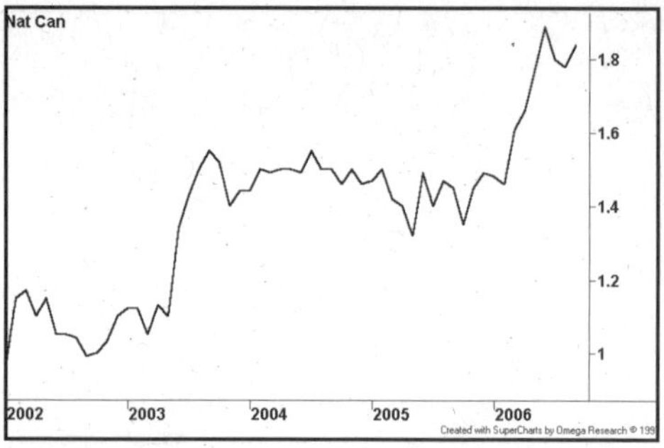

www.nci-ltd.com

Melbourne-based National Can was established in 1954, and has grown steadily to become Australia's third-largest can manufacturer. It comprises two operating businesses – NCI Packaging is engaged in metal and plastic manufacturing; and Pacmetal Services supplies highly decorated, coated and plain tinplate and aluminium, ready for use by local and international packaging manufacturers. It operates eight plants in Australia, three in New Zealand and one each in Fiji and Papua New Guinea, supplying the paint, chemical, aerosol, industrial and food packaging markets.

Latest business results (June 2006, full year)

A modest rise in sales translated into a big jump in profits, as the company achieved success in its drive to cut costs and boost margins. Australian revenues, about three-quarters of the total, rose 6%, with the pre-tax profit surging 65%, which the company attributed to improved margins, containment of operating costs and a reduction in inventories built up in the previous year. These inventories had been accumulated to mitigate the risks associated with raw materials shortages. New Zealand sales rose 1% in local currency, but fell 2% in Australian dollars, with stronger domestic sales largely offset by export weakness. However, New Zealand profits rose 26%. Higher prices and lower costs were factors that helped the small PNG and Fiji operations to record double-digit sales and profit growth.

Outlook

National Can occupies a strong position in the competitive domestic packaging industry. With its business highly geared to levels of economic activity its best potential for growth comes from cost cutting, new technology, new products or moves abroad. With raw materials costs increasing, it is also important for the company to be able to pass these on to customers. The company is working on a strategic plan to become one of the industry's lowest cost producers, and this has involved a series of capital investments in new equipment and tooling, along with product innovations. In July 2006 its New Zealand business acquired monobloc manufacturing equipment in order to expand into the aluminium aerosol market. National Can has said that it expects modest revenue growth in the June 2007 year, providing economic conditions do not deteriorate, with profits largely flat.

NCI Year to 30 June	2005	2006
Revenues ($mn)	180.4	188.4
EBIT ($mn)	12.4	19.0
EBIT margin (%)	6.9	10.1
Profit before tax ($mn)	12.6	19.9
Profit after tax ($mn)	9.1	13.9
Earnings per share (¢)	13.6	20.9
Cash flow per share (¢)	28.3	34.5
Dividend (¢)	7.5	10
Percentage franked	100	100
Net tangible assets per share ($)	1.72	1.82
Interest cover (times)	–	–
Return on equity (%)	8.0	11.7
Debt-to-equity ratio (%)	–	–
Current ratio	4.7	4.4

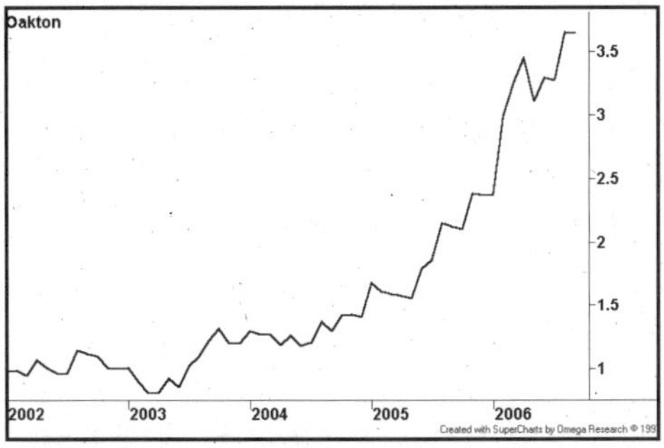

www.oakton.com.au

OAKTON LIMITED

Share price ($)	3.58	
12-month high ($)	3.70	
12-month low ($)	1.92	
Market capitalisation ($mn)	293.7	
Price-to-NTA-per-share ratio	18.6	
5-year share price return (% p.a.)	46.1	
Sector: Information technology	**Company**	**Sector**
Price-earnings ratio (times)	20.3	22.8
Dividend yield (%)	4.7	2.2

Melbourne-based technology consultant Oakton was established in 1988. It has grown rapidly through acquisition, and now serves a wide variety of blue-chip corporate and government clients. Working in partnership with leading business system product vendors, it provides guidance on information technology (IT) requirements, covering the full lifecycle of planning and design, custom software development, packaged software implementation, information management and system integration processes. It also provides a service fully managing organisations' operational systems. Oakton has offices in Melbourne, Sydney and Brisbane. In August 2006 it acquired the IT services company Clickstream, and it plans to open an offshore development centre in India.

Latest business results (June 2006, full year)

Oakton achieved another excellent result, with sales and profits again up strongly, achieved solely through organic growth. Sydney was again the standout region, with profits up more than 75%. The Sydney office is now responsible for 39% of company profits, compared to 32% a year earlier. There was also a successful start for the new office in Brisbane. Altogether, clients in the financial services sector accounted for 30.6% of total revenues, followed by products and services (28.4%), public sector (17.6%), resources (16.6%) and communications and high tech (6.8%).

Outlook

Oakton continues to grow rapidly. At June 2006, staff numbers had grown to 457, up from 363 a year earlier, with a further rise to 515 in August 2006, following the Clickstream acquisition. With strong demand continuing for IT services in Australia, the company is working to boost client numbers in Melbourne, Sydney and Brisbane, and to increase the number of services it provides to each of its clients. It is also looking to expand geographically, and is considering opening a new office in Canberra. The Clickstream acquisition is expected to add more than $6 million in revenues to Oakton in the June 2007 year, and to help establish Oakton as a leading participant in the information management IT services field. The company believes that its planned offshore development in India will enable it to become more competitive. With no debt and some $8 million in cash, Oakton is evaluating further acquisition opportunities.

OKN Year to 30 June	2005	2006
Revenues ($mn)	54.0	76.8
EBIT ($mn)	13.1	20.5
EBIT margin (%)	24.3	26.7
Profit before tax ($mn)	13.3	20.7
Profit after tax ($mn)	9.2	14.4
Earnings per share (¢)	11.4	17.6
Cash flow per share (¢)	12.6	18.6
Dividend (¢)	10	16.75
Percentage franked	100	100
Net tangible assets per share ($)	0.15	0.19
Interest cover (times)	–	–
Return on equity (%)	32.6	44.7
Debt-to-equity ratio (%)	–	–
Current ratio	2.2	2.5

OAMPS LIMITED

Share price ($)	4.53
12-month high ($)	4.60
12-month low ($)	2.79
Market capitalisation ($mn)	669.5
Price-to-NTA-per-share ratio	12.4
5-year share price return (% p.a.)	33.7

Sector: Financials	Company	Sector
Price-earnings ratio (times)	16.8	15.7
Dividend yield (%)	4.0	4.3

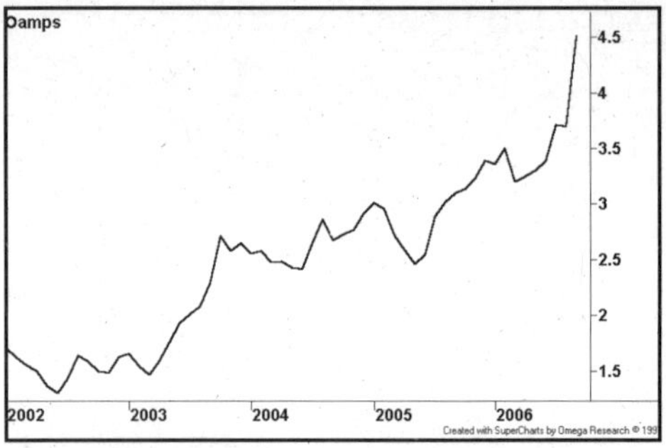

www.oamps.com.au

Melbourne-based OAMPS, established in 1976 as the Oil Agents Mutual Provident Society, is one of Australia's largest insurance brokers and underwriters. It specialises in providing services to domestic businesses, particularly in niche markets, and has grown rapidly through acquisition. It also operates in other related businesses, including financial planning, asset finance, superannuation investment and funds management. In addition, it operates an insurance broking and underwriting business in the United Kingdom, where it specialises in oil, tanker and hazardous goods risks. In July 2006 it sold its premium funding business.

Latest business results (June 2006, full year)

OAMPS enjoyed another good year, with earnings up strongly, despite just a modest increase in revenues, as a competitive insurance environment sent rates lower. The key was the company's underwriting business, with profits up nearly 60%, despite a small dip in revenues. Insurance broking was also strong, particularly in the United Kingdom, where profits jumped nearly 20%. The small British operation is responsible for only about 7% of company revenues, but contributes around 14% of profit. The company's financial services division, a very small part of its business, enjoyed an excellent year, with funds under management up 18% to $305 million. But the agencies business – managing a number of specialist underwriting agencies – saw profits tumble, despite a rise in written premiums and in commission and fee income.

OMP Year to 30 June	2005	2006
Revenues ($mn)	268.1	277.5
Underwriting (%)	46	45
Broking – Australia (%)	32	35
Agencies (%)	11	11
Broking – UK (%)	6	7
EBIT ($mn)	38.4	46.2
EBIT margin (%)	14.3	16.7
Profit before tax ($mn)	48.6	57.3
Profit after tax ($mn)	33.3	39.7
Earnings per share (¢)	23.7	26.9
Cash flow per share (¢)	25.7	30.3
Dividend (¢)	15.1	18
Percentage franked	100	100
Net tangible assets per share ($)	0.31	0.37
Interest cover (times)	–	–
Return on equity (%)	19.5	19.7
Debt-to-equity ratio (%)	–	–
Current ratio	1.2	1.2

Outlook

OAMPS had $200 million in net cash holdings in June 2006, and it plans a vigorous program of acquisition during 2006–07. As a result, despite continuing pressure on the rates that it can charge, it expects EPS growth of 5% to 10% in the June 2007 year. It will also book a pre-tax profit of around $18 million from the sale of its premium funding business. The company's particular strategy is to identify niche markets where it believes it can add value to the services being offered to clients, and to enter these markets through acquisition, and it made eight acquisitions between March and August 2006, adding more than $65 million to annual revenues. As this book was going to press, Wesfarmers had made a takeover bid for OAMPS.

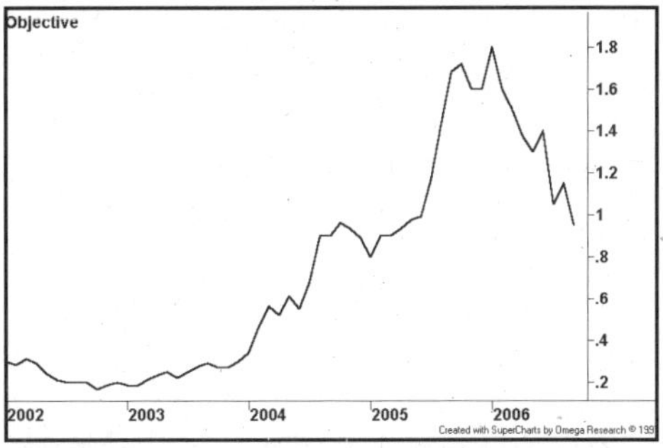

www.objective.com

OBJECTIVE CORPORATION LIMITED

Share price ($)	1.05
12-month high ($)	1.90
12-month low ($)	0.99
Market capitalisation ($mn)	145.2
Price-to-NTA-per-share ratio	6.3
5-year share price return (% p.a.)	26.7

Sector: Information technology	Company	Sector
Price-earnings ratio (times)	19.8	22.8
Dividend yield (%)	2.1	2.2

Founded in 1987, Sydney-based Objective develops and provides enterprise content management (ECM) software, designed to help clients electronically manage their records and their data retrieval systems. It targets government organisations and large corporations, particularly those operating within regulatory regimes requiring strict recordkeeping, and it derives its revenues from the sale of its product, consulting fees from implementation services, and ongoing maintenance and support services. European business is responsible for about a third of company turnover, and the company is also strong in New Zealand.

Latest business results (June 2006, full year)

Sales were up, but profits declined, as business in Europe fell below expectations. Asia Pacific saw revenues surge 45% to $24.7 million, with profits up 37%. But European sales fell 26% to $12.2 million, and profits tumbled 59%. During the year the company signed new contracts with the New Zealand central government and most Australian state governments, and with new customers in the energy, education and local government sectors.

Outlook

The ECM software business is growing worldwide, as government bodies, private companies and others must manage the collection, storage and delivery of a fast-growing amount of data. Objective is a leader in the field, with an estimated 26% market share in Australia, 35% in New Zealand, and a growing presence abroad. Its key product is Objective 7, released in 2005, which is a module-based system that allows ready access to data by a wide variety of potential users. In the UK, Objective has in hand major contracts for the Scottish Executive and for the housing and urban regeneration specialist Places for People. During 2005–06 the company's software was re-certified to the UK National Archives electronic recordkeeping standard, TNA2, which will open considerably more opportunities for the company. Objective spends heavily on research and development – $5.7 million in the June 2006 year, up 33% on the previous year – in order to stay at the forefront of trends in its business. With virtually no debt and more than $17 million in net cash holdings it has funds available to invest for future growth and it is also able to grow by acquisition.

OCL Year to 30 June	2005	2006
Revenues ($mn)	33.3	36.9
EBIT ($mn)	10.2	8.5
EBIT margin (%)	30.5	23.1
Profit before tax ($mn)	10.7	9.4
Profit after tax ($mn)	8.0	7.2
Earnings per share (¢)	5.9	5.3
Cash flow per share (¢)	6.1	5.6
Dividend (¢)	2	2.25
Percentage franked	100	100
Net tangible assets per share ($)	0.13	0.17
Interest cover (times)	–	–
Return on equity (%)	53.1	35.3
Debt-to-equity ratio (%)	–	–
Current ratio	2.8	3.3

ONESTEEL LIMITED

Share price ($)	4.29	
12-month high ($)	4.40	
12-month low ($)	3.15	
Market capitalisation ($mn)	2391.0	
Price-to-NTA-per-share ratio	2.0	
5-year share price return (% p.a.)	41.6	
Sector: Materials	**Company**	**Sector**
Price-earnings ratio (times)	14.1	12.3
Dividend yield (%)	4.0	2.3

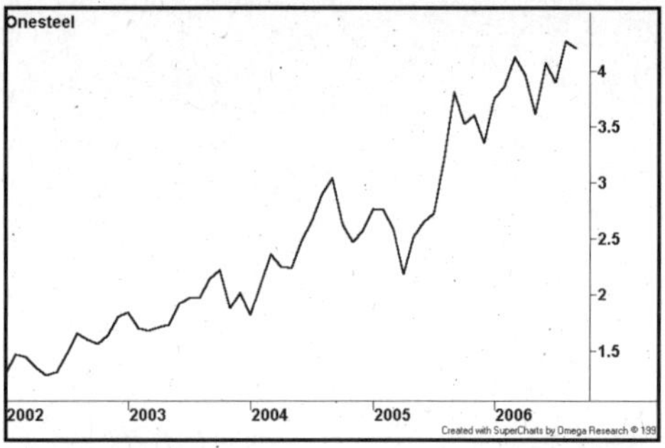

www.onesteel.com

Sydney-based OneSteel was formed in 2000 from various BHP steel businesses. It is today Australia's leading manufacturer of such steel products as rails, rods, bars, reinforcing wire, tubes and pipes. It is also a prominent metals distribution company. The majority of its products are used in the construction, manufacturing, housing, mining and agricultural industries. It has announced plans for the acquisition of Smorgon Steel.

Latest business results (June 2006, full year)

Price rises and productivity gains gave OneSteel a good boost to its profits, despite sluggish demand for its products. During the year the company dispatched 2.29 tonnes of steel, a 1% rise on the previous year, at an average price 6.9% higher than the year before. Strong demand from the engineering, resources and non-residential construction sectors offset weakness in certain manufacturing, rural automotive and residential construction segments. Exports to New Zealand represented 10% of total steel sales, up from 4%.

Outlook

OneSteel has achieved successive profit increases for five straight years, thanks to the strength of the domestic economy, heavy infrastructure investment in Australia and the company's continuing efforts to boost productivity. It has launched Project Magnet, costing $355 million, to commercialise its magnetite ore reserves for producing steel, along with the sale of surplus hematite ore reserves. The capital works are due to be substantially completed during 2006–07, and the project is expected to generate additional revenues for OneSteel of more than $1.5 billion over 20 years. Otherwise, the company's long-term future is very much tied to its agreement to acquire Smorgon Steel, which the two companies believe should deliver cost savings of $70 million per year. The agreement must be approved by the Australian Competition and Consumer Commission, and as this book was being published BlueScope Steel had bought a 20% stake in Smorgon Steel, which some observers viewed as an attempt to block the OneSteel acquisition. For the near term, OneSteel's business will be strongly linked to trends in the domestic economy, with turmoil in the car industry a possible negative factor. Rising input costs and cheap imports are further concerns.

OST Year to 30 June	2005	2006
Revenues ($mn)	3938.5	4004.6
Distribution (%)	54	54
Manufacturing (%)	45	45
EBIT ($mn)	277.2	300.3
EBIT margin (%)	7.0	7.5
Gross margin (%)	20.0	19.9
Profit before tax ($mn)	226.0	246.0
Profit after tax ($mn)	153.1	171.6
Earnings per share (¢)	27.4	30.5
Cash flow per share (¢)	43.9	47.1
Dividend (¢)	13.5	17
Percentage franked	100	100
Net tangible assets per share ($)	1.96	2.16
Interest cover (times)	5.4	5.5
Return on equity (%)	11.6	12.4
Debt-to-equity ratio (%)	46.5	42.5
Current ratio	1.8	1.8

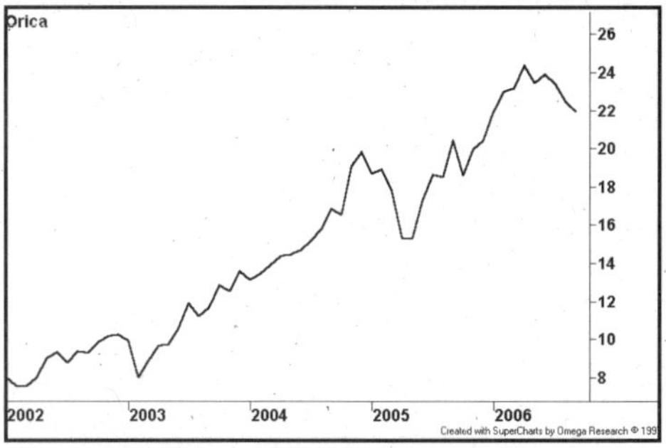

www.orica.com.au

ORICA LIMITED

Share price ($)	22.70	
12-month high ($)	26.45	
12-month low ($)	17.77	
Market capitalisation ($mn)	6981.2	
Price-to-NTA-per-share ratio	4.0	
5-year share price return (% p.a.)	43.8	
Sector: Materials	**Company**	**Sector**
Price-earnings ratio (times)	18.5	12.3
Dividend yield (%)	3.1	2.3

Melbourne-based Orica was founded some 130 years ago as a supplier of explosives for the mining industry, and for many years it was a subsidiary of Britain's Imperial Chemical Industries. It is now a leading manufacturer of a range of industrial and consumer products. These include one of the world's largest mining explosives businesses and a major chemicals operation, as well as Dulux paints and Selleys home handyman and car care products. It has sold its 70% stake in Incitec Pivot, Australia's foremost producer of fertilisers.

Latest business results (March 2006, half year)

In a good result, Orica saw sales and profits rise, driven by its growing strength in mining explosives. The mining services division saw sales up 23%, with EBIT rising 15%. The now-sold Incitec Pivot business also saw strong profit growth, despite a decline in revenues. Sales of consumer products edged up, but profits dipped, largely reflecting difficult market conditions in the retail sector. Chemical services recorded a 15% rise in sales with EBIT up 27%, thanks to productivity improvements, along with higher volumes and prices. But the Orica Chemnet chemicals distribution business was hurt by softer market conditions and integration problems with some recent acquisitions, and profits were down sharply.

Outlook

The sale during 2006 of its shares in its fertiliser subsidiary Incitec Pivot and its chemicals joint venture Qenos has set Orica on a new path, with a heavy emphasis on mining explosives. It has spent nearly $1 billion to acquire global assets of Dyno Nobel, and it is now working to integrate these with its existing operations. The company expects considerable cost-saving and synergy to derive from this acquisition over a period of two years. It has launched a big restructuring of its Chemnet business, which distributes thousands of products to customers in many countries, in order to boost flagging profitability.

ORI Year to 30 September	2004	2005
Revenues ($mn)	4610.5	5126.7
EBIT ($mn)	553.3	563.1
EBIT margin (%)	12.0	11.0
Profit before tax ($mn)	481.0	460.0
Profit after tax ($mn)	325.6	334.9
Earnings per share (¢)	119.1	122.8
Cash flow per share (¢)	181.5	187.3
Dividend (¢)	68	71
Percentage franked	41	32
Interest cover (times)	7.7	5.5
Return on equity (%)	23.2	23.2
Half year to 31 March	**2005**	**2006**
Revenues ($mn)	2384.3	2598.6
Mining services (%)	38	43
Chemnet (%)	20	19
Consumer products (%)	16	15
Fertilisers (%)	18	15
Chemical services (%)	8	8
Profit before tax ($mn)	197.8	212.1
Profit after tax ($mn)	137.2	153.2
Earnings per share (¢)	50.3	49.0
Dividend (¢)	25	26
Percentage franked	32	35
Net tangible assets per share ($)	2.50	5.74
Debt-to-equity ratio (%)	96.0	54.3
Current ratio	1.1	1.4

ORIGIN ENERGY LIMITED

Share price ($)	6.48
12-month high ($)	7.68
12-month low ($)	6.30
Market capitalisation ($mn)	5108.9
Price-to-NTA-per-share ratio	3.5
5-year share price return (% p.a.)	19.7

Sector: Energy	**Company**	**Sector**
Price-earnings ratio (times)	15.5	14.8
Dividend yield (%)	2.8	2.6

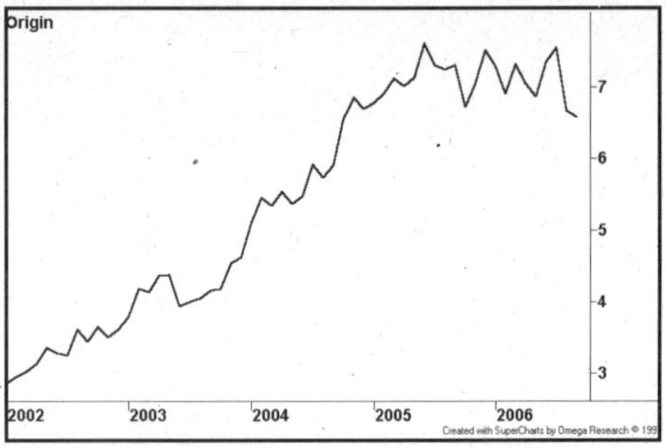

www.originenergy.com.au

Origin Energy, formerly the energy arm of the Boral group, was de-merged in 2000. Today it is one of Australia's leading energy companies, supplying natural gas, electricity and liquefied petroleum gas to more than two million business and residential customers in Australia, New Zealand and the Pacific. It operates under five core business units: exploration and production, retail, generation, networks, and the Contact Energy business, which is based on Origin's 51% equity stake in the New Zealand power company.

Latest business results (June 2006, full year)

Sales and profits rose, with a full-year contribution from Contact Energy and stronger domestic retail business offsetting a sharp decline in exploration and production earnings. Contact, which generates about 25% of New Zealand's electricity, as well as selling gas, benefited from high power prices in that country, with a significant boost to profits. In Australia, Origin was able to overcome the impact of continuing high levels of customer churn in the retail gas and electricity market to post a 5% gain in sales revenues and a 10% profit rise. The generation business also boosted profits. However, higher oil prices could not offset the impact of lower oil and condensate production, higher operating costs and a big increase in exploration write-offs, and the exploration and production division saw EBIT fall 25%.

Outlook

Origin's particular strength is that it operates across the entire energy supply chain, and it continues to expand. Its long-term target is for annual EPS growth of 10% to 15%. Nevertheless, it forecasts little growth in the June 2007 year, due to continued high levels of capital spending and a more challenging environment for Contact Energy, which faces a big escalation in gas costs. Beyond that, however, Origin sees a significant increase in its high-margin exploration and production business, thanks in particular to the BassGas and Otway Gas projects, which will contribute for only part of the 2006–07 period, but will then start to play a much larger role in the company's business. Coal seam gas developments too will become increasingly significant, and the Kupe gas project is expected to contribute to profits from mid-2009.

ORG Year to 30 June	**2005**	**2006**
Revenues ($mn)	4870.0	5879.8
EBIT ($mn)	645.1	773.0
EBIT margin (%)	13.2	13.1
Profit before tax ($mn)	508.6	623.2
Profit after tax ($mn)	301.2	331.9
Earnings per share (¢)	42.1	41.9
Cash flow per share (¢)	78.7	79.4
Dividend (¢)	15	18
Percentage franked	100	100
Net tangible assets per share ($)	1.60	1.84
Interest cover (times)	4.7	5.2
Return on equity (%)	13.5	12.7
Debt-to-equity ratio (%)	77.9	66.1
Current ratio	1.0	1.0

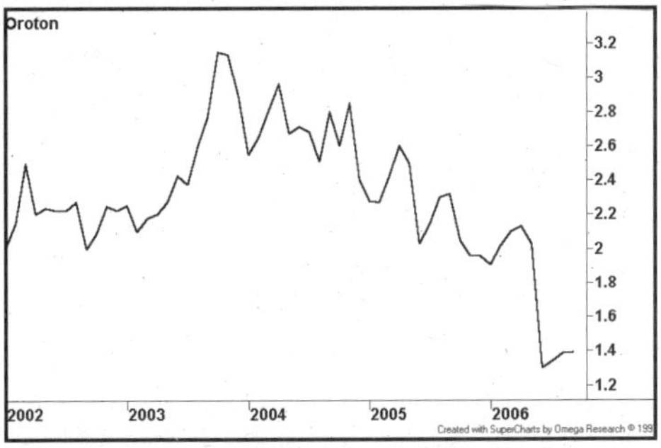

www.orotongroup.com.au

OROTONGROUP LIMITED

Share price ($)	1.35	
12-month high ($)	2.35	
12-month low ($)	1.13	
Market capitalisation ($mn)	57.8	
Price-to-NTA-per-share ratio	3.5	
5-year share price return (% p.a.)	8.3	
Sector: Consumer discretionary	**Company**	**Sector**
Price-earnings ratio (times)	18.5	18.8
Dividend yield (%)	3.7	4.0

Sydney-based fashion company OrotonGroup was established in 1938. It operates through four premium brands – Polo Ralph Lauren, Oroton, Morrissey and Marcs – with a total of 92 stores. The company is still majority-owned by the founding Lane family. It has sold its Aldo footwear business.

Latest business results (July 2006, full year)

High levels of discounting and a sluggish performance from the Marcs, Morrissey and Aldo brands led to another decline in profits, despite a rise in sales. In addition, the company made a substantial one-off write-down of assets, and it declared an operating loss for the year (significant items such as a write-down of assets are not included in the tables in this book). The Polo Ralph Lauren brand (representing 42% of total company turnover) had a good year, with retail sales up 9% and wholesale business surging 17%. The Oroton brand (26% of turnover) was also firm, with retail sales growth of 3% and wholesale growth of 14%. Morrissey sales grew, but with a minimal contribution to profits, and Marcs products saw a sharp decline in sales. A total of six new stores were opened during the year.

Outlook

OrotonGroup has been struggling for two years with computer and inventory problems, along with limping sales for some of its brands, and this has hurt profits and the share price. It has now launched a major restructuring, with the aim of putting the focus on its two core brands, Oroton and Polo Ralph Lauren. The sale in September 2006 of its Aldo footwear brand – acquired only in 2004 – for its written-down value was an initial step in this plan. It is also seeking buyers for its Marcs and Morrissey businesses. It plans a significant expansion of its Oroton business, including the opening of new stores, particularly outside New South Wales. It will also develop new store formats and introduce new product categories. The company sees significant growth potential for Polo Ralph Lauren, including selective store expansion opportunities, and it plans to simplify and restructure its operations in order to reduce costs. It has appointed a new chief executive.

ORL Year to 29 July*	2005	2006
Revenues ($mn)	148.5	159.3
EBIT ($mn)	6.5	6.1
EBIT margin (%)	4.4	3.8
Gross margin (%)	62.2	60.2
Profit before tax ($mn)	5.3	4.7
Profit after tax ($mn)	3.5	3.1
Earnings per share (¢)	8.4	7.3
Cash flow per share (¢)	20.9	17.9
Dividend (¢)	12.5	5
Percentage franked	100	100
Net tangible assets per share ($)	0.43	0.38
Interest cover (times)	5.3	4.3
Return on equity (%)	9.3	12.1
Debt-to-equity ratio (%)	65.1	65.4
Current ratio	1.2	1.9

* 30 July 2005

PERPETUAL LIMITED

Share price ($)	71.80	
12-month high ($)	76.39	
12-month low ($)	61.20	
Market capitalisation ($mn)	2888.6	
Price-to-NTA-per-share ratio	10.3	
5-year share price return (% p.a.)	21.0	
Sector: Financials	**Company**	**Sector**
Price-earnings ratio (times)	22.4	15.7
Dividend yield (%)	4.5	4.3

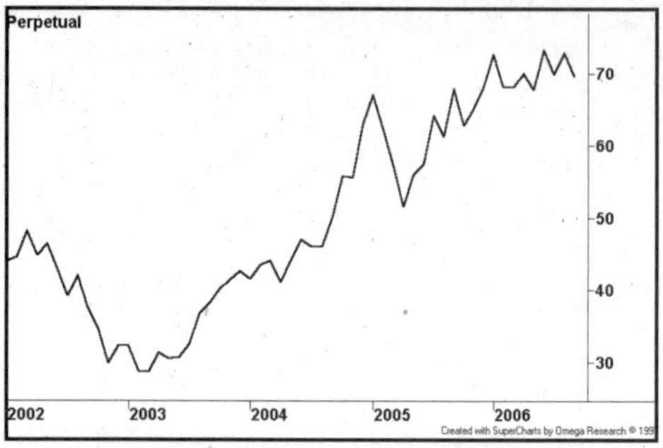

www.perpetual.com.au

Sydney-based Perpetual was established in 1885 and is now a dynamic financial services company. It divides its operations into four broad areas: Perpetual Investments offers a range of managed investment products to the retail, wholesale and institutional markets; the private clients business gives clients access to tailored financial, tax, legal and estate planning advice; the corporate trust operation offers securitisation, trust and responsible entity services, as well as acting as trustee for corporate debt issues, infrastructure projects, security agencies, development capital, management buyouts and property trusts; and PI Investment Management Limited is a global investment manager, based in Dublin.

Latest business results (June 2006, full year)

Strong financial markets helped Perpetual record another good result. Perpetual Investments funds under management jumped 23% to $32.8 billion, while Perpetual Private Clients funds under advice rose 14% to $6.6 billion. Perpetual Corporate Trust securitisation funds under administration grew 24% to $178.6 billion, thanks to the strength of the mortgage-lending market and new issuance volumes in residential mortgage-backed securities.

Outlook

Perpetual has become a leading stock market beneficiary of the continuing growth in superannuation funds in Australia and the strength of the local equity market. It expects new initiatives announced in the May 2006 Federal Budget to further stimulate the superannuation business. It views its private client business as a key growth area, and is also seeking opportunities in the inter-generational wealth transfer sector and in private philanthropy. However, its business success has become quite dependent on the local stock market, and the company itself has conceded that it could be hurt by any sharp fall in Australian equities. In order to diversify, in 2004 it established PI Investment Management, based in Dublin, as a global equities firm, and it is now expanding this business to the US and the Netherlands. It has also been moving into property securities management and direct property investment. It has successfully launched a credit fixed-interest business, which has attracted funds under management totalling $2.8 billion, including net inflows of $1.9 billion in the June 2006 year, and it has been working to streamline and diversify its corporate trust operations.

PPT Year to 30 June	2005	2006
Revenues ($mn)	353.7	420.2
EBIT ($mn)	136.8	169.3
EBIT margin (%)	38.7	40.3
Profit before tax ($mn)	141.5	178.0
Profit after tax ($mn)	95.8	122.4
Earnings per share (¢)	254.4	320.6
Cash flow per share (¢)	279.8	340.1
Dividend (¢)	260	326
Percentage franked	100	100
Net tangible assets per share ($)	5.60	6.95
Interest cover (times)	–	–
Return on equity (%)	32.8	40.8
Debt-to-equity ratio (%)	–	–
Current ratio	2.3	1.2

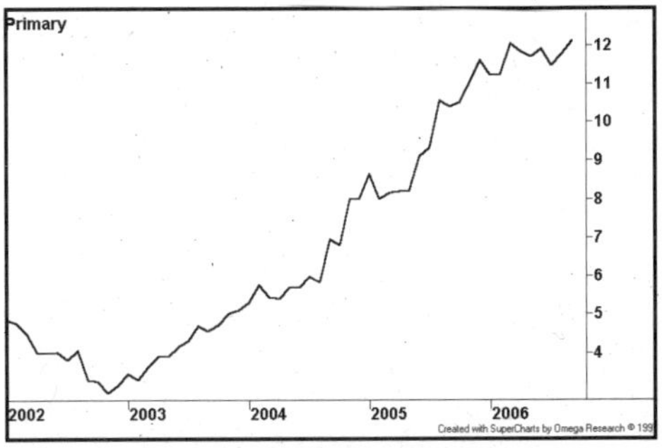

www.primaryhealthcare.com.au

PRIMARY HEALTH CARE LIMITED

Share price ($)	11.30
12-month high ($)	12.25
12-month low ($)	9.60
Market capitalisation ($mn)	1380.2
Price-to-NTA-per-share ratio	55.1
5-year share price return (% p.a.)	26.9

Sector: Health care	Company	Sector
Price-earnings ratio (times)	28.7	31.1
Dividend yield (%)	3.7	1.8

Sydney-based Primary Health Care operates 31 medical centres in NSW, Queensland, Victoria, South Australia and the ACT. It also manages SDS Pathology, with business mainly in NSW, though with moves into other states. In 2005 it acquired Australia's largest medical software company, Health Communication Network (HCN).

Latest business results (June 2006, full year)

The strength of Primary Health Care's medical centre business and a full year of operations for the HCN acquisition helped the company report another strong result. Medical centre revenues were up 21% and profits (before interest, depreciation and amortisation) rose 24%, reflecting the growing efficiency of this operation. Seven new centres were opened during the year, two each in Victoria and the ACT, and one each in South Australia, New South Wales and Queensland, though these made just a modest contribution to the result. The pathology division realised 16% sales growth, with profits up 7%. Margins for this business were hurt by the company's expansion into new markets. Turnover more than doubled for the health technology division, thanks to a full year of revenues for HCN, and this business moved healthily into profit, after a tiny loss in the previous year.

Outlook

Primary Health Care is a leading participant in the continuing consolidation of the private medical sector in Australia. It claims that its model of aggregating individual doctors' practices into large medical centres provides the scope for considerable cost saving and organic growth. With just 3% of the national market, it still sees enormous potential for expansion. Its target is to have 40 medical centres by December 2007, and it believes it is on track to meet this goal. It is establishing infrastructure to support the extension of its pathology business into Victoria, South Australia, Queensland and the ACT, and as business grows it expects margins to improve. The HCN acquisition gives the company access to more than three-quarters of Australia's GPs, who use the Medical Director software developed by that business. In September 2006 Primary Health announced that it had rejected an offer from Symbion Health to buy the SDS Pathology business.

PRY Year to 30 June	2005	2006
Revenues ($mn)	190.9	240.7
Medical centres (%)	58	56
Pathology operations (%)	34	32
Health technology (%)	6	12
EBIT ($mn)	58.2	74.9
EBIT margin (%)	30.5	31.1
Profit before tax ($mn)	53.0	67.7
Profit after tax ($mn)	37.6	47.5
Earnings per share (¢)	33.8	39.4
Cash flow per share (¢)	46.2	55.3
Dividend (¢)	25	42
Percentage franked	100	100
Net tangible assets per share ($)	0.14	0.21
Interest cover (times)	11.3	10.4
Return on equity (%)	13.8	12.8
Debt-to-equity ratio (%)	24.6	31.1
Current ratio	0.7	0.9

PRO MEDICUS LIMITED

Share price ($)	1.29	
12-month high ($)	1.77	
12-month low ($)	1.14	
Market capitalisation ($mn)	129.0	
Price-to-NTA-per-share ratio	10.7	
5-year share price return (% p.a.)	10.1	
Sector: Health care	**Company**	**Sector**
Price-earnings ratio (times)	21.1	31.1
Dividend yield (%)	3.1	1.8

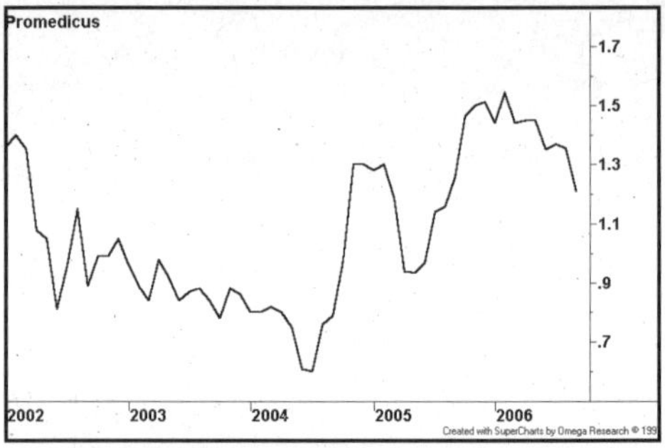

www.promedicus.com.au

Melbourne-based Pro Medicus, established in 1983, provides software and internet services to the medical profession. Its Pro Medicus Practice Management System is a software package designed to manage the administration of a clinic. Its Promedicus.net network allows secure internet delivery of diagnostic results, and is used by around 80% of Australian GPs. It has entered the GP clinical desktop market with the acquisition of software technology which is being marketed as ProMed Clinical. In an alliance with Agfa-Gevaert, the company is at the forefront of digital imaging technology for medical – principally radiology – applications.

Latest business results (June 2006, full year)

Continuing acceptance in Australia of its products and further good growth in North America handed Pro Medicus another excellent result. Domestically, revenues rose 9% to $9.1 million, with EBIT up 12%. The Promedicus.net network carried 2.9 million transactions, an 8% rise over the previous year, with 22 000 doctors registered to use it. North American sales rose 15% to $2.3 million, with profits up 13%, as the company achieved growing success marketing its digital imaging technology.

Outlook

Pro Medicus has strong positions in several niche markets with high levels of profitability and very attractive growth prospects. It is working to boost the Promedicus.net network by promoting it more widely to specialist doctors, where it has yet to achieve a high penetration. It is also trying to leverage its relationship with GPs into boosting demand for its medical software products. The company believes its digital imaging technology offers clear clinical and cost benefits to radiology practices, and domestically it now has 25 sites using the technology, with more contracts expected during 2006–07, and it is also seeing good growth in North America. In the US it has a three-year, $10 million contract with Agfa HealthCare, giving Agfa exclusive rights to market both its technology and its Pro Medicus Practice Management software in the rapidly growing private imaging centre market in North America. It is also working to establish itself in Europe. Pro Medicus has no debt and with more than $11 million in cash holdings it is able to finance further expansion.

PME Year to 30 June	2005	2006
Revenues ($mn)	10.3	11.4
EBIT ($mn)	7.2	8.0
EBIT margin (%)	69.7	70.5
Profit before tax ($mn)	7.7	8.6
Profit after tax ($mn)	5.5	6.1
Earnings per share (¢)	5.5	6.1
Cash flow per share (¢)	5.6	6.2
Dividend (¢)	4.25	4
Percentage franked	100	100
Net tangible assets per share ($)	0.12	0.12
Interest cover (times)	–	–
Return on equity (%)	46.0	47.0
Debt-to-equity ratio (%)	–	–
Current ratio	6.2	8.0

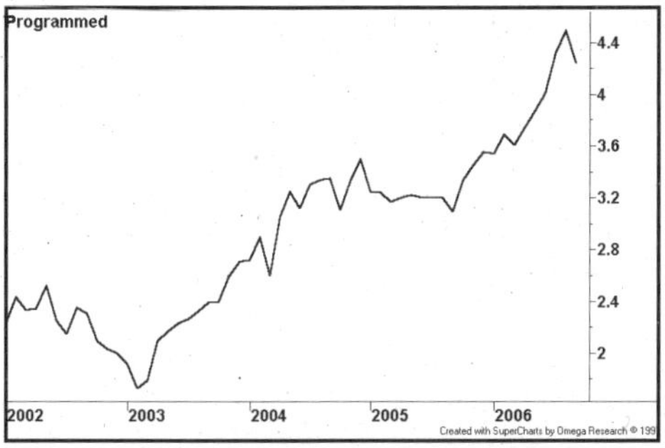

www.pmsltd.com.au

PROGRAMMED MAINT. SERVICES LIMITED

Share price ($)	4.44
12-month high ($)	4.53
12-month low ($)	2.99
Market capitalisation ($mn)	314.5
Price-to-NTA-per-share ratio	2.8
5-year share price return (% p.a.)	20.1

Sector: Industrials	Company	Sector
Price-earnings ratio (times)	15.6	13.6
Dividend yield (%)	3.8	4.3

Melbourne-based Programmed Maintenance Services was established in 1951 to provide contract painting services. Today it has over 5000 commercial, industrial and institutional clients on long-term contracts, covering 60 000 buildings and properties throughout Australia and New Zealand. Services have expanded from painting to a wide variety of building and property servicing and maintenance work. Its Barry Bros. Specialised Services subsidiary is involved in drain and sewer system maintenance work. The company has also entered the UK market, where it has a growing contract painting business.

Latest business results (March 2006, full year)

The company recorded its eighth straight year of profit growth. However, revenues grew much faster than profits, reflecting the lower margins prevailing on some of the company's new services. The core domestic property maintenance business, responsible for about 70% of company turnover, saw revenues surge 25%, but with profits little changed. This followed depressed demand in the painting business in NSW and the loss of the company's NSW schools contract. The Barry Bros. Specialised Services business, accounting for about 10% of company turnover, saw revenues up 35% while profits surged 87%, thanks especially to greater utilisation of equipment and tighter operating cost controls. This division has been a particular beneficiary of increased investment in infrastructure projects in the eastern states. New Zealand business enjoyed another excellent year, and British operations were also strong.

Outlook

The company has reported that business has been picking up during 2006, and it expects March 2007 profits to grow at levels similar to previous years. In Victoria, where grounds management revenue is complemented by landscaping services, performance has been particularly strong, and the company expects its decision to introduce landscaping services nationally to contribute to further growth in 2006–07. The October 2005 acquisition of facilities management provider Tungsten Group made a small contribution to March 2006 results, but is expected to provide a bigger boost in 2007. Programmed Maintenance has made a significant investment in boosting the capabilities of its Barry Bros. business, and it expects high growth to continue. New contracts suggest continuing strong results from New Zealand and the UK.

PRG Year to 31 March	2005	2006
Revenues ($mn)	231.6	282.9
EBIT ($mn)	30.1	33.9
EBIT margin (%)	13.0	12.0
Profit before tax ($mn)	26.8	29.7
Profit after tax ($mn)	18.3	20.2
Earnings per share (¢)	26.3	28.5
Cash flow per share (¢)	37.8	41.6
Dividend (¢)	15	17
Percentage franked	71	100
Net tangible assets per share ($)	1.60	1.61
Interest cover (times)	9.2	8.2
Return on equity (%)	16.5	16.5
Debt-to-equity ratio (%)	39.9	59.0
Current ratio	3.0	2.7

PUBLISHING AND BROADCASTING LIMITED

Share price ($)	18.55
12-month high ($)	19.27
12-month low ($)	15.52
Market capitalisation ($mn)	12340.3
Price-to-NTA-per-share ratio	11.5
5-year share price return (% p.a.)	19.4

Sector: Consumer discretionary	Company	Sector
Price-earnings ratio (times)	20.2	18.8
Dividend yield (%)	3.2	4.0

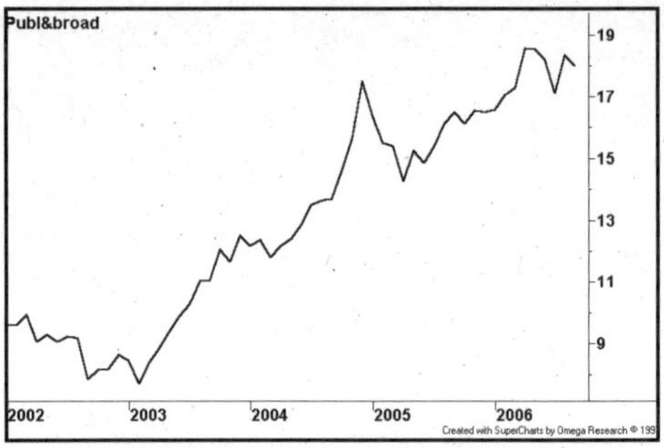

www.pbl.com.au

Publishing and Broadcasting (PBL), under chairman James Packer, operates television's Nine Network as well as Melbourne's Crown casino and Perth's Burswood casino. It also owns ACP Magazines, which publishes many of Australia's best-known magazines, including *The Australian Women's Weekly*, *Woman's Day*, *TV Week*, *Cleo* and *The Bulletin*. It owns the Ticketek ticketing agency, as well as 25% of Foxtel cable television, 50% of the Premier Media Group (formerly Fox Sports), 50% of the Ninemsn internet service, 33.3% of Sky News Australia, 25% of the SEEK online jobs service, 41% of carsales.com.au, 50% of the Hoyts cinema business, and 25% of the Hollywood production company New Regency.

Latest business results (June 2006, full year)

Once again the PBL casino business was the main factor behind a solid rise in company profits. Revenues for the gaming division rose 16.8% – in part reflecting the inclusion of a full year of results for Burswood, compared to just 10 months in the previous year – with profits jumping 27.5%. Part of this rise was attributed to an above-average win rate during the year, after a below-average rate in the previous year. The company said that, on a normalised basis, gaming profits rose 14.7%. Television revenues edged down 3.7%, while profits tumbled 20.3%, with this business hit by a combination of rising costs and a slippage in viewer numbers. Magazine revenues and profits both rose nearly 7%. There was a $19.9 million equity-accounted profit from Ninemsn, $36.3 million from Premier Media, $12.8 million from Hoyts, $8.5 million from SEEK, and the first profit from Foxtel.

PBL Year to 30 June	2005	2006
Revenues ($mn)	3276.2	3551.8
Gaming (%)	45	48
Magazines (%)	25	25
Television (%)	27	24
EBIT ($mn)	757.7	816.2
EBIT margin (%)	23.1	23.0
Gross margin (%)	10.1	10.5
Profit before tax ($mn)	634.3	698.8
Profit after tax ($mn)	520.0	619.2
Earnings per share (¢)	78.2	91.8
Cash flow per share (¢)	101.1	115.7
Dividend (¢)	52	59
Percentage franked	100	100
Net tangible assets per share ($)	0.84	1.61
Interest cover (times)	6.1	7.0
Return on equity (%)	13.3	16.0
Debt-to-equity ratio (%)	48.1	42.1
Current ratio	1.3	1.2

Outlook

For the medium term, until its internet and cable TV businesses grow substantially, it would seem that PBL's best growth prospects are its casino interests. It has launched a joint venture with Melco International Development of Hong Kong to build three major casino complexes at Macau. The first of these, Crown Macau, is scheduled to open in April 2007, followed by City of Dreams in late 2008 and Trinity in 2009. The company's publishing and television businesses remain highly profitable, but growth potential appears modest.

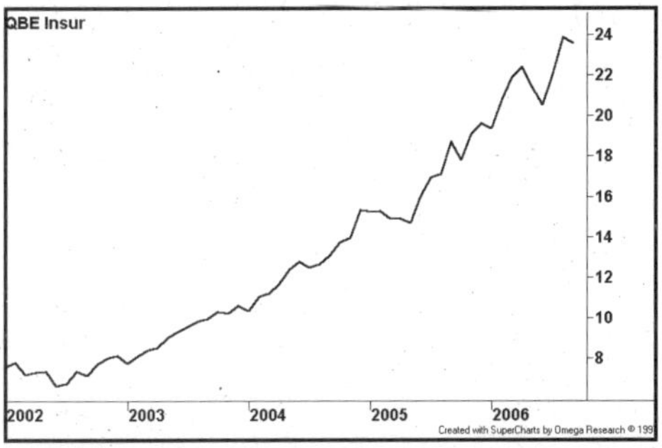

www.qbe.com.au

QBE INSURANCE GROUP LIMITED

Share price ($)	24.20
12-month high ($)	24.30
12-month low ($)	17.16
Market capitalisation ($mn)	19130.6
Price-to-NTA-per-share ratio	4.7
5-year share price return (% p.a.)	37.1

Sector: Financials	**Company**	**Sector**
Price-earnings ratio (times)	16.8	15.7
Dividend yield (%)	2.9	4.3

Sydney-based QBE – founded as North Queensland Insurance Company in 1886 – is one of Australia's best-regarded insurance companies, specialising in general insurance and reinsurance. It has expanded globally, with operations in 42 countries, and over three-quarters of business comes from abroad, with particular strength in Europe. It has become the second-largest underwriter at Lloyd's of London.

Latest business results (June 2006, half year)

QBE reported another excellent result, on the back of better-than-expected premium rate increases and a continuation of a low frequency of claims. The pre-tax insurance profit of $748 million represented 18.7% of net earned premium, a big jump from 15.8% a year earlier. All major areas of business showed higher insurance profits, and most of the 42 countries in which QBE operates were profitable. Recent acquisitions also helped the result, more than offsetting lower realised and unrealised after-tax gains on equities of $11 million, down from $39 million in the June 2005 half. During the period the company acquired a general aviation business in Denmark, a new general aviation team for its Lloyd's operations, and a farm and agricultural portfolio in the US.

Outlook

QBE forecasts that 2006 full-year profit will be at least 15% up on 2005. However, for the longer term, many analysts are speculating that the insurance cycle is due to enter a downturn, with lower premiums, subdued economic growth and higher reinsurance rates. This could lead to a period of consolidation within the industry, and QBE has said it is actively seeking further growth through acquisition. There has also been speculation that it could merge with a major domestic insurer such as IAG or Promina, or that it could acquire the non-life insurance business of Suncorp. With a relatively low exposure to equity markets, QBE benefits from rising interest rates.

QBE Year to 31 December	**2004**	**2005**
Net earned premium ($mn)	6781.0	7386.0
Profit before tax ($mn)	1115.0	1523.0
Profit after tax ($mn)	857.0	1091.0
Earnings per share (¢)	123.1	144.1
Dividend (¢)	54	71
Percentage franked	50	50
Return on equity (%)	23.3	23.9
Half year to 30 June	**2005**	**2006**
Net earned premium ($mn)	3506.0	3998.0
Profit before tax ($mn)	675.0	809.0
Profit after tax ($mn)	491.0	591.0
Earnings per share (¢)	64.6	73.9
Dividend (¢)	33	40
Percentage franked	50	60
Net tangible assets per share ($)	4.47	5.19
Debt-to-equity ratio (%)	5.5	7.3
Current ratio	1.4	1.4

REBEL SPORT LIMITED

Share price ($)	3.60	
12-month high ($)	3.79	
12-month low ($)	2.24	
Market capitalisation ($mn)	282.2	
Price-to-NTA-per-share ratio	3.0	
5-year share price return (% p.a.)	22.6	
Sector: Consumer discretionary	**Company**	**Sector**
Price-earnings ratio (times)	12.9	18.8
Dividend yield (%)	4.2	4.0

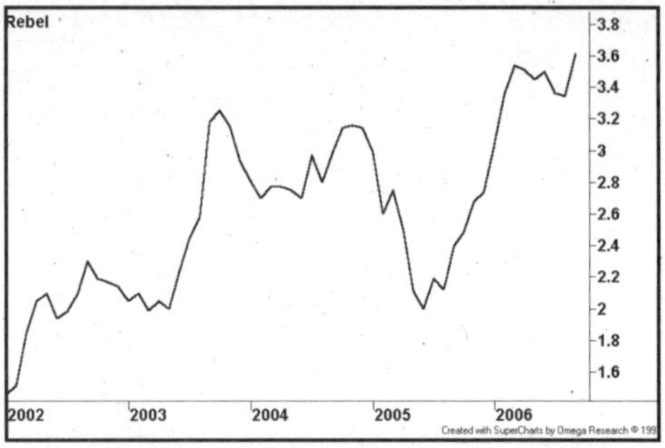

www.rebelsport.com.au

Rebel Sport, one of Australia's leading sporting goods retailers, began trading as a single store in Sydney's west in 1985. It has grown into a large chain of retail outlets across Australia, and also manages the small Glue chain of 'athleisure' stores, which sell fashionable sporting and leisure wear. Harvey Norman Holdings owns a majority of Rebel Sport's equity. At the end of August 2006 the company operated 61 Rebel Sport stores and 10 Glue stores.

Latest business results (July 2006, full year)

Rebel enjoyed an excellent year, with a strong rise in sales translating into an even bigger boost to profits. In part this was due to new stores. Six new Rebel Sport stores were opened during the year, with one closed, and two new Glue stores were opened. However, even on a same-store basis, sales rose a healthy 10.8% from the previous year, reflecting the company's efforts to refine its product mix, to cut inventories and to boost margins. Each of Rebel's key merchandise categories – footwear (25% of total sales), apparel (35%) and sporting equipment (40%) – showed double-digit revenues growth, and most stores delivered record sales. There was a particular boost from merchandise sales for the soccer World Cup.

Outlook

Rebel Sport has been engaged in a major restructuring of its business, with the particular aim of changing from a head office–driven operation to one where major decisions are made at the local level, with store managers sharing in their particular store's profits. This has involved some large expenses, but the result is a reduced cost base, no debt and more than $34 million in cash holdings. It continues to expand, and plans around six new stores in 2006–07. It sees the growth of soccer in Australia and the Ashes cricket series as offering particularly good business potential. It is developing a 'home brand' range of products, and these have achieved strong sales, to the extent that the company has been obliged to obtain additional warehouse space. It is also seeing good growth for its Rebel Direct program of direct sales to schools and sports clubs.

REB Year to 1 July*	2005	2006
Revenues ($mn)	316.9	371.2
EBIT ($mn)	21.9	29.9
EBIT margin (%)	6.9	8.1
Gross margin (%)	42.4	43.7
Profit before tax ($mn)	23.0	31.8
Profit after tax ($mn)	15.9	22.0
Earnings per share (¢)	20.7	28.0
Cash flow per share (¢)	34.7	41.4
Dividend (¢)	10	15
Percentage franked	100	100
Net tangible assets per share ($)	1.06	1.21
Interest cover (times)	–	–
Return on equity (%)	19.8	24.4
Debt-to-equity ratio (%)	–	–
Current ratio	2.6	2.4

* 2 July 2005

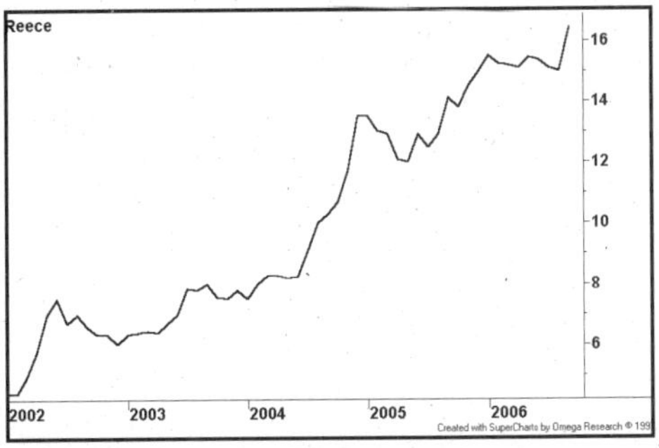

www.reece.com.au

REECE AUSTRALIA LIMITED

Share price ($)	16.34
12-month high ($)	16.40
12-month low ($)	12.55
Market capitalisation ($mn)	1618.5
Price-to-NTA-per-share ratio	4.4
5-year share price return (% p.a.)	36.4

Sector: Industrials	**Company**	**Sector**
Price-earnings ratio (times)	18.7	13.6
Dividend yield (%)	2.7	4.3

Melbourne-based plumbing supplies company Reece Australia traces its origins back to 1919, when Harold Reece started selling his products from the back of a truck. It has gradually expanded from its Victorian roots, and is today one of the country's leading suppliers of plumbing products, with 267 stores and showrooms nationwide. It has also expanded into related fields. Its four operating divisions are plumbing and bathroom, Reece HVAC (heating, ventilation, air conditioning), industrial, and irrigation. It operates a National Training Centre in Melbourne, for plumbers wishing to enhance their technical and business skills. In March 2006 it began operations in New Zealand. The controlling Wilson family own more than 75% of the company's equity.

Latest business results (June 2006, full year)

Reece overcame the housing slowdown and an environment of rising costs to post another excellent result, with sales and profit both up by double-digit amounts. Again the company's emphasis on inventory management and cost control showed success, with profits growing at a faster rate than sales. Reece opened 30 new stores during the period.

Outlook

Reece is heavily geared to the housing and renovations market, and again it is not prepared to make a forecast for the year ahead, other than to say that it anticipates moderate growth. However, it is concerned that interest rate rises, cost pressures and subdued housing activity could have a negative impact on business. In addition, the plumbing supplies market is increasingly competitive. Nevertheless, Reece remains a conservatively managed company that occupies a central position in the hardware supply business. It sells mainly to plumbers and builders, but also engages in some high-margin retail business. It has a policy of steady expansion, and plans to open around 24 new stores in the June 2007 year. With more than $50 million in net cash holdings it is also ready to consider business acquisitions if opportunities arise. It has acquired the assets and business of L.G. Carder, a long-established New Zealand plumbing company operating from two locations in Auckland, and it will use this business as the base for a planned new network of stores throughout New Zealand.

REH Year to 30 June	2005	2006
Revenues ($mn)	1009.6	1113.4
EBIT ($mn)	107.5	123.1
EBIT margin (%)	10.6	11.1
Gross margin (%)	27.2	28.4
Profit before tax ($mn)	108.5	124.6
Profit after tax ($mn)	75.8	86.9
Earnings per share (¢)	76.1	87.2
Cash flow per share (¢)	86.8	100.6
Dividend (¢)	38	44
Percentage franked	100	100
Net tangible assets per share ($)	3.30	3.75
Interest cover (times)	–	–
Return on equity (%)	24.8	24.6
Debt-to-equity ratio (%)	–	–
Current ratio	2.0	1.9

RINKER GROUP LIMITED

Share price ($)	14.23	
12-month high ($)	21.44	
12-month low ($)	12.52	
Market capitalisation ($mn)	12 795.2	
Price-to-NTA-per-share ratio	7.3	
3-year share price return (% p.a.)	35.0	
Sector: Materials	**Company**	**Sector**
Price-earnings ratio (times)	17.7	12.3
Dividend yield (%)	3.0	2.3

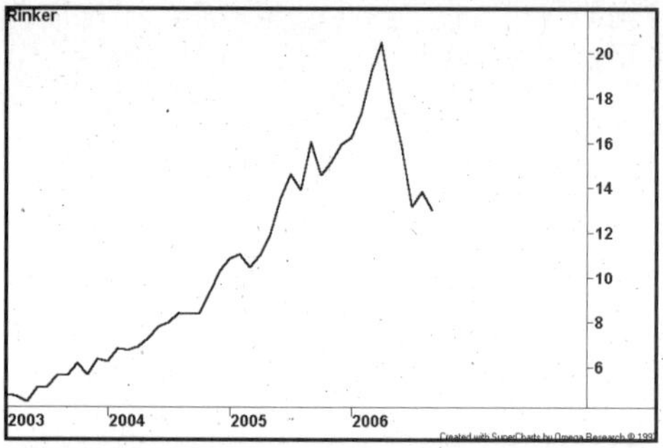

www.rinkergroup.com

Sydney-based Rinker Group was part of CSR until de-merged in 2003 (companies de-merged from another entity are eligible for inclusion in this book after two years of profits and dividends, instead of the five years that is the rule for all other companies). It is among the world's largest manufacturers and distributors of heavy building materials, such as cement, concrete, aggregates and concrete blocks and pipes. In America it operates through Rinker Materials Corporation, and around 80% of total company turnover derives from the US. In Australia it is one of the leading heavy building materials groups.

Latest business results (March 2006, full year)

Rinker now reports its results in US dollars. For the purposes of this book, these have been converted into Australian dollars, at the rate of US$1 = A$1.3 for the March 2005 results, and US$1 = A$1.4 for the March 2006 results. However, this means that the figures in this book are unofficial, and are for general guidance only. The company reported a superb profit increase, driven by continuing strong growth in construction activity in its major US markets – particularly Florida, Arizona and Nevada – together with higher prices and cost reduction initiatives, easily offsetting rises in costs, especially for fuel. All areas of US business were strong. In Australia, the company reported single-digit increases in revenues and profits, with higher infrastructure and commercial activity compensating for the fall-off in housing, and price rises offsetting higher costs.

RIN Year to 31 March	2005	2006
Revenues ($mn)	5602.6	7151.8
EBIT ($mn)	1007.6	1603.8
EBIT margin (%)	23.4	31.4
Gross margin (%)	44.3	47.8
Profit before tax ($mn)	966.0	1575.7
Profit after tax ($mn)	641.2	1036.3
Earnings per share (¢)	52.4	80.5
Cash flow per share (¢)	73.1	103.2
Dividend (¢)	21	42
Percentage franked	73	60
Net tangible assets per share ($)	1.84	1.95
Interest cover (times)	31.5	79.8
Return on equity (%)	20.3	28.3
Debt-to-equity ratio (%)	11.0	13.5
Current ratio	1.8	1.9

Outlook

Rinker remains a stock market powerhouse, thanks to its strength in the US. With construction activity remaining buoyant in all its major markets, it expects further growth in the March 2007 year. It occupies the number one market position for its products in Florida and Arizona, where economic growth continues at a pace higher than the national average, and it is investing heavily to expand. Plans include a one-million tonne, US$220 million cement plant in Florida, scheduled for completion in 2008, and a major new aggregates quarry in NSW to supply up to five million tonnes a year. However, cost pressures remain a concern.

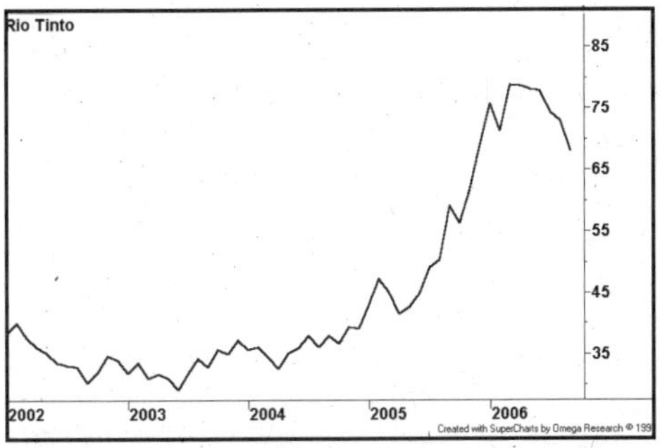

www.riotinto.com

RIO TINTO LIMITED

Share price ($)	74.65
12-month high ($)	88.10
12-month low ($)	50.03
Market capitalisation ($mn)	34169.8
Price-to-NTA-per-share ratio	5.2
5-year share price return (% p.a.)	19.8

Sector: Materials	**Company**	**Sector**
Price-earnings ratio (times)	15.8	12.3
Dividend yield (%)	1.4	2.3

British-based Rio Tinto, one of the world's largest mining companies, retains its ASX presence in a dual-listing structure, and continues to pay franked dividends to Australian shareholders. Australian subsidiaries include Coal and Allied Industries and Energy Resources of Australia. It has sold its 14.5% stake in Lihir Gold. Among its major products, it mines copper, gold, industrial minerals, iron ore, diamonds and coal, and is a large aluminium producer.

Latest business results (June 2006, half year)

Rio Tinto reported another stunning result, exceeding most market forecasts. The surging copper price boosted the company's copper sales by 71% to US$3.6 billion, with after-tax profit more than doubling to US$2 billion. However, all major areas of business were strong. The iron ore profit rose 40% to US$955 million, energy was up 23% to US$377 million, aluminium rose 82% to US$368 million, industrial minerals rose 10% to US$137 million, and diamonds were up 14% to US$113 million. China accounted for about 14% of total sales, and Japan 20%. (Note that Rio Tinto reports its results in US dollars. The figures in the tables on this page are based on Australian dollar figures supplied by the company.)

Outlook

The resources boom continues, and Rio Tinto forecasts a strong second half. In particular, it expects to benefit from higher copper and iron ore prices, as well as from its heavy investment program aimed at boosting output. At present the company has projects costing US$5 billion under way, including a major expansion of Western Australian iron ore capacity, with a further $10 billion worth of projects in the planning stage. However, rising costs – which reduced first-half profit by US$513 million – are a continuing concern. Thanks to its strong balance sheet, there is speculation that Rio Tinto plans major acquisitions. A share buyback and a special dividend are also seen as possible.

RIO Year to 31 December	**2004**	**2005**
Revenues ($mn)	19786.0	27195.0
EBIT ($mn)	4026.8	9366.3
EBIT margin (%)	20.4	34.4
Profit before tax ($mn)	3864.0	9247.0
Profit after tax ($mn)	3094.0	6497.0
Earnings per share (¢)	224.3	471.1
Cash flow per share (¢)	339.5	597.8
Dividend (¢)	103.82	105.42
Percentage franked	100	100
Interest cover (times)	24.7	78.5
Return on equity (%)	22.7	36.6

Half year to 30 June	**2005**	**2006**
Revenues ($mn)	12258.0	16366.0
Profit before tax ($mn)	3979.0	6593.0
Profit after tax ($mn)	2710.0	5069.0
Earnings per share (¢)	197.4	376.6
Dividend (¢)	50.56	52.48
Percentage franked	100	100
Net tangible assets per share ($)	10.99	14.38
Debt-to-equity ratio (%)	28.8	18.4
Current ratio	1.5	1.2

THE ROCK BUILDING SOCIETY LIMITED

Share price ($)	5.00
12-month high ($)	5.59
12-month low ($)	4.43
Market capitalisation ($mn)	90.6
Price-to-NTA-per-share ratio	2.4
5-year share price return (% p.a.)	20.7

Sector: Financials	Company	Sector
Price-earnings ratio (times)	19.6	15.7
Dividend yield (%)	4.9	4.3

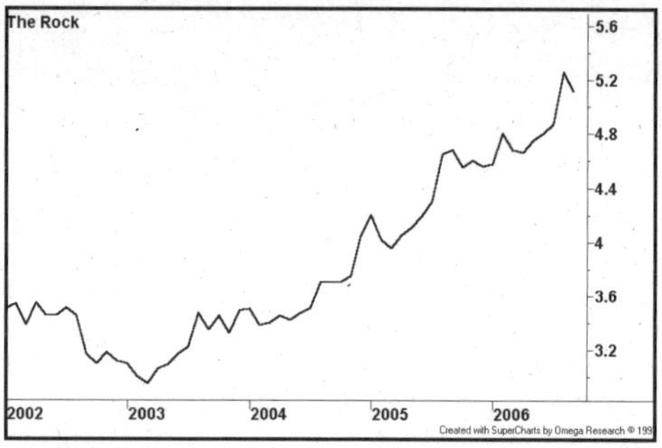

www.therock.com.au

The Rock Building Society was established in 1967 and is based in Rockhampton. Its main role has been to take retail deposits and provide housing finance for Queensland residents, and it is the leading home lender in central Queensland. It operates 10 branches in Queensland – including a new one in Brisbane – and nine agencies in the state. It also has lending agencies in Sydney, Melbourne, Brisbane, Perth and Adelaide. It has sold its financial planning business.

Latest business results (June 2006, full year)

Profits marked time, as a weakening housing market and strong competition hit the company's business. Loan approvals plunged 31% to $219 million, and the year-end loan balance stood at $946 million, down 9% from the previous year. Total deposits stood at $491 million, up 2% from a year earlier. The interest margin continued to edge up. The sale in early 2006 of its financial planning business realised an after-tax profit of $297 000, which is included in the June 2006 profit figure.

Outlook

The Rock had been striving to diversify away from its heavy dependence on home lending, and its financial planning operations were a key element of that plan. With this business now sold, it is hoping to boost its insurance and business banking activities. However, these remain small, and the bank's present focus is on expanding its retail banking operations beyond their central Queensland base. The opening of its first Brisbane branch in December 2005 is part of this strategy. It is also working to achieve more balance in how loans are originated and how they are funded, and the aim is for more direct loan origination and higher levels of retail deposits. If achieved, this would lead to a boost in the profitability of its home mortgage business. But with Queensland a highly competitive market – thanks to the presence of the big four national banks, Suncorp-Metway, Bank of Queensland and several other building societies – it is difficult to achieve growth in a housing downturn. Speculation that The Rock could become a takeover target has helped support the share price.

ROK Year to 30 June	2005	2006
Operating income ($mn)	25.4	26.2
Net interest income ($mn)	17.7	18.6
Operating expenses ($mn)	18.8	19.6
Profit before tax ($mn)	6.6	6.6
Profit after tax ($mn)	4.6	4.6
Earnings per share (¢)	29.1	25.5
Dividend (¢)	23.5	24.5
Percentage franked	100	100
Non-interest income to total income (%)	30.2	28.7
Net tangible assets per share ($)	2.05	2.06
Cost-to-income ratio (%)	74.0	74.7
Return on equity (%)	13.8	12.1
Return on assets (%)	0.5	0.4

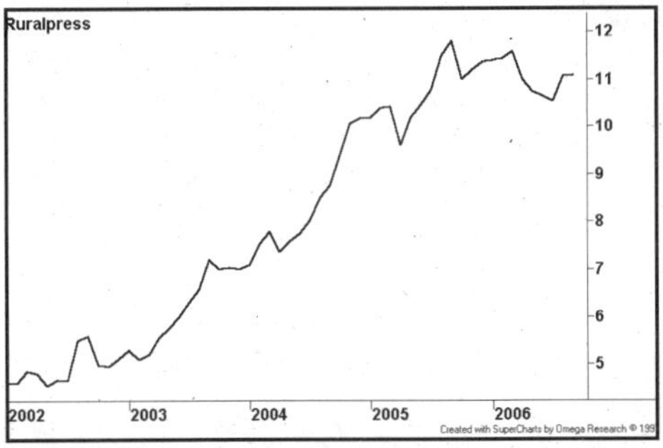

www.ruralpress.com.au

RURAL PRESS LIMITED

Share price ($)	11.00
12-month high ($)	12.10
12-month low ($)	10.20
Market capitalisation ($mn)	1319.6
Price-to-NTA-per-share ratio	25.7
5-year share price return (% p.a.)	26.1

Sector: Consumer discretionary	Company	Sector
Price-earnings ratio (times)	11.5	18.8
Dividend yield (%)	4.9	4.0

Rural Press, based in country New South Wales, was established in 1911, and is today one of the world's leading agricultural publishers, with 63 specialist newspapers and magazines in Australia, America and New Zealand. It also manages a string of 160 regional and metropolitan newspapers and magazines – including *The Canberra Times* – throughout Australia. In addition, it operates 16 major printing businesses in all Australian states, and it owns Star Broadcasting Network, which operates radio stations in South Australia and Queensland. The Fairfax family own more than 50% of the equity.

Latest business results (June 2006, full year)

Rural Press absorbed the costs of significant press upgrades at its large printing facilities to record another sound increase in sales and profits. It was largely organic growth, achieved without the benefit of major acquisitions, and in the face of more competitive markets and a more subdued economic climate than in the previous two years. Strength was across the board. The Australasian publishing business – responsible for nearly three-quarters of total company turnover – saw revenues up 2%, with EBIT rising 7%. Australasian printing revenues grew by 4%, but with profits ahead by less than 1%, reflecting the cost of the press upgrades. There was a major turnaround in US publishing operations, after the slump of the previous year, with profits soaring threefold on an 8% sales rise. The relatively tiny broadcasting division also saw sales and profits up.

Outlook

With its high fixed costs, Rural Press, like other media and printing companies, is a major beneficiary of the continuing firmness of the economy. It targets growth for 2006–07, though notes that uncertainties over interest rates and petrol prices could hurt business. The company is also affected by the weather, with drought conditions able to exert quite a negative influence on advertising revenues. Nevertheless, it is a beneficiary of the strength of rural publishing, with regional newspapers enjoying an extremely high rate of household penetration. In addition, alternative news sources, such as online media, are far less popular in rural areas than in the city. Rural Press has expressed interest in moving into the television business.

RUP Year to 30 June	2005	2006
Revenues ($mn)	564.6	583.0
EBIT ($mn)	148.5	174.4
EBIT margin (%)	26.3	29.9
Profit before tax ($mn)	138.9	162.5
Profit after tax ($mn)	101.1	113.4
Earnings per share (¢)	85.2	95.4
Cash flow per share (¢)	100.5	113.4
Dividend (¢)	51.5	54
Percentage franked	100	100
Net tangible assets per share ($)	0.39	0.43
Interest cover (times)	15.5	14.7
Return on equity (%)	18.9	27.1
Debt-to-equity ratio (%)	42.8	44.1
Current ratio	1.5	1.5

SANTOS LIMITED

Share price ($)	11.34	
12-month high ($)	13.68	
12-month low ($)	10.26	
Market capitalisation ($mn)	6804.7	
Price-to-NTA-per-share ratio	2.1	
5-year share price return (% p.a.)	18.3	
Sector: Energy	**Company**	**Sector**
Price-earnings ratio (times)	8.7	14.8
Dividend yield (%)	3.4	2.6

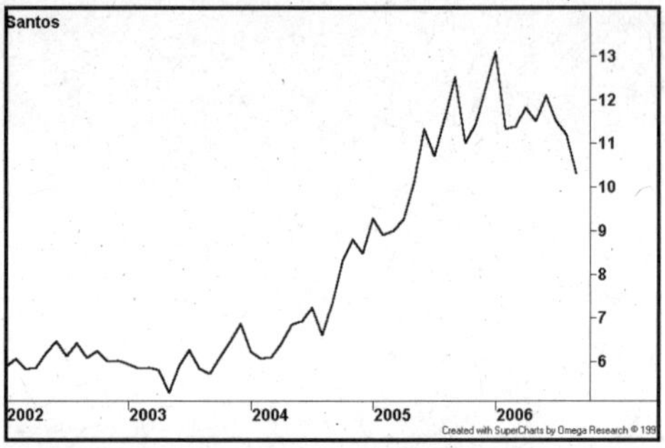

www.santos.com.au

Adelaide-based Santos, established in 1954, is one of Australia's leading producers of oil and gas. Most of its output is from the Cooper/Eromanga basin in central Australia, though it has additional interests in other parts of Australia, as well as in the US, North Africa, the Middle East, and Central and South East Asia. It supplies gas to all mainland Australian states and territories, ethane to Sydney, and oil and liquids to domestic and international customers.

Latest business results (June 2006, half year)

Profits continued to rise for Santos, as it reaped further benefits from soaring energy prices. Total production volume of 28.7 million barrels of oil equivalent (MMboe) was 9% up on the figure for the 2005 first half. Sales volume was up 5% to 30.1 million MMboe. The average oil price that the company received rose 40%, and the average condensate price was up 22%. The result included a $24.3 million provision for costs that might be incurred from a massive mud blow-out at the Banjar Panji exploration well in East Java. Santos has an 18% stake in this project.

STO Year to 31 December	**2004**	**2005**
Revenues ($mn)	1500.9	2462.8
EBIT ($mn)	566.4	1206.8
EBIT margin (%)	37.7	49.0
Gross margin (%)	35.1	50.5
Profit before tax ($mn)	518.8	1135.5
Profit after tax ($mn)	354.7	762.1
Earnings per share (¢)	60.6	129.6
Cash flow per share (¢)	141.8	225.0
Dividend (¢)	33	38
Percentage franked	100	100
Interest cover (times)	11.9	16.9
Return on equity (%)	13.0	28.6
Half year to 30 June	**2005**	**2006**
Revenues ($mn)	1019.5	1313.3
Profit before tax ($mn)	421.9	520.7
Profit after tax ($mn)	289.5	369.5
Earnings per share (¢)	46.9	59.5
Dividend (¢)	18	20
Percentage franked	100	100
Net tangible assets per share ($)	4.33	5.42
Debt-to-equity ratio (%)	50.6	46.8
Current ratio	1.4	1.6

Outlook

Santos has an active development program and expects continuing growth in output. It is forecasting production rising from 56 MMboe in 2005 to 60–61 MMboe in 2006 and 62–63 MMboe in 2007. Santos views the start during 2006 of LNG production at Bayu-Undan in the Timor Gap as marking a turning point in its history, as it will not only boost company profits for up to 20 years, but will also provide great potential for future growth. At the Cooper Oil Project, which started in February 2006, the company will drill 1000 wells over five years. By August 2006 it had drilled 42, with 37 of them successful. In another development with long-term potential, Santos is involved in negotiations on the construction of a natural gas pipeline from Papua New Guinea to Queensland. It has lost out to Beach Petroleum in a bid to acquire Delhi Petroleum.

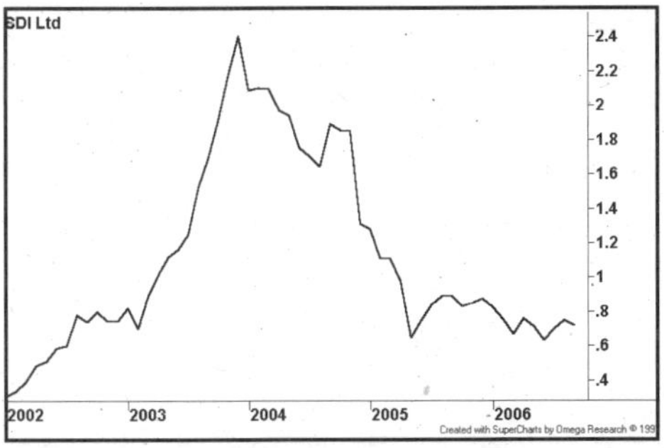

www.sdi.com.au

SDI LIMITED

Share price ($)	0.77
12-month high ($)	0.94
12-month low ($)	0.58
Market capitalisation ($mn)	88.7
Price-to-NTA-per-share ratio	4.8
5-year share price return (% p.a.)	38.1

Sector: Health care	Company	Sector
Price-earnings ratio (times)	17.5	31.1
Dividend yield (%)	0.8	1.8

Melbourne-based SDI (formerly Southern Dental Industries), founded in 1972, develops and manufactures specialist dental restorative materials. It classifies its businesses into two major product groups: alloy materials for dental fillings; and aesthetic materials, such as composites, adhesives, sealants and tooth whitening systems. All SDI's manufacturing is done in Melbourne, and the company sells its products through distributors and retailers in over 70 countries, with more than 90% of sales overseas. It has offices and warehouses in Chicago, Cologne and Sao Paulo.

Latest business results (June 2006, full year)

Profits came racing back again, after the sudden decline in 2005, which had followed five straight years of earnings growth exceeding 35%. Sales slipped a little, but the company was able to benefit from substantially higher margins and a sharp decline in low-margin international tender sales. It also gained from some new, high-margin products, as well as from measures introduced during the year to micro-manage its exposure to currency fluctuations and raw material prices. All regions showed growth.

Outlook

SDI has established a firm position in the Australian market for its products, and it is also among the top 10 worldwide, with high market shares. It devotes a large percentage of revenues to research and development work, and has been releasing a steady stream of new items. Two products in particular are seen as having the potential to make a strong contribution to future profit growth. One of these is the Pola tooth whitening system, which is seeing excellent growth in sales as tooth whitening develops as a popular oral health treatment. SDI has been continually expanding the Pola product range. The other product seen as having particular potential is Riva glass ionomer cement for dental fillings. Glass ionomer cement technology is gaining steady international acceptance. SDI is also seeing good sales of its Radii Plus second-generation light-curing device for dental work, and of many Radii accessory products such as composites, adhesives and tooth whitening treatments. Rising silver prices are a concern, although the company has hedged its exposure for 2006–07. SDI's target in coming years is for annual sales growth of 10% to 15%.

SDI Year to 30 June	2005	2006
Revenues ($mn)	45.9	45.2
EBIT ($mn)	3.7	7.4
EBIT margin (%)	8.1	16.3
Gross margin (%)	57.1	64.6
Profit before tax ($mn)	2.9	6.4
Profit after tax ($mn)	3.0	5.1
Earnings per share (¢)	2.5	4.4
Cash flow per share (¢)	4.4	5.7
Dividend (¢)	0.9	0.6
Percentage franked	100	100
Net tangible assets per share ($)	0.15	0.16
Interest cover (times)	4.6	7.8
Return on equity (%)	11.1	18.2
Debt-to-equity ratio (%)	50.5	44.0
Current ratio	2.6	2.8

SELECT HARVESTS LIMITED

Share price ($)	13.50
12-month high ($)	15.01
12-month low ($)	11.65
Market capitalisation ($mn)	530.1
Price-to-NTA-per-share ratio	7.4
5-year share price return (% p.a.)	58.0

Sector: Consumer staples	Company	Sector
Price-earnings ratio (times)	20.1	15.5
Dividend yield (%)	4.7	3.2

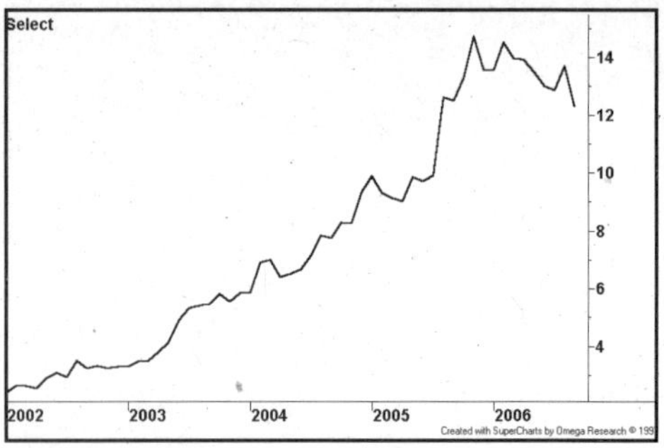

www.selectharvests.com.au

Melbourne-based Select Harvests is Australia's biggest almond grower and processor – managing more than 50% of Australia's almond orchards – and one of the three largest growers in the world. As well as its own almond orchards, in Victoria's Sunraysia district, it has a thriving business managing orchards owned by external investors, from which it derives set-up fees and annuity-style income. It is also a leading supplier to Australian supermarkets of processed and packaged nuts, dried fruits and associated products, through the Lucky, Sunsol, Ni-Vit, Meriram and Soland brands. It has sold its small pesticides business.

Latest business results (June 2006, full year)

Profits continued to grow, but not at the same pace as in previous years. The high-margin almond growing operation was dented by unfavourable climatic conditions, and the total crop of 6230 tonnes was up only marginally from the previous year. In addition, world almond prices slipped from their record highs of 2005. Nevertheless, the company saw revenues from its almond operations jump 54%, with EBIT up 44%. By contrast, the food products business achieved sales growth of 16%, but cost increases and lower margins forced profits down. This business is responsible for 70% of company turnover, but contributes less than a quarter of company profit. In addition, there was a $4.1 million profit from the sale of the company's pesticide business (not included in the figures in the table).

Outlook

Select Harvests has had a sensational run of rising profits, which has been reflected in the share price. The company continues to expand, and though world almond prices have eased, they still remain at high levels, while global almond demand continues to grow. During the June 2006 year, Select completed the development of three new almond projects for external investors totalling 8300 acres, its largest annual planting to date. During the June 2007 year the company plans to develop a further 11 000 acres of new orchards. However, there have been concerns that the government might decide to phase out some of the tax deductions it grants for agribusiness managed investment schemes, which would diminish the attractions of Select's orchard investments.

SHV Year to 30 June	2005	2006
Revenues ($mn)	173.9	217.9
Food products (%)	74	70
Almond operations (%)	24	30
EBIT ($mn)	33.1	38.4
EBIT margin (%)	19.0	17.6
Gross margin (%)	26.4	24.0
Profit before tax ($mn)	31.8	37.9
Profit after tax ($mn)	22.1	26.5
Earnings per share (¢)	56.9	67.2
Cash flow per share (¢)	65.1	76.2
Dividend (¢)	42	63
Percentage franked	100	100
Net tangible assets per share ($)	1.52	1.83
Interest cover (times)	26.1	82.3
Return on equity (%)	26.4	27.9
Debt-to-equity ratio (%)	–	–
Current ratio	1.5	1.8

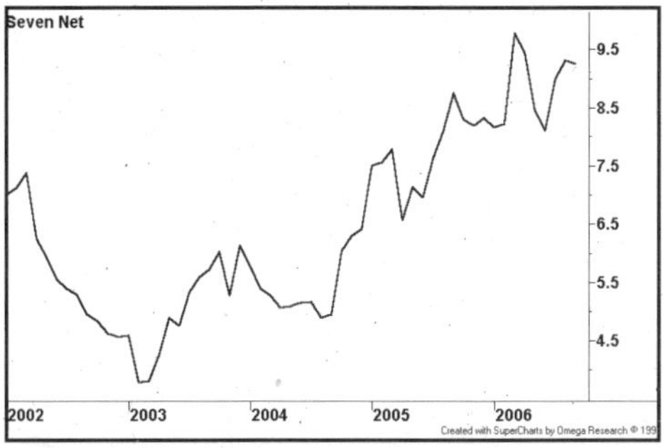

www.sevencorporate.com.au

SEVEN NETWORK LIMITED

Share price ($)	9.38
12-month high ($)	9.90
12-month low ($)	7.65
Market capitalisation ($mn)	2068.2
Price-to-NTA-per-share ratio	na
5-year share price return (% p.a.)	10.7

Sector: Consumer discretionary	**Company**	**Sector**
Price-earnings ratio (times)	19.1	18.8
Dividend yield (%)	2.9	4.0

The Seven Network, with its headquarters in Sydney, was formed from television stations owned by the Fairfax group and the Herald and Weekly Times. It is now one of Australia's big three commercial networks. It owns five stations in capital cities and one in regional Queensland, and it also broadcasts through independently owned affiliates. It owns 50% of Yahoo!7, with Yahoo! Australia, and a third of Sky News Australia. It also operates Pacific Magazines, which publishes leading titles that include *Better Homes and Gardens*, *marie claire*, *New Idea*, *That's Life* and *Men's Health*. It has sold its interest in the Telstra Dome stadium. Entrepreneur Kerry Stokes is the chairman and leading shareholder.

Latest business results (June 2006, full year)

A continuing string of hit television programs delivered Seven a big boost in the ratings and a surge in its annual profits. The result came from just a 9.6% increase in television advertising revenues, which was achieved in an overall television market that was down 1.5%. The magazine business achieved a 13% rise in revenues, thanks to circulation revenue growth of 11% and advertising growth of 14%. However, magazine profits were down, in large part due to expenditure of $5.3 million to launch two new titles, *Famous* and *Diabetic Living*.

Outlook

Seven's television business has achieved considerable growth in viewer numbers through a wave of hit programs that include *Desperate Housewives*, *Lost*, *Grey's Anatomy*, *Prison Break*, *Dancing with the Stars*, *Border Security* and *Medical Emergency*. Its news programs have also enjoyed growing popularity, and it has benefited from a degree of instability at its main rival Channel Nine. However, the television business is notoriously fickle, with high fixed costs, and just small declines in advertising revenues can translate into a sharp drop in profits. With Channel Ten it will broadcast AFL matches from the 2007 season, and it sees great potential in its plans to televise V8 supercar racing. It views its Yahoo!7 venture – launched in January 2006 – as offering enormous scope for growth in digital media. Its new *Famous* magazine has enjoyed a strong opening three months. In September 2006 Seven Network announced plans to invest $26 million for a 33% stake in Engin Limited, a leading Australian internet phone company.

SEV Year to 30 June	**2005**	**2006**
Revenues ($mn)	1180.4	1285.7
Television (%)	81	80
Magazines (%)	19	20
EBIT ($mn)	140.6	214.5
EBIT margin (%)	11.9	16.7
Profit before tax ($mn)	89.3	174.1
Profit after tax ($mn)	55.6	107.7
Earnings per share (¢)	25.7	49.2
Cash flow per share (¢)	114.1	136.6
Dividend (¢)	23.5	27.5
Percentage franked	100	100
Net tangible assets per share ($)	–	–
Interest cover (times)	2.7	5.3
Return on equity (%)	6.6	15.5
Debt-to-equity ratio (%)	66.9	69.5
Current ratio	1.5	1.8

SIMS GROUP LIMITED

Share price ($)	20.50
12-month high ($)	21.12
12-month low ($)	14.03
Market capitalisation ($mn)	2604.9
Price-to-NTA-per-share ratio	3.8
5-year share price return (% p.a.)	39.9

Sector: Materials	Company	Sector
Price-earnings ratio (times)	11.8	12.3
Dividend yield (%)	5.1	2.3

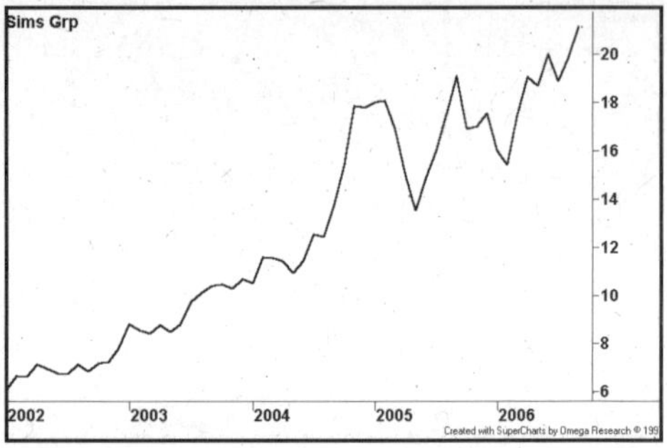

www.simsmetal.com.au

Sydney-based Sims, formerly called Simsmetal, was founded in 1917, and is today Australia's largest metals recycler. It has become the world's largest producer of ferrous scrap metal, used in steel making, and a leading producer of non-ferrous scrap, particularly copper and aluminium. It also operates a significant non-metals recycling operation. Some 70% of revenues and profits come from overseas activities, primarily in America, Britain and New Zealand. Following its 2005 merger with US metals recycler Hugo Neu Corporation, 26% of the equity in Sims is held by the Neu family.

Latest business results (June 2006, full year)

Profits marked time, despite a big rise in revenues as a result of an eight-month contribution from Sims Hugo Neu. Earnings for Sims are heavily dependent on highly volatile scrap metal prices, and a weak first half was followed by a powerful recovery in the second half. America now accounts for nearly half of company revenues, although profit growth there was constrained by the expense of integrating Hugo Neu. Domestic business saw profits little changed. However, British earnings fell sharply. The company's small but flourishing products recycling business recorded an 89% jump in profits.

Outlook

With China responsible for 21% of Sims Group's sales, and Japan and Korea taking a further 12% – up from 14% and 8% respectively in the June 2005 year – the company is highly geared to the continuing boom in that region. However, with extreme volatility evident in the scrap metals markets, the company must also be astute in the timing of sales. It has reported that the new financial year started extremely strongly. Sims sees particular potential in its fast-growing recycling business, which has operations in several countries and is involved in recycling products such as tyres, plastics, computers and electrical appliances. The acquisition of the Dutch-based Mirec group of companies, Europe's leading electronic and electrical equipment recycler, has given a boost to this business, and Sims also has a major kerbside recycling contract for New York City that it views as offering big prospects. However, it expects to expand its other businesses too, and is believed to be evaluating further acquisitions in several countries.

SGM Year to 30 June	2005	2006
Revenues ($mn)	2565.0	3752.4
EBIT ($mn)	289.6	301.9
EBIT margin (%)	11.3	8.0
Gross margin (%)	100.0	100.0
Profit before tax ($mn)	284.2	285.6
Profit after tax ($mn)	197.0	196.6
Earnings per share (¢)	216.3	174.2
Cash flow per share (¢)	252.3	211.0
Dividend (¢)	140	105
Percentage franked	57	49
Net tangible assets per share ($)	4.47	5.47
Interest cover (times)	54.0	18.5
Return on equity (%)	40.8	22.9
Debt-to-equity ratio (%)	10.2	24.0
Current ratio	1.8	1.8

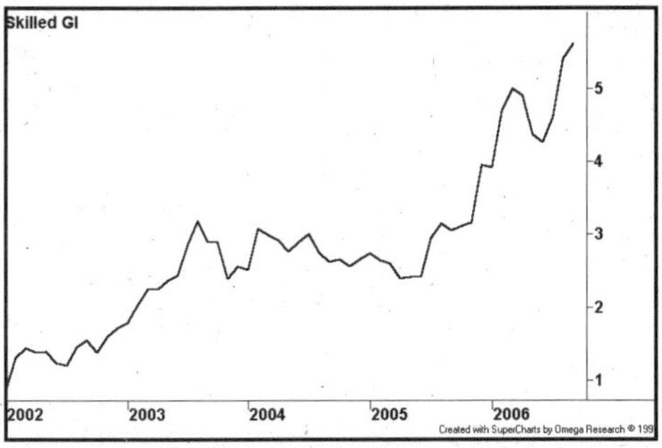

www.skilled.com.au

SKILLED GROUP LIMITED

Share price ($)	5.60
12-month high ($)	5.64
12-month low ($)	2.88
Market capitalisation ($mn)	575.7
Price-to-NTA-per-share ratio	20.1
5-year share price return (% p.a.)	63.0

Sector: Industrials	Company	Sector
Price-earnings ratio (times)	24.0	13.6
Dividend yield (%)	3.4	4.3

Melbourne-based Skilled, with a history dating back 40 years, provides skilled and semi-skilled labour to Australian companies, specialising in the blue collar, call centre and nursing sectors. Its core Skilled brand represents about three-quarters of its business. Other brands include Origin Healthcare, Excelior, Extraman, PeopleCo and SEM Fire & Rescue. It operates through more than 90 offices around Australia. In August 2006 it announced plans to acquire rival skilled labour provider Tesa Group, and it has launched a takeover bid for Catalyst Recruitment Systems.

Latest business results (June 2006, full year)

A combination of recent acquisitions, a tight labour market and Skilled's exposure to the resources industry handed the company a strong profit gain. The Skilled brand increased revenues by 13%, with EBIT up 20%. The company's other brands reported a 25% rise in revenues, with EBIT moving from a small loss to a healthy profit. This result included a full year of reporting for the Extraman business, acquired in July 2005.

Outlook

Skilled is one of the big beneficiaries of the firm domestic economy and an increasingly tight labour market, and it forecasts continued profit growth in the 2006–07 year. About 20% of its turnover derives from the mining and resources industry, and this business is expected to support continuing future growth. The company also enjoys a healthy exposure to rail and road infrastructure spending. It is seeing good business for its new Extraman subsidiary, which provides labour to the mining, resources and marine industries. Among its growth initiatives, it has established the Skilled Services Group, to undertake dedicated shutdowns, contract maintenance, rail services and plant relocation and expansion. After refurbishing and expanding its call centre business in Burnie Tasmania, it has started construction of a second call centre in Melbourne. In February 2006 it acquired ProSafe Personnel, a small West Australian agency providing health and safety professionals to the offshore oil and gas industry. Its planned $62 million acquisition of Tesa Group reinforces Skilled's position in the mining and resources sector, and it views its bid to buy Catalyst Recruitment as an opportunity to further strengthen its position in blue collar recruitment.

SKE Year to 30 June	2005	2006
Revenues ($mn)	793.4	961.4
EBIT ($mn)	24.4	37.7
EBIT margin (%)	3.1	3.9
Profit before tax ($mn)	21.6	35.6
Profit after tax ($mn)	14.5	24.0
Earnings per share (¢)	14.7	23.3
Cash flow per share (¢)	24.9	31.9
Dividend (¢)	16	19
Percentage franked	100	100
Net tangible assets per share ($)	0.27	0.28
Interest cover (times)	8.6	17.6
Return on equity (%)	16.2	22.4
Debt-to-equity ratio (%)	25.3	2.8
Current ratio	1.3	1.2

SONIC HEALTHCARE LIMITED

Share price ($)	12.81	
12-month high ($)	16.12	
12-month low ($)	11.12	
Market capitalisation ($mn)	3720.3	
Price-to-NTA-per-share ratio	na	
5-year share price return (% p.a.)	12.9	
Sector: Health care	**Company**	**Sector**
Price-earnings ratio (times)	21.4	31.1
Dividend yield (%)	3.2	1.8

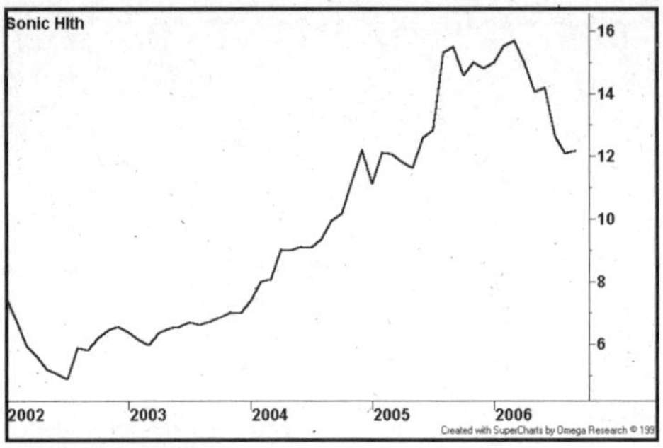

www.sonichealthcare.com.au

Sydney-based Sonic Healthcare is one of the world's largest medical diagnostics companies, providing pathology and radiology services to medical practitioners, hospitals, community medical services and their patients. It is Australia's largest private provider of pathology services, with a growing presence overseas. Its many businesses include Douglass Hanly Moir Pathology, Barratt & Smith Pathology, Sullivan Nicolaides Pathology, Queensland X-Ray, Capital Pathology, Clinpath Laboratories, Castlereagh Imaging, Lifescreen Australia and Melbourne Pathology.

Latest business results (June 2006, full year)

Revenues and profits were up, with the company's eleventh straight year of double-digit EPS growth. Pathology revenues and EBIT were both up 23%, to $1.24 billion and $259 million respectively, though this largely reflected acquisition activity during the year, and organic growth was substantially more modest. Radiology revenues were up 6% to $314 million, while EBIT edged up less than 1% to $52 million. There was a good result from Sonic's main Australian pathology practices.

Outlook

Sonic has achieved sustained success through its drive to consolidate the once-fragmented Australian pathology industry, which has become one of the high-growth medical sectors. It now holds a domestic market share that is estimated to be approaching 40%, followed by Symbion Health (formerly Mayne Group) with around a third of the market, and Gribbles Pathology, with less than 10%. It is also prominent in New Zealand, and is now moving strongly into Northern Hemisphere markets. In Europe it has acquired two British pathology practices, The Doctors Laboratory Group and Omnilabs, and a 55% stake in Schottdorf Group in Germany. In August 2005 it bought 82% of the shares in Texas-based Clinical Pathology Laboratories, which was the largest privately owned pathology business in the US. It is now working to integrate this business into its existing operations, and says that it is in advanced negotiations on further significant offshore acquisitions. In America and in many European countries, the pathology sector is as fragmented as it once was in Australia, and Sonic believes it can replicate abroad the success it has enjoyed in Australia consolidating numerous small pathology businesses. The company's own guidance is for EPS growth of around 10% in the June 2007 year.

SHL Year to 30 June	2005	2006
Revenues ($mn)	1374.8	1645.2
Pathology (%)	73	75
Radiology (%)	21	19
EBIT ($mn)	251.3	304.2
EBIT margin (%)	18.3	18.5
Profit before tax ($mn)	209.8	263.8
Profit after tax ($mn)	135.4	172.0
Earnings per share (¢)	49.8	59.8
Cash flow per share (¢)	68.1	79.2
Dividend (¢)	36	41
Percentage franked	100	100
Net tangible assets per share ($)	–	–
Interest cover (times)	6.1	7.5
Return on equity (%)	15.1	15.4
Debt-to-equity ratio (%)	66.1	57.0
Current ratio	1.0	1.3

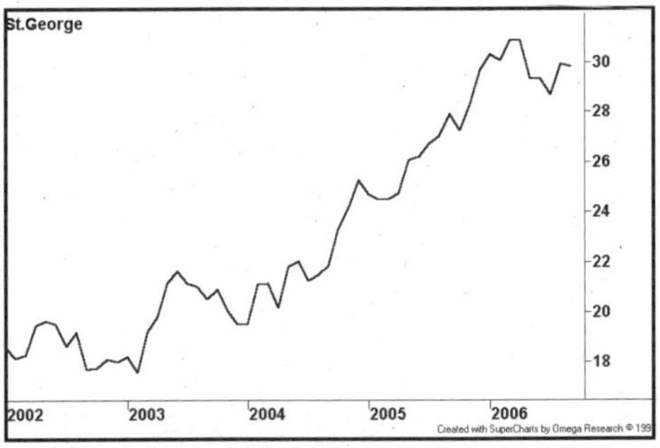

www.stgeorge.com.au

ST GEORGE BANK LIMITED

Share price ($)	30.24	
12-month high ($)	31.39	
12-month low ($)	26.31	
Market capitalisation ($mn)	15765.8	
Price-to-NTA-per-share ratio	4.8	
5-year share price return (% p.a.)	19.8	
Sector: Financials	**Company**	**Sector**
Price-earnings ratio (times)	17.6	15.7
Dividend yield (%)	4.5	4.3

Sydney-based St George, originally a building society founded in 1937, has grown from a series of mergers and acquisitions to become Australia's fifth-largest retail bank. Though operating in most states and territories, it has particular strength in South Australia, where it owns BankSA, and in New South Wales. It owns the financial services company Asgard Wealth Solutions (formerly known as Sealcorp).

Latest business results (March 2006, half year)

St George recorded another strong result. Home lending grew 13% to $59.7 billion, despite the bank's high exposure to the weak New South Wales housing market. Commercial lending was up 15% to $21.4 billion. Retail funds increased 13.5% to $41.8 billion, with particularly strong growth in online banking. Funds under management rose 33.6% to $37.2 billion, with Asgard recording its fastest-growing six-month period, thanks to a 40% increase in net inflows. Successful cost containment initiatives meant that the bank's cost-to-income ratio fell even further in the half, to 44.1%.

Outlook

St George continues its organic growth strategy, which it believes offers less risk than growth through acquisition. It believes it is on target to achieve EPS growth of at least 10% in the September 2006 and 2007 years, though much will depend on global economies and interest rates. It maintains a particular focus on customer service, and generally achieves higher customer satisfaction ratings than most rivals. It is working to diversify its home lending activities away from its heavy exposure to New South Wales and South Australia, and 28% of this business is now in the non-core states of Victoria, Queensland and Western Australia. The bank's wealth management operation – including funds management and margin lending – continues to perform strongly, although it could be hurt by any stock market volatility. Wealth management now contributes 13% of the bank's profit, up from just 7% in 2003.

SGB Year to 30 September	2004	2005
Operating income ($mn)	2570.0	2775.0
Net interest income ($mn)	1612.0	1707.0
Operating expenses ($mn)	1222.0	1263.0
Profit before tax ($mn)	1135.0	1300.0
Profit after tax ($mn)	767.0	891.0
Earnings per share (¢)	150.4	172.1
Dividend (¢)	122	137
Percentage franked	100	100
Non-interest income to total income (%)	37.3	38.5
Cost-to-income ratio (%)	47.5	45.5
Return on equity (%)	17.7	18.5
Return on assets (%)	1.2	1.2

Half year to 31 March	2005	2006
Operating income ($mn)	1367.0	1434.0
Profit before tax ($mn)	704.0	736.0
Profit after tax ($mn)	449.0	502.0
Earnings per share (¢)	89.1	96.0
Dividend (¢)	67	74
Percentage franked	100	100
Net tangible assets per share ($)	5.71	6.30

STW COMMUNICATIONS GROUP LIMITED

Share price ($)	2.76
12-month high ($)	3.50
12-month low ($)	2.66
Market capitalisation ($mn)	574.3
Price-to-NTA-per-share ratio	3.5
5-year share price return (% p.a.)	−2.3

Sector: Consumer discretionary	Company	Sector
Price-earnings ratio (times)	15.5	18.8
Dividend yield (%)	5.3	4.0

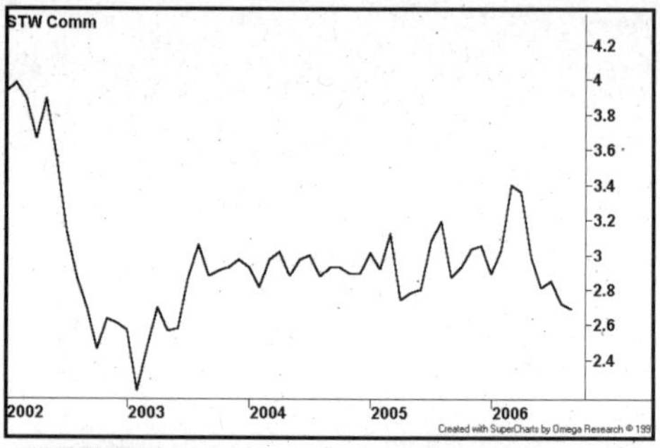

www.stwgroup.com.au

Sydney-based STW Communications Group, formerly called Singleton Group, was founded by entrepreneur John Singleton. It is a holding company, owning two-thirds of Singleton Ogilvy & Mather Holdings, as well as a 49% interest in the Australian and New Zealand operations of the advertising company J. Walter Thompson. Thanks to its policy of growth by acquisition, the traditional advertising business now accounts for only about half its turnover, and it has direct or indirect ownership of over 50 other smaller businesses. These are in such diverse fields as internet design and marketing, ethnic advertising, market research, public relations, sponsorship, branding and direct marketing.

Latest business results (June 2006, half year)

STW presents its financial results in varying ways, and it can be difficult sometimes to make valid comparisons. Sales and profits rose strongly, with the company attributing acquisitions for 38% of the sales growth. Advertising businesses saw sales up 15% and profits up 13%. The company terms the remainder of its businesses as Diversified Marketing and Communications Entities, and as a group they saw after-tax profit up 32%. Among the specialist categories of the latter grouping, a stand-out performance came from the five entities labelled Information and Insight, with revenues up 196% and profits surging 278%.

SGN Year to 31 December	2004	2005
Revenues ($mn)	144.4	176.1
EBIT ($mn)	20.8	38.9
EBIT margin (%)	14.4	22.1
Profit before tax ($mn)	18.3	36.5
Profit after tax ($mn)	8.3	32.2
Earnings per share (¢)	4.9	17.8
Cash flow per share (¢)	5.1	18.4
Dividend (¢)	13.4	14.7
Percentage franked	100	100
Interest cover (times)	8.3	16.1
Return on equity (%)	4.0	15.4
Half year to 30 June	**2005**	**2006**
Revenues ($mn)	79.9	101.6
Profit before tax ($mn)	14.1	17.6
Profit after tax ($mn)	12.8	15.6
Earnings per share (¢)	7.3	7.9
Dividend (¢)	4.8	4.8
Percentage franked	100	100
Net tangible assets per share ($)	0.71	0.80
Debt-to-equity ratio (%)	53.2	27.1
Current ratio	1.5	1.0

Outlook

STW retains a string of high-paying blue-chip domestic and international clients, and this underpins its business. Thanks to its holding company structure, it is able to attract rival corporations as clients, each dealing with different arms of the company. It continues to expand, with a rising number of acquired companies providing numerous synergies and cross-selling opportunities. It claims to be a direct beneficiary of the fragmentation of large corporations' media spend and to be less subject to cyclical swings in this spending. It expects 2006 full-year after-tax profit to be 17% to 22% higher than 2005.

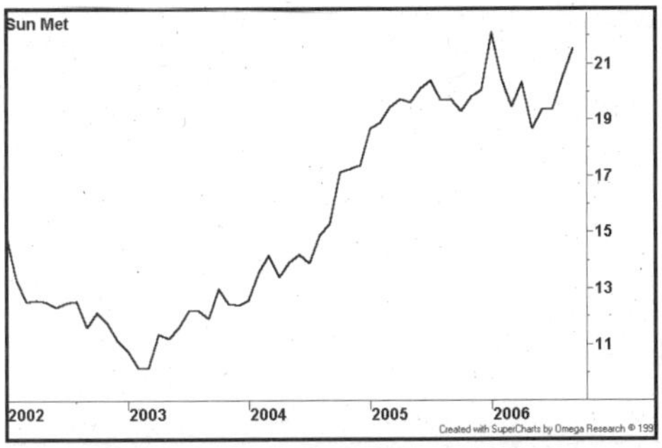

www.suncorp.com.au

SUNCORP-METWAY LIMITED

Share price ($)	21.15
12-month high ($)	22.30
12-month low ($)	18.40
Market capitalisation ($mn)	11553.0
Price-to-NTA-per-share ratio	3.6
5-year share price return (% p.a.)	17.8

Sector: Financials	Company	Sector
Price-earnings ratio (times)	12.7	15.7
Dividend yield (%)	4.6	4.3

Brisbane-based Suncorp-Metway, Queensland's largest company, was formed from the 1996 merger of Metway Bank, the Queensland Industry Development Corporation and the insurance company Suncorp. It divides its businesses into three core areas – banking, insurance and wealth management. It is Australia's sixth-largest bank and one of the largest insurers – the latter business under the GIO brand – with some 4.3 million customers. It has 229 retail and business banking outlets, mainly in Queensland, and GIO has 34 agencies in New South Wales and Victoria.

Latest business results (June 2006, full year)

Profits rose modestly, based on a strong result from the banking section, which saw pre-tax profit up 11.5%. Total lending was up 11% to $38.8 billion, with a notable increase in the growth rate in the latter part of the year. Housing loans of $20.8 billion grew 10.3%, below the industry growth rate of 13.3%. Retail deposits were up 11% to $16.9 billion. The general insurance pre-tax profit rose 4.7% in a highly competitive market environment. A focus on driving profitable insurance growth helped offset the impact of Cyclone Larry, which caused widespread damage in areas of northern Queensland. The wealth management business saw profits down, reflecting the impact of lower investment earnings for the year. Funds under management grew 9.3% to $13 billion, and funds under administration were up 19.8% to $6.2 billion.

Outlook

Suncorp-Metway occupies a powerful position in its home state, and is active nationwide. Because of its span of businesses it is able to achieve a product cross-selling ratio that is higher than for most other banks. It sees continuing strong growth for its banking side, and forecasts profit growth for this business of around 10% in the June 2007 year. Continuing cost reductions in its insurance operation are expected to help deliver a good 2007 profit, providing no major insurance event occurs. Suncorp-Metway has increasingly been seen as a takeover target, which has supported the share price. There has been considerable speculation that the company might be acquired and its banking and insurance divisions separated. Bank management have said that the bank itself is also evaluating various merger and acquisition opportunities in the financial services sector.

SUN Year to 30 June	2005	2006
Operating income ($mn)	5321.0	5580.0
Net interest income ($mn)	787.0	848.0
Operating expenses ($mn)	3945.0	4228.0
Profit before tax ($mn)	1377.0	1346.0
Profit after tax ($mn)	882.0	916.0
Earnings per share (¢)	163.5	166.6
Dividend (¢)	87	97
Percentage franked	100	100
Non-interest income to total income (%)	85.2	84.8
Net tangible assets per share ($)	6.25	5.94
Cost-to-income ratio (%)	74.1	75.8
Return on equity (%)	20.7	20.5
Return on assets (%)	1.8	1.7

TABCORP HOLDINGS LIMITED

Share price ($)	15.05
12-month high ($)	17.35
12-month low ($)	14.78
Market capitalisation ($mn)	7906.2
Price-to-NTA-per-share ratio	na
5-year share price return (% p.a.)	16.5

Sector: Consumer discretionary	Company	Sector
Price-earnings ratio (times)	14.5	18.8
Dividend yield (%)	5.9	4.0

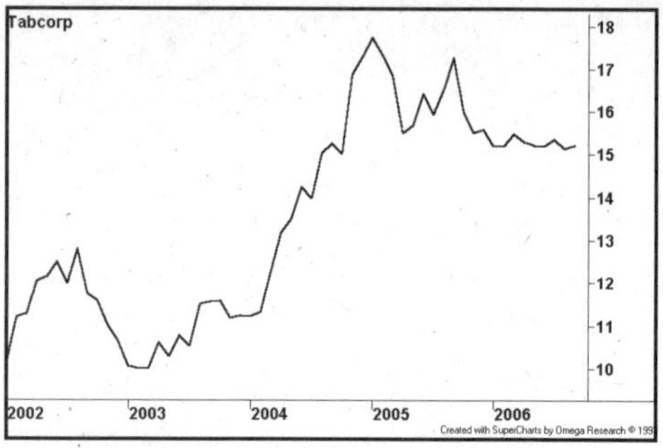

www.tabcorp.com.au

Melbourne-based Tabcorp was established in 1994 with the privatisation of Victoria's TAB operations. It has since grown substantially through acquisition, and now claims to be the fourth-largest gambling and entertainment business in the world. It operates four hotel and casino complexes – Star City in Sydney, Conrad Jupiters on the Gold Coast, Conrad Treasury in Brisbane, and Jupiters Townsville. It runs TAB operations in New South Wales and Victoria. It manages poker machines in Victoria and operates Keno games in Victoria, New South Wales and Queensland. Its media division runs the Sky horse racing television channel and Sky 2KY radio.

Latest business results (June 2006, full year)

Tabcorp overcame various hiccups in its many businesses to post a gain in profits. The casinos division enjoyed a good year with EBIT up 8%, despite some new smoking bans and disruptions during the refurbishment of Conrad Jupiters. This business accounts for about a third of company turnover, but contributes half of total profit. Wagering EBIT fell by 2%, with business hurt by a dispute over the broadcasting of horse races. The gaming and network games division was hit by an increase in the Victorian electronic gaming machines levy, and EBIT edged up less than 1%.

Outlook

With fears that consumer spending could start to slide, leading to a decline in gambling, Tabcorp is struggling to boost growth. In addition, as its various licences come up for renewal, it faces a continuing squeeze from state governments wanting to increase their take from gambling while simultaneously trying to limit Australia's burgeoning gambling industry. In mid-2006, Tabcorp announced a takeover offer for UNiTAB of Brisbane, but this was opposed by the Australian Competition and Consumer Commission. It is now seeking to expand overseas, and has established an international division, with the aim of taking advantage of global opportunities in gambling entertainment. It has entered into a joint venture with China LotSynergy to provide support services for the lottery market in China, with an initial trial Keno project launched in January 2006, although it has conceded that it has encountered technical problems. Escalating costs led to the withdrawal from a proposed casino development in Singapore.

TAH Year to 30 June	2005	2006
Revenues ($mn)	3760.6	3776.9
Wagering (%)	35	35
Casinos (%)	34	35
Gaming & network games (%)	27	28
EBIT ($mn)	806.6	851.5
EBIT margin (%)	21.4	22.5
Profit before tax ($mn)	636.1	695.0
Profit after tax ($mn)	433.4	543.4
Earnings per share (¢)	83.9	103.6
Cash flow per share (¢)	112.2	130.1
Dividend (¢)	81	89
Percentage franked	100	100
Net tangible assets per share ($)	–	–
Interest cover (times)	4.7	5.4
Return on equity (%)	16.6	16.4
Debt-to-equity ratio (%)	71.3	65.8
Current ratio	0.4	0.3

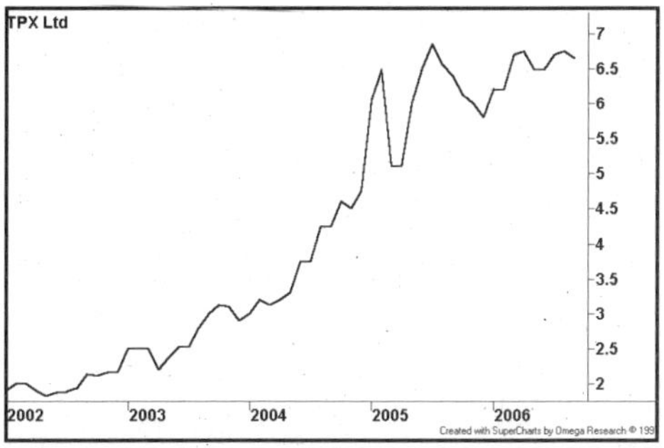

www.tasmanianperpetual.com.au

TASMANIAN PERPETUAL TRUSTEES LIMITED

Share price ($)	6.64
12-month high ($)	7.00
12-month low ($)	5.75
Market capitalisation ($mn)	144.5
Price-to-NTA-per-share ratio	7.9
5-year share price return (% p.a.)	32.4

Sector: Financials	Company	Sector
Price-earnings ratio (times)	19.1	15.7
Dividend yield (%)	4.5	4.3

Tasmanian Perpetual Trustees, with its headquarters in Launceston, was formed from the merger in December 2001 of Tasmanian Trustees and Perpetual Trustees Tasmania. Both companies had been founded in 1887. It engages in traditional trustee services, such as estate planning, will preparation, estate management and powers of attorney, and also offers a range of financial planning and wealth management services. In addition it runs managed funds and it jointly owns Tasmanian Banking Services, in a 50–50 partnership with Bendigo Bank.

Latest business results (June 2006, full year)

Revenues and profits rose again, in another firm result. The rate of growth was considerably more modest than in recent years, although the June 2005 figures included a one-off $0.87 million profit from the restructuring of the Tattersall's estate to prepare it for public listing. Total funds under management were up 6% to $1.379 billion. The company's share of the after-tax profit of Tasmanian Banking Services rose 3% to $749 000.

Outlook

Tasmanian Perpetual Trustees enjoys a strong reputation in its home state, and together with its Tasmanian Banking Services joint venture it is a powerful force in Tasmanian finance, with seven branch offices. It services a quarter of all adult Tasmanian residents, and it has more than 5000 business and community clients. It is seen as having particular strength in rural services. The joint venture Tasmanian Banking Services is making steady progress, and as well as making a strong and growing contribution to Tasmanian Perpetual's profits, it also provides considerable synergies, including five shared branch offices and the ability to gain new clients. Tasmanian Perpetual is opening its eighth branch, in Kingston in southern Tasmania, and this will also act as a new branch for Tasmanian Banking Services. In other initiatives, the company will launch two new investment funds, one providing exposure mainly to listed property trusts and the other investing in international equities. Tasmanian Perpetual has stated that despite growing competition it believes it is on track for an increase in EPS of at least 8% in the June 2007 year. Takeover speculation has at times been an incentive for the share price.

TPX Year to 30 June	2005	2006
Revenues ($mn)	18.3	20.4
EBIT ($mn)	9.5	10.3
EBIT margin (%)	51.5	50.3
Profit before tax ($mn)	9.5	10.3
Profit after tax ($mn)	6.9	7.5
Earnings per share (¢)	31.6	34.7
Cash flow per share (¢)	33.1	36.8
Dividend (¢)	22	30
Percentage franked	100	100
Net tangible assets per share ($)	0.79	0.85
Interest cover (times)	–	–
Return on equity (%)	23.1	23.6
Debt-to-equity ratio (%)	–	–
Current ratio	4.2	4.5

TECHNOLOGY ONE LIMITED

Share price ($)	0.75
12-month high ($)	0.77
12-month low ($)	0.52
Market capitalisation ($mn)	227.0
Price-to-NTA-per-share ratio	7.5
5-year share price return (% p.a.)	6.0

Sector: Information technology	**Company**	**Sector**
Price-earnings ratio (times)	18.2	22.8
Dividend yield (%)	4.5	2.2

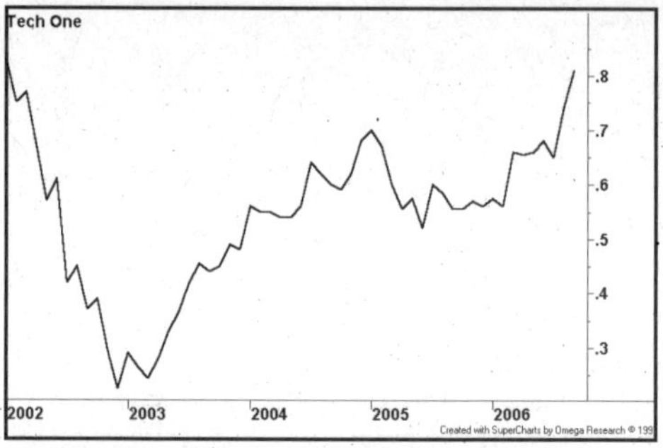

www.technologyone.com.au

Brisbane-based Technology One, founded in 1987, designs, develops, implements and supports financial management and accounting software. It has gained success with its Finance One software product, and enjoys particular strength in local government. Its software is also used by many colleges and universities, and the company has a thriving business developing custom software for clients. It operates from offices in Australia, New Zealand, Malaysia and the UK.

Latest business results (June 2006, full year)

Technology One returned to double-digit profit growth with an excellent result based on a successful reception for its new Connected Intelligence (Ci) suite of products. The company won substantial new business from large multinational companies as well as from government departments and universities. Initial licence fees to new customers showed impressive 58% growth to $12.8 million. During the year the company boosted research and development (R&D) spending by 24% to $12.7 million, representing nearly 20% of total revenues.

Outlook

Technology One is one of the high-tech companies that listed on the ASX late in 1999, near the height of the dot-com boom. However, unlike virtually all the others, it not only has prospered but has managed a record of continuing good profits and dividend payouts. It is a conservatively managed company. It devotes considerable amounts towards R&D, and this money is fully expensed as it is incurred – thus providing a realistic picture of its financial position – rather than being capitalised, as is common among many companies. It has a strong balance sheet and maintains high dividend payouts to its shareholders. It is devoting considerable resources to moving its customer base to the new Ci platform, with successive releases of new software products planned for 2006 and 2007, and it has said that it expects profit growth of 15% to 20% in the June 2007 year. It expects New South Wales, Victoria and New Zealand to be the key regions fuelling this growth. In March 2006 it opened its first office in the UK, and it sees Europe as a market with great potential. It is also considering further expansion to China and the US.

TNE Year to 30 June	**2005**	**2006**
Revenues ($mn)	53.7	65.2
Service delivery (%)	72	74
Software engineering (%)	26	25
EBIT ($mn)	13.3	15.1
EBIT margin (%)	24.7	23.2
Profit before tax ($mn)	14.4	16.3
Profit after tax ($mn)	10.6	12.3
Earnings per share (¢)	3.5	4.1
Cash flow per share (¢)	3.9	4.5
Dividend (¢)	3.1	3.41
Percentage franked	100	100
Net tangible assets per share ($)	0.10	0.10
Interest cover (times)	–	–
Return on equity (%)	28.2	31.7
Debt-to-equity ratio (%)	–	–
Current ratio	3.5	3.4

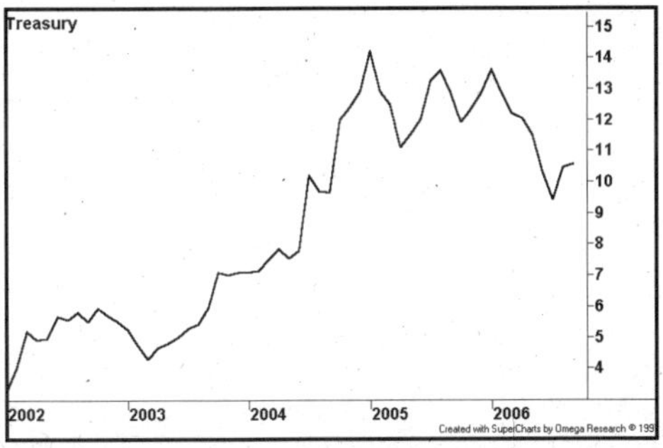

www.treasury-group.com

TREASURY GROUP LIMITED

Share price ($)	11.00	
12-month high ($)	13.80	
12-month low ($)	9.09	
Market capitalisation ($mn)	243.3	
Price-to-NTA-per-share ratio	6.6	
5-year share price return (% p.a.)	53.0	
Sector: Financials	**Company**	**Sector**
Price-earnings ratio (times)	17.5	15.7
Dividend yield (%)	4.5	4.3

Melbourne company Treasury Group provides specialist back-office services for boutique fund management companies. Not only does it take a fee for its services – based on the amount of funds under management – but it also takes an equity stake in the companies with which it works. It owns 67% of the equity of Global Value Investors, 50% of Investors Mutual, 47% of Treasury Asia Asset Management, 42% of Orion Asset Management and 35% of Confluence Asset Management. It has sold its 50% stake in Armytage Private.

Latest business results (June 2006, full year)

Total funds under management in Treasury Group's stable of investment managers rose 16.9% to $10.1 billion, delivering to the company another solid increase in revenues and profits. There was a third straight year of very strong performance from Orion Asset Management, with its funds under management up 52% to $4.1 billion. By contrast, Investors Mutual funds edged down from $5.5 billion to $5.4 billion, reflecting the loss of some institutional mandates. The comparatively tiny fund holdings of Confluence and Global Value showed good growth.

Outlook

Treasury Group has enjoyed big success and has become a stock market superstar, with a soaring share price. Thanks to the rapid growth in Australia of the boutique funds management business, the company has had many requests to provide back-room services, and it has been able to select only those fund managers it believes offer the best long-term growth potential. The main risk to its business is that it is heavily dependent on highly talented individuals, and if any of them chose to quit they might be difficult to replace. It also faces the possibility of a sluggish stock market and a slowdown of inflows to its funds. However, it anticipates that such conditions could make many of the funds – which take a value approach – more attractive. It has seen a successful launch of its new Treasury Asia Asset Management business, and in July 2006 it launched RARE Infrastructure, a fund to invest in listed infrastructure assets. It is seeing growing interest from international investors, and by early 2007 it plans to launch Dublin-based funds for European investors.

TRG Year to 30 June	2005	2006
Revenues ($mn)	43.1	50.2
EBIT ($mn)	30.7	33.6
EBIT margin (%)	71.1	66.9
Profit before tax ($mn)	31.9	34.9
Profit after tax ($mn)	11.8	13.9
Earnings per share (¢)	56.5	63.0
Cash flow per share (¢)	57.5	64.5
Dividend (¢)	40	50
Percentage franked	100	100
Net tangible assets per share ($)	1.36	1.67
Interest cover (times)	–	–
Return on equity (%)	48.3	39.4
Debt-to-equity ratio (%)	–	–
Current ratio	2.8	3.8

TROY RESOURCES NL

Share price ($)	2.52	
12-month high ($)	3.54	
12-month low ($)	2.37	
Market capitalisation ($mn)	128.8	
Price-to-NTA-per-share ratio	2.4	
5-year share price return (% p.a.)	28.2	
Sector: Materials	**Company**	**Sector**
Price-earnings ratio (times)	8.7	12.3
Dividend yield (%)	2.8	2.3

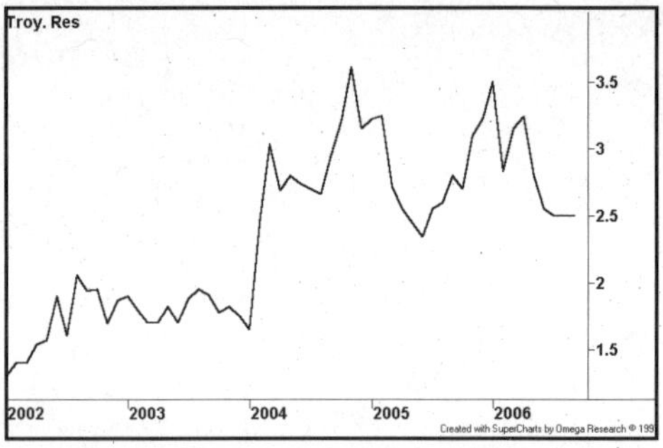

www.try.com.au

Perth-based Troy Resources, founded in 1984, is among the 10 largest Australian-owned gold mining companies. It has two gold mining operations – at Sandstone in Western Australia and a 70% holding in the Sertão mine in the state of Goiás in central Brazil. It also has exploration ventures domestically and in Brazil and Mongolia.

Latest business results (June 2006, full year)

Increased production and the strength of the gold price combined to give a major boost to Troy's revenues and profits. Total production of 110 263 ounces of gold was up sharply from 71 851 ounces in the June 2005 year, thanks to the successful launch of production at the Lord Henry and Lord Nelson mines at Sandstone. However, the company's share of Brazilian output fell from 48 706 ounces to 41 514 ounces. The total average cost of production was $240 per ounce, with a steep rise in average costs at Sertão, from $129 per ounce to $232, as it came to the end of its life. The average amount received was $687 per ounce.

Outlook

Troy forecasts gold production in the June 2007 year of around 100 000 ounces – down on the previous year due to mine scheduling and the processing of lower grade ore – at an average cost of about $325 per ounce. It expects continuing good production at Sandstone. In Brazil, with the Sertão mine at the end of its life, the company has moved to production at satellite bodies of ore in the region. With more than $32 million in net cash holdings, Troy maintains an active exploration program. It is exploring around both its Sandstone and Sertão mines. In addition, Troy has a project generation team based in Brazil, and plans to launch two exploration ventures in different parts of the country. It is also active in Mongolia, looking for gold, coal and uranium. It has made a $3.3 million investment in Birim Goldfields of Canada, and plans a strategic alliance with that company to explore for gold in Ghana. Troy has also acquired a strategic 17% equity stake in Adelaide Resources, which maintains large exploration areas in South Australia. The company's goal is to secure a one-million ounce orebody capable of delivering about 100 000 ounces of gold annually for at least 10 years.

TRY Year to 30 June	2005	2006
Revenues ($mn)	54.6	85.7
EBIT ($mn)	13.5	30.0
EBIT margin (%)	24.6	35.0
Gross margin (%)	50.0	55.7
Profit before tax ($mn)	14.9	31.9
Profit after tax ($mn)	7.7	16.1
Earnings per share (¢)	14.0	29.1
Cash flow per share (¢)	29.5	42.0
Dividend (¢)	6.5	7
Percentage franked	100	100
Net tangible assets per share ($)	0.80	1.06
Interest cover (times)	–	–
Return on equity (%)	18.8	31.2
Debt-to-equity ratio (%)	–	–
Current ratio	3.7	3.6

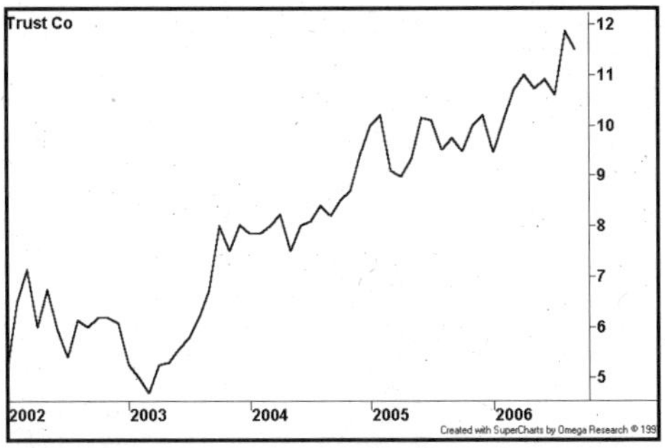

www.trust.com.au

TRUST COMPANY OF AUSTRALIA LIMITED

Share price ($)	11.50
12-month high ($)	11.95
12-month low ($)	9.35
Market capitalisation ($mn)	373.8
Price-to-NTA-per-share ratio	3.7
5-year share price return (% p.a.)	26.6

Sector: Financials	Company	Sector
Price-earnings ratio (times)	20.6	15.7
Dividend yield (%)	3.6	4.3

Melbourne-based Trust Company of Australia was founded in 1885, and is one of Australia's oldest trustee companies. In 2002 it merged with Permanent Trustee Company, which had been established in 1887. Its services include funds management, estates and trusts, financial planning, property and infrastructure custody, superannuation, charitable services, securitisation and structured finance. It has offices in Sydney, Melbourne, Brisbane and Townsville. It operates a new joint venture securitisation business with the Bank of New York.

Latest business results (February 2006, full year)

The company reported a good result, with profits up strongly. However, because of a major restructuring of its operations, comparisons with the previous year are difficult. The company now divides its businesses into two broad groupings. The first of these, financial services, saw revenue growth of 11% for private clients and 9% for estates and trusts, with assets under control growing to $3.4 billion. The second division, institutional services, realised an excellent result from its corporate services business, with revenues up 30% and assets under control soaring 29% to $82.5 billion. The company reported a profit before interest, taxation, depreciation and amortisation of $2.4 million from its new joint venture with the Bank of New York. There was also an $8.6 million one-off pre-tax profit from the sale of businesses.

Outlook

Trust Company has completed a major restructuring of its operations – including the sale of non-strategic businesses – in order to focus on those areas where it believes it has competitive strengths. It is investing heavily in marketing and staff training, and believes this will underpin its long-term growth prospects. It has a particular strength in the provision of fiduciary services to the property sector, and plans to open offices in Hong Kong and Singapore to service the Asian real estate investment trust market, which is expected to grow significantly in coming years. It has announced that it expects further profit growth in the February 2007 year, though this is dependent on the local equity market remaining firm and on the progress of the Bank of New York joint venture.

TRU Year to 28 February	2005	2006
Revenues ($mn)	49.8	51.2
Corporate services (%)	18	23
Estates & trusts (%)	28	23
Funds management (%)	22	21
Private clients (%)	14	15
Superannuation (%)	11	9
Investment portfolio (%)	4	6
EBIT ($mn)	8.1	21.8
EBIT margin (%)	16.4	42.6
Profit before tax ($mn)	8.6	22.4
Profit after tax ($mn)	8.2	18.0
Earnings per share (¢)	25.6	55.9
Cash flow per share (¢)	33.9	62.8
Dividend (¢)	38	41
Percentage franked	100	100
Net tangible assets per share ($)	2.33	3.08
Interest cover (times)	–	–
Return on equity (%)	6.7	13.5
Debt-to-equity ratio (%)	–	–
Current ratio	2.9	4.7

UNITED GROUP LIMITED

Share price ($)	14.10
12-month high ($)	14.96
12-month low ($)	9.60
Market capitalisation ($mn)	1909.0
Price-to-NTA-per-share ratio	54.4
5-year share price return (% p.a.)	54.1

Sector: Industrials	Company	Sector
Price-earnings ratio (times)	22.1	13.6
Dividend yield (%)	3.1	4.3

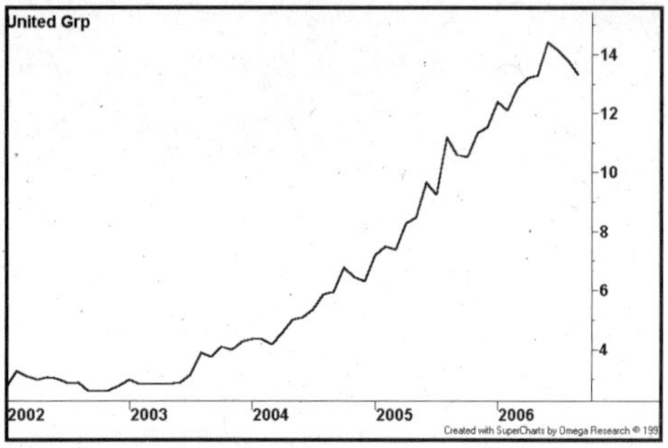

www.unitedgroup.com.au

Sydney-based United Group is one of Australia's leading engineering companies, with specialties in power supply, water and waste management, defence, resources engineering, telecommunications and heavy haulage railways. It is also active in facilities and property management. Its operations are primarily in Australia and New Zealand, though it is steadily expanding elsewhere.

Latest business results (June 2006, full year)

In an excellent result, United achieved its fifth successive year of profit expansion exceeding 30%. Strong domestic infrastructure spending by both the government and private sectors was one of the keys, with revenues for the company's infrastructure division more than doubling and profits up more than threefold. The resources boom was another factor, and United's resources division saw profits double, on a 50% jump in revenues. The company's core rail business continued to grow, and was another beneficiary of the buoyant resources sector, with strong demand for coal wagons in Queensland and New South Wales, and for iron ore wagons and locomotives in Western Australia. This division also benefited from the acquisition of transportation assets from engineering giant Alstom, and it is now undertaking maintenance for Melbourne's passenger train and tram fleet. The service division was helped by the mid-2005 acquisition of PREMAS International, Singapore's leading property services company.

Outlook

With a $4.3 billion order book at June 2006, United is on track for continuing strong growth. It is a particular beneficiary of high infrastructure and resources spending in Australia, with new projects that include a $250 million scheme to construct high-voltage power lines across southern Queensland, and a $650 million joint venture with Thiess to upgrade rail infrastructure in south-east Queensland. Its rail division is hopeful of winning major long-term work supplying passenger trains for Sydney and it is also pursuing opportunities in China and elsewhere in Asia. The services division has been successful in negotiating a string of major facilities management contacts, and the mid-2006 $163 million acquisition of the American real estate service company Equis Corporation is part of United's strategy to expand globally. However, the company has conceded that a skills shortage in Australia is a challenge.

UGL Year to 30 June	2005	2006
Revenues ($mn)	1254.9	2232.4
Rail (%)	43	43
Infrastructure (%)	18	24
Resources (%)	25	21
Services (%)	14	12
EBIT ($mn)	65.7	123.0
EBIT margin (%)	5.2	5.5
Profit before tax ($mn)	57.3	105.8
Profit after tax ($mn)	47.5	78.7
Earnings per share (¢)	45.8	63.7
Cash flow per share (¢)	63.7	85.6
Dividend (¢)	30	44
Percentage franked	100	100
Net tangible assets per share ($)	1.61	0.26
Interest cover (times)	7.9	7.2
Return on equity (%)	18.7	18.5
Debt-to-equity ratio (%)	–	31.7
Current ratio	1.3	1.3

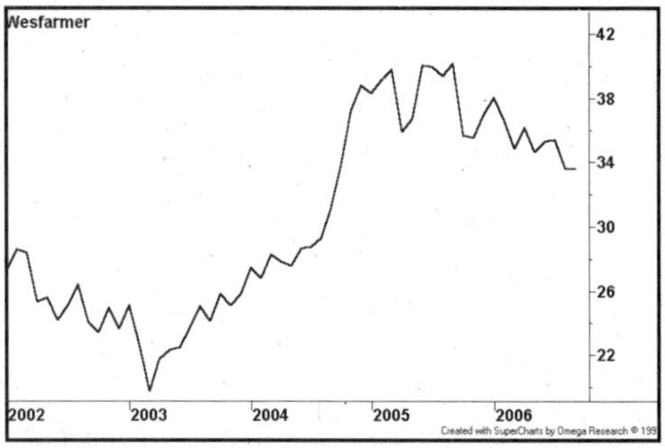

www.wesfarmers.com.au

WESFARMERS LIMITED

Share price ($)	33.90
12-month high ($)	40.49
12-month low ($)	32.65
Market capitalisation ($mn)	12766.5
Price-to-NTA-per-share ratio	7.4
5-year share price return (% p.a.)	10.7

Sector: Industrials	Company	Sector
Price-earnings ratio (times)	14.4	13.6
Dividend yield (%)	6.3	4.3

Perth-based Wesfarmers, founded in 1914 as a farmers' cooperative, is now a conglomerate with many major areas of operation. It runs the Bunnings chain of hardware stores, it is a coal miner and a supplier of liquefied petroleum, and it manufactures fertilisers and agricultural chemicals. It has a large insurance business and it distributes industrial safety products. It owns 50% of the investment bank Gresham Partners Group and 50% of the forestry company Wespine Industries.

Latest business results (June 2006, full year)

Wesfarmers turned in another excellent result, due almost entirely to its booming energy business. Sharply higher coal prices and increased output from the company's Curragh coal mine in Queensland boosted energy division turnover by 44%, while EBIT almost doubled. This business, though just 19% of total company revenues, represents nearly 40% of profit. The Bunnings home improvement business had a rocky first half, but a recovery in the second half meant that sales and profits for the year edged up. The company opened 12 new warehouse stores and closed one. At June 2006 it operated 142 warehouse stores and 84 smaller stores across Australia and New Zealand. The industrial and safety business saw revenues largely unchanged, but profits fell 11%, reflecting a big restructuring of the division. Strong competition and margin pressures forced insurance profits down, and a sharp decline in fertiliser demand, following the lowest June rainfall in Western Australia on record, hurt chemicals and fertilisers division profits. The company also recorded a $178.7 million after-tax profit on the sale of its 50% stake in Australian Railroad Group.

Outlook

Company profits look set to fall in the June 2007 year as coal prices decline and production and transportation costs continue to rise. Wesfarmers plans to open 10 to 14 new Bunnings warehouse stores each year, and this should underpin home improvement division growth. But the underperforming industrial and safety business remains a challenge, while competition remains high in the insurance industry. Wesfarmers has a reputation for big moves, and there is intense speculation that it plans a major acquisition to stimulate renewed growth. In September 2006 it announced a takeover bid for insurance broker OAMPS.

WES Year to 30 June	2005	2006
Revenues ($mn)	8101.1	8818.3
Home improvement (%)	50	48
Energy (%)	14	19
Industrial & safety distribution (%)	14	13
Insurance (%)	14	13
Chemicals & fertilisers (%)	7	7
EBIT ($mn)	1018.0	1330.6
EBIT margin (%)	12.6	15.1
Gross margin (%)	34.6	36.6
Profit before tax ($mn)	966.6	1232.1
Profit after tax ($mn)	701.8	869.4
Earnings per share (¢)	186.0	235.6
Cash flow per share (¢)	236.1	312.4
Dividend (¢)	180	215
Percentage franked	100	100
Net tangible assets per share ($)	3.37	4.59
Interest cover (times)	19.8	13.5
Return on equity (%)	23.1	29.4
Debt-to-equity ratio (%)	62.6	45.9
Current ratio	1.2	1.2

WESTPAC BANKING CORPORATION

Share price ($)	23.30	
12-month high ($)	25.35	
12-month low ($)	20.14	
Market capitalisation ($mn)	42 649.5	
Price-to-NTA-per-share ratio	4.0	
5-year share price return (% p.a.)	16.1	
Sector: Financials	**Company**	**Sector**
Price-earnings ratio (times)	15.3	15.7
Dividend yield (%)	4.3	4.3

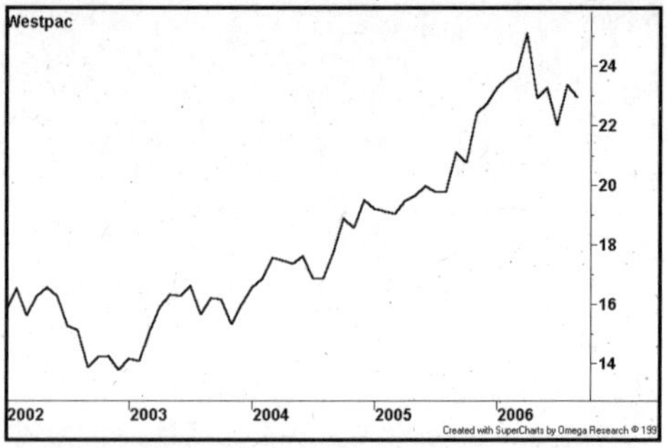

www.westpac.com.au

Westpac, which began trading in 1817 as the Bank of New South Wales, is one of Australia's big four banks, with interests in most areas of financial services. Around 15% of revenues and profit come from New Zealand, where Westpac Trust is one of that country's leading banks. It is also active in the Pacific region. It has moved strongly into wealth management, with the acquisition of BT Financial Group, Rothschild Australia Asset Management and Hastings Funds Management.

Latest business results (March 2006, half year)

A firm domestic economy helped Westpac to another solid rise in profits. Most areas of business were strong. The main driver of the good result was domestic retail banking, with profits up 12%. Lending growth of 11% easily offset expense growth of 2%, and there was particularly strong credit card business. A particular highlight was a 20% jump in profits from BT Financial Group, with funds under administration up 27%. BT now contributes 11% of total company profit, up from 8% three years earlier. Thanks to Westpac's buoyant funds management business, along with continuing strength in insurance, margin lending and discount broking, the bank's advice business to its customer base saw sales volumes up 21%. New Zealand business grew, but was restrained by a weakening economy and a highly competitive banking environment.

WBC Year to 30 September	2004	2005
Operating income ($mn)	8010.0	8805.0
Net interest income ($mn)	4755.0	5245.0
Operating expenses ($mn)	3940.0	4105.0
Profit before tax ($mn)	3492.0	4150.0
Profit after tax ($mn)	2539.0	2818.0
Earnings per share (¢)	137.5	152.2
Dividend (¢)	86	100
Percentage franked	100	100
Non-interest income to total income (%)	40.6	40.4
Cost-to-income ratio (%)	49.2	46.6
Return on equity (%)	17.6	18.0
Return on assets (%)	1.1	1.1
Half year to 31 March	**2005**	**2006**
Operating income ($mn)	4161.0	4563.0
Profit before tax ($mn)	1887.0	2243.0
Profit after tax ($mn)	1261.0	1469.0
Earnings per share (¢)	71.9	79.7
Dividend (¢)	49	56
Percentage franked	100	100
Net tangible assets per share ($)	5.37	5.78

Outlook

With its focus on Australia and New Zealand, Westpac continues to work at boosting efficiency across all areas of its operations. It is placing particular stress on wealth management and the BT business, expecting continuing strong growth, including further gains in cross-sales to its large customer base. Its institutional banking arm is picking up strength, and business lending remains strong. However, Westpac could be hurt by rising interest rates and any economic slowdown. Its exposure to New Zealand makes it vulnerable to weakness in that country's economy. Westpac expects its September 2006 profit to be about 10% up on the September 2005 year.

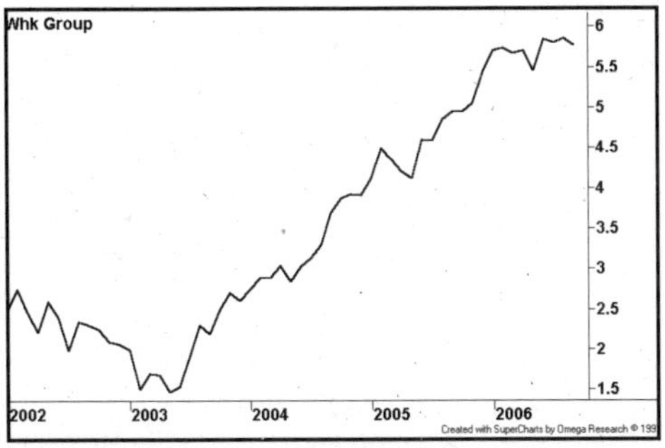

www.whkgroup.com.au

WHK GROUP LIMITED

Share price ($)	5.77
12-month high ($)	6.00
12-month low ($)	4.87
Market capitalisation ($mn)	440.0
Price-to-NTA-per-share ratio	14.9
5-year share price return (% p.a.)	25.5

Sector: Financials	**Company**	**Sector**
Price-earnings ratio (times)	19.9	15.7
Dividend yield (%)	2.4	4.3

Melbourne-based WHK, formerly known as Investor Group, manages a network of 20 accountancy and financial planning businesses in Australia and New Zealand, and has grown to become Australia's fifth-largest accounting business. It operates from more than 100 offices, employs some 2300 staff and specialises in providing advice to small and medium-sized enterprises and to high-net-worth individuals. It divides its operations into two divisions: the business services division provides a full range of traditional accounting and specialist services including accounting, taxation, audit and assurance, estate planning, business advisory and corporate advisory services; and the financial services division provides financial planning, risk insurance, self-managed superannuation and finance broking services.

Latest business results (June 2006, full year)

WHK enjoyed another good year, thanks to both organic growth and continued acquisitions. The business services division was a particular beneficiary of acquisitions, and margins were maintained despite the cost pressures incurred from integrating the new businesses. The financial services division, which is more dependent on organic growth, was a particular beneficiary of ongoing annuity-type fees based on funds being managed by WHK. The results also included a $0.6 million profit on the sale of a non-core superannuation fund and a $0.8 million loss from the fraudulent misappropriation of a member firm's funds. At June 2006, WHK held funds under advice of $6.72 billion, a 19% rise from a year earlier.

Outlook

WHK has expanded strongly by acquisition, and it continues to seek out new growth opportunities. Its strategy is to operate a number of stand-alone firms – at June 2006 it had 19 accounting firms and one specialist financial planning firm – and to strengthen these and boost their efficiency through internal mergers and what it terms 'tuck-in' acquisitions. It sees particular growth potential in financial planning, and is moving into new long-term growth areas such as risk insurance and finance broking. However, the weakening of the New Zealand dollar could hurt company profits – New Zealand represents about 8% of company turnover – and business could also be affected by the move of Count Financial to launch countplus, a rival network of accountancy and financial planning practices.

WHG Year to 30 June	2005	2006
Revenues ($mn)	201.0	251.5
Business services (%)	75	75
Financial services (%)	25	25
EBIT ($mn)	25.7	33.1
EBIT margin (%)	12.8	13.2
Profit before tax ($mn)	24.4	31.3
Profit after tax ($mn)	16.5	21.8
Earnings per share (¢)	23.1	28.9
Cash flow per share (¢)	27.3	33.2
Dividend (¢)	12.5	14
Percentage franked	100	100
Net tangible assets per share ($)	0.46	0.39
Interest cover (times)	20.2	18.7
Return on equity (%)	12.3	13.7
Debt-to-equity ratio (%)	0.3	13.2
Current ratio	1.9	2.1

WIDE BAY AUSTRALIA LIMITED

Share price ($)	11.40
12-month high ($)	11.80
12-month low ($)	7.50
Market capitalisation ($mn)	236.2
Price-to-NTA-per-share ratio	2.6
5-year share price return (% p.a.)	29.3

Sector: Financials	Company	Sector
Price-earnings ratio (times)	16.1	15.7
Dividend yield (%)	4.5	4.3

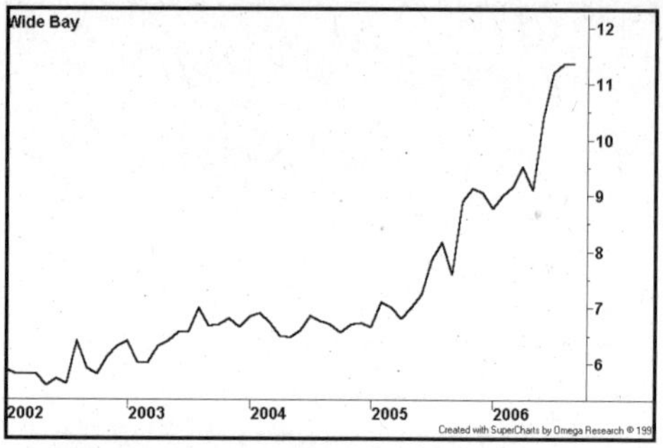

www.widebaycap.com.au

Based in Bundaberg in Queensland, Wide Bay Australia – formerly known as Wide Bay Capricorn Building Society – was founded in 1979 from the merger of two smaller building societies. It is a leading provider of financial services in south-east and central Queensland, with a network of 35 branches and agencies, and is one of Queensland's largest non-bank deposit-taking institutions. It has expanded interstate, with one branch in Sydney and another in Melbourne, as well as lending operations in Adelaide.

Latest business results (June 2006, full year)

Wide Bay overcame the housing slowdown to post another solid result. Loan approvals fell for the second straight year – from $449.6 million to $417 million – but the total loan book continued to grow, up 8% to $1.425 billion. Altogether, assets and funds under management were up 7.9% to $1.645 billion. Stringent cost control led to a further decline in the cost-to-income ratio. The company's captive lenders' mortgage insurance company, Mortgage Risk Management, made another strong contribution, with an after-tax surplus of $2.15 million.

Outlook

Wide Bay is developing a series of initiatives to stimulate continued growth. In July 2006 it launched a $47 million takeover bid for the Pioneer Permanent Building Society, which operates a network of branches centred on Mackay in northern Queensland. However, as this book was going to press it appeared more likely that Bank of Queensland would succeed with its own counter-offer to acquire Pioneer. Wide Bay is also working to develop a network of mortgage brokers, which it believes will boost its total lending figure in the June 2007 year. It expects lending through brokers to rise to 25% of its total lending, up from 12% to 16% at present, though this could place pressure on margins. In addition, new branches are planned during 2006–07 for Gympie and Robina, and the company is considering further interstate expansion. Wide Bay has acquired a 25% equity stake in the financial planning firm Financial Technology Securities in order to strengthen its presence in the financial planning industry and expand the range of services available to its customers.

WBB Year to 30 June	2005	2006
Operating income ($mn)	39.6	46.6
Net interest income ($mn)	26.9	32.0
Operating expenses ($mn)	24.1	26.4
Profit before tax ($mn)	17.6	20.2
Profit after tax ($mn)	12.4	14.5
Earnings per share (¢)	60.8	70.6
Dividend (¢)	42	51.5
Percentage franked	100	100
Non-interest income to total income (%)	32.0	31.4
Net tangible assets per share ($)	4.05	4.32
Cost-to-income ratio (%)	60.7	56.7
Return on equity (%)	15.2	16.9
Return on assets (%)	1.0	0.9

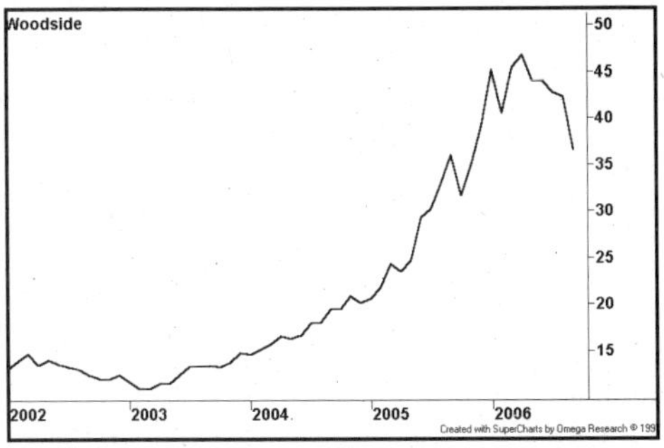

www.woodside.com.au

WOODSIDE PETROLEUM LIMITED

Share price ($)	41.08
12-month high ($)	49.80
12-month low ($)	29.10
Market capitalisation ($mn)	27 273.3
Price-to-NTA-per-share ratio	7.5
5-year share price return (% p.a.)	27.0

Sector: Energy	Company	Sector
Price-earnings ratio (times)	25.9	14.8
Dividend yield (%)	2.3	2.6

Perth-based Woodside, founded in 1954, is Australia's largest listed specialist energy company. Its major interest is the North West Shelf project off Western Australia, which supplies liquefied natural gas for Asia, natural gas for the domestic market, and liquefied petroleum gas, crude oil and condensate for international markets. It also has major exploration and development interests in Western Australia. It is operator of oil and gas discoveries in offshore Mauritania and has other exploration and production interests in the US, North Africa and elsewhere. Shell Australia owns 34% of Woodside's equity.

Latest business results (June 2006, half year)

The continuing oil price surge helped deliver another strong mid-year profit gain to Woodside. Production volume of 29.9 million barrels of oil equivalent (MMboe) was in line with the 2005 first half, with Gulf of Mexico production and the start-up of the Chinguetti oil project in Mauritania offsetting the effects of cyclones in Western Australia. The sales volume of 29.1 MMboe was slightly down from a year earlier. However, the company realised an average price of US$65.42 per barrel, a 32.8% jump from the June 2005 half. In May 2006 the company made its initial LNG shipment to the new Chinese LNG terminal at Guangdong. Woodside forecasts 2006 full-year production of 72 MMboe, up from 59.7 MMboe in 2005.

Outlook

Woodside has three major projects that are expected to contribute to growth in 2006 and 2007. They are: the Chinguetti oil field, which is its first self-operated international project; the Enfield oil project in Western Australia, which launched production in July 2006; and the Otways gas project in Victoria. It is also very active in the Gulf of Mexico. For the longer term, the company's Pluto gas field off Western Australia has enormous potential, with production scheduled for late in 2010. In August 2006 Woodside announced a takeover bid for the US oil and gas producer Energy Partners, which operates in the Gulf of Mexico.

WPL Year to 31 December	2004	2005
Revenues ($mn)	2124.8	2746.7
EBIT ($mn)	1006.9	1416.6
EBIT margin (%)	47.4	51.6
Gross margin (%)	64.9	68.9
Profit before tax ($mn)	1006.4	1407.7
Profit after tax ($mn)	671.8	1037.7
Earnings per share (¢)	102.8	158.4
Cash flow per share (¢)	108.5	164.9
Dividend (¢)	59	93
Percentage franked	100	100
Interest cover (times)	2046.5	159.9
Return on equity (%)	25.8	33.1
Half year to 30 June	**2005**	**2006**
Revenues ($mn)	1241.5	1567.9
Profit before tax ($mn)	635.5	755.3
Profit after tax ($mn)	437.4	542.9
Earnings per share (¢)	65.6	81.4
Dividend (¢)	35	49
Percentage franked	100	100
Net tangible assets per share ($)	4.94	5.46
Debt-to-equity ratio (%)	14.0	43.4
Current ratio	1.9	0.8

PART II – THE TABLES

Table A

Market capitalisation

A company's market capitalisation is determined by multiplying the share price by the number of shares. To be included in this book, a company must (with a few exceptions, noted in the preface) be in the All Ordinaries Index, which comprises the 500 largest companies by market capitalisation.

	$mn		$mn		$mn
BHP Billiton	97006.5	Seven Network	2068.2	Commander Communications	428.4
Commonwealth Bank	58785.9	United Group	1909.0	GUD Holdings	418.2
National Australia Bank	58268.5	Bendigo Bank	1849.3	Trust Company of Australia	373.8
ANZ	49713.5	Downer EDI	1696.5	Fleetwood Corporation	334.8
Westpac Banking	42649.5	Reece Australia	1618.5	Programmed Maint. Services	314.5
Rio Tinto	34169.8	Bank of Queensland	1602.9	Oakton	293.7
Woodside Petroleum	27273.3	David Jones	1541.6	Fantastic Holdings	286.3
QBE Insurance	19130.6	Coates Hire	1470.6	Rebel Sport	282.2
Coles Myer	16337.1	Adelaide Bank	1443.6	Infomedia	250.6
Macquarie Bank	16204.4	Primary Health Care	1380.2	Treasury Group	243.3
St George Bank	15765.8	Rural Press	1319.6	K&S Corporation	240.8
Rinker Group	12795.2	Adelaide Brighton	1252.4	Wide Bay Australia	236.2
Wesfarmers	12766.5	Jubilee Mines	1189.5	Blackmores	232.4
Publishing & Broadcasting	12340.3	Flight Centre	1136.5	ARB Corporation	228.3
Suncorp-Metway	11553.0	Campbell Brothers	964.7	Hunter Hall International	227.5
Brambles Industries	11410.1	Gunns	949.5	Technology One	227.0
AXA Asia Pacific	11191.8	Macarthur Coal	910.1	Housewares International	203.7
CSL	9284.3	Corporate Express Australia	905.2	Ausdrill	187.0
Tabcorp Holdings	7906.2	GWA International	860.0	HPAL	183.0
Orica	6981.2	Cabcharge Australia	853.0	CVC	176.0
Santos	6804.7	Beach Petroleum	840.5	Candle Australia	169.6
Lend Lease Corporation	6299.8	Great Southern Plantations	821.4	Gazal Corporation	157.3
Leighton Holdings	5613.3	Hills Industries	794.1	Objective Corporation	145.2
Australian Stock Exchange	5601.7	OAMPS	669.5	Tasmanian Perpetual Trustees	144.5
Origin Energy	5108.9	IRESS Market Technology	667.4	Pro Medicus	129.0
Computershare	4590.6	Crane Group	659.6	Troy Resources	128.8
Boral	4213.3	Alesco	629.8	National Can Industries	118.9
Fairfax (John) Holdings	3990.6	Amalgamated Holdings	604.6	HGL	98.5
Sonic Healthcare	3720.3	Skilled Group	575.7	MaxiTRANS Industries	94.5
Harvey Norman Holdings	3670.5	STW Communications	574.3	Rock Building Society	90.6
Metcash	3231.9	Select Harvests	530.1	SDI	88.7
Billabong International	3003.6	Monadelphous Group	525.3	Institute of Drug Technology	62.3
CSR	2951.0	Count Financial	516.3	OrotonGroup	57.8
Perpetual	2888.6	Kingsgate Consolidated	473.9	CMI	43.5
Cochlear	2853.3	Colorado Group	445.9	Adcorp Australia	35.6
Sims Group	2604.9	WHK Group	440.0	Magna Pacific	22.7
OneSteel	2391.0				

Table B

Revenues

This list ranks the companies in the book according to their most recent full-year revenues figures (operating income for the banks). The figures include revenues from sales and services, but other revenues – such as interest receipts and investment income – are not generally included.

	$mn
BHP Billiton	42 870.7
Coles Myer	34 212.0
Rio Tinto	27 195.0
National Australia Bank	13 856.0
Commonwealth Bank	12 286.0
Lend Lease Corporation	11 903.3
ANZ	9 350.0
Wesfarmers	8 818.3
Westpac Banking	8 805.0
Leighton Holdings	8 502.6
Metcash	8 192.5
QBE Insurance	7 386.0
Rinker Group	7 151.8
Origin Energy	5 879.8
Suncorp-Metway	5 580.0
Orica	5 126.7
AXA Asia Pacific	4 918.0
Boral	4 756.1
Brambles Industries	4 696.1
Downer EDI	4 619.2
Macquarie Bank	4 393.0
OneSteel	4 004.6
Tabcorp Holdings	3 776.9
Sims Group	3 752.4
Publishing & Broadcasting	3 551.8
CSR	2 946.1
CSL	2 848.9
St George Bank	2 775.0
Woodside Petroleum	2 746.7
Santos	2 462.8
United Group	2 232.4
Harvey Norman Holdings	2 172.4
Crane Group	1 941.5
Fairfax (John) Holdings	1 906.8
David Jones	1 821.6
Sonic Healthcare	1 645.2
Computershare	1 604.2
Seven Network	1 285.7
Corporate Express Australia	1 115.2
Reece Australia	1 113.4
Billabong International	1 023.5
Flight Centre	973.7
Skilled Group	961.4
Hills Industries	931.8
Cabcharge Australia	870.4
Commander Communications	764.0
Adelaide Brighton	723.2
Coates Hire	715.0
Gunns	637.5
GWA International	620.0
Alesco	600.5
Rural Press	583.0
Amalgamated Holdings	563.1
Macarthur Coal	534.8
Monadelphous Group	532.0
Campbell Brothers	522.7
Great Southern Plantations	485.1
Bendigo Bank	477.4
Colorado Group	466.0
GUD Holdings	462.4
Cochlear	452.3
Housewares International	424.2
Perpetual	420.2
Rebel Sport	371.2
K&S Corporation	367.1
Bank of Queensland	356.7
Ausdrill	317.1
Adelaide Bank	311.7
Australian Stock Exchange	305.6
Jubilee Mines	293.7
Programmed Maint. Services	282.9
OAMPS	277.5
CMI	275.7
Candle Australia	270.0
Fleetwood Corporation	252.4
WHK Group	251.5
MaxiTRANS Industries	245.0
Primary Health Care	240.7
Fantastic Holdings	233.8
Select Harvests	217.9
Gazal Corporation	215.8
National Can Industries	188.4
HPAL	180.1
STW Communications	176.1
OrotonGroup	159.3
Blackmores	148.0
ARB Corporation	125.9
Beach Petroleum	121.4
HGL	116.6
Count Financial	104.8
Troy Resources	85.7
Oakton	76.8
Kingsgate Consolidated	72.8
IRESS Market Technology	71.6
Technology One	65.2
Infomedia	55.6
Trust Company of Australia	51.2
Treasury Group	50.2
Wide Bay Australia	46.6
SDI	45.2
Objective Corporation	36.9
Hunter Hall International	36.4
CVC	35.1
Adcorp Australia	32.6
Magna Pacific	30.0
Rock Building Society	26.2
Institute of Drug Technology	24.9
Tasmanian Perpetual Trustees	20.4
Pro Medicus	11.4

Table C

Year-on-year revenues growth

Companies generally strive for growth, though profit growth is usually of far more significance than a boost in revenues. In fact, it is possible for a company to increase its revenues by all kinds of means – including cutting profit margins or acquiring other companies – and YOY revenues growth is of little relevance if other ratios are not also improving.

	%
Beach Petroleum	98.3
United Group	77.9
Santos	64.1
Great Southern Plantations	63.1
Troy Resources	56.8
Ausdrill	56.3
Computershare	50.8
Sims Group	46.3
Macarthur Coal	44.5
Oakton	42.4
Hunter Hall International	38.3
Rio Tinto	37.4
Monadelphous Group	36.2
Leighton Holdings	36.0
Coates Hire	35.5
Lend Lease Corporation	32.7
Cochlear	29.6
Woodside Petroleum	29.3
Rinker Group	27.7
Commander Communications	27.4
Primary Health Care	26.1
Count Financial	25.6
Select Harvests	25.3
WHK Group	25.1
Downer EDI	24.0
Jubilee Mines	23.9
CSR	22.8
Bank of Queensland	22.2
Programmed Maint. Services	22.2
STW Communications	22.0
Technology One	21.3
Skilled Group	21.2
Billabong International	21.1
Origin Energy	20.7
BHP Billiton	20.3
Campbell Brothers	20.0
Sonic Healthcare	19.7
Perpetual	18.8
Hills Industries	18.4
Wide Bay Australia	17.7
GUD Holdings	17.2
IRESS Market Technology	17.2
Metcash	17.2
Macquarie Bank	17.1
Rebel Sport	17.1
Candle Australia	16.5
Treasury Group	16.5
Harvey Norman Holdings	14.2
Cabcharge Australia	13.6
Corporate Express Australia	13.5
Kingsgate Consolidated	13.2
Flight Centre	11.8
Gazal Corporation	11.7
Tasmanian Perpetual Trustees	11.3
Orica	11.2
Pro Medicus	11.1
Bendigo Bank	10.9
Objective Corporation	10.9
Boral	10.7
Reece Australia	10.3
Adelaide Bank	10.1
Blackmores	10.1
HPAL	9.9
Westpac Banking	9.9
MaxiTRANS Industries	9.8
ARB Corporation	9.7
Australian Stock Exchange	9.3
Commonwealth Bank	8.9
QBE Insurance	8.9
Seven Network	8.9
Wesfarmers	8.9
Publishing & Broadcasting	8.4
ANZ	8.2
St George Bank	8.0
K&S Corporation	7.7
Brambles Industries	7.5
HGL	7.4
OrotonGroup	7.3
National Australia Bank	6.3
Fantastic Holdings	5.8
Adelaide Brighton	5.0
Suncorp-Metway	4.9
Alesco	4.8
National Can Industries	4.4
Housewares International	3.9
Coles Myer	3.6
CSL	3.6
OAMPS	3.5
Rural Press	3.3
Rock Building Society	3.1
Trust Company of Australia	2.8
Crane Group	2.0
Fairfax (John) Holdings	1.8
OneSteel	1.7
Amalgamated Holdings	1.2
David Jones	1.2
Tabcorp Holdings	0.4
Gunns	-0.1
AXA Asia Pacific	-0.4
Colorado Group	-0.6
GWA International	-1.1
SDI	-1.7
CMI	-1.8
Fleetwood Corporation	-3.6
Adcorp Australia	-3.7
Infomedia	-6.0
Institute of Drug Technology	-6.6
Magna Pacific	-18.2
CVC	-39.1

Table D

EBIT margin

A company's earnings before interest and taxation (EBIT) is sometimes regarded as a better measure of its profitability than the straight pre-tax or post-tax profit figure. EBIT is derived by adding net interest payments (that is, interest payments minus interest receipts) to the pre-tax profit. Different companies choose different methods of financing their operations; by adding back interest payments to their profits we can help minimise these differences and make comparisons between companies more valid.

The EBIT margin is the EBIT figure as a percentage of annual sales. Clearly a high figure is to be desired, though of course this can be achieved artificially by inflating borrowings (and hence interest payments). And it is noteworthy that efficient companies like some of the giant retailers can operate most satisfactorily on low margins.

The EBIT margin figure has little relevance for banks – whose high interest payments to their customers mean they have virtually no EBIT – and they have been excluded, as have the insurance companies.

	%		%		%
CVC	72.0	Coates Hire	22.2	Flight Centre	11.4
Pro Medicus	70.5	STW Communications	22.1	Reece Australia	11.1
Treasury Group	66.9	Brambles Industries	21.9	Orica	11.0
Australian Stock Exchange	58.1	Billabong International	21.5	Colorado Group	10.4
Woodside Petroleum	51.6	Campbell Brothers	20.5	Ausdrill	10.1
Tasmanian Perpetual Trustees	50.3	Institute of Drug Technology	20.2	National Can Industries	10.1
Hunter Hall International	50.1	Adelaide Brighton	18.5	Gazal Corporation	9.1
Jubilee Mines	50.1	Sonic Healthcare	18.5	Fantastic Holdings	8.7
Santos	49.0	ARB Corporation	18.1	Corporate Express Australia	8.6
Beach Petroleum	47.2	CSL	18.1	Rebel Sport	8.1
BHP Billiton	45.6	Harvey Norman Holdings	18.0	David Jones	8.0
Great Southern Plantations	42.6	Select Harvests	17.6	K&S Corporation	8.0
Trust Company of Australia	42.6	Computershare	16.9	Sims Group	8.0
Perpetual	40.3	OAMPS	16.7	Hills Industries	7.9
Infomedia	40.1	Seven Network	16.7	Monadelphous Group	7.8
Macarthur Coal	39.6	Magna Pacific	16.4	OneSteel	7.5
IRESS Market Technology	39.3	SDI	16.3	CMI	7.2
Troy Resources	35.0	GWA International	15.4	MaxiTRANS Industries	6.9
Rio Tinto	34.4	Wesfarmers	15.1	Housewares International	6.6
Rinker Group	31.4	Amalgamated Holdings	15.0	Candle Australia	6.3
Primary Health Care	31.1	Blackmores	14.2	Cabcharge Australia	6.1
Rural Press	29.9	CSR	14.1	United Group	5.5
Oakton	26.7	Adcorp Australia	13.9	Downer EDI	5.1
Cochlear	24.7	GUD Holdings	13.8	Lend Lease Corporation	5.1
Gunns	24.2	HPAL	13.6	Commander Communications	5.0
Count Financial	23.5	WHK Group	13.2	Crane Group	4.7
Technology One	23.2	Origin Energy	13.1	Leighton Holdings	4.5
Objective Corporation	23.1	Boral	12.9	Coles Myer	4.4
Kingsgate Consolidated	23.0	Fleetwood Corporation	12.3	Skilled Group	3.9
Publishing & Broadcasting	23.0	Programmed Maint. Services	12.0	OrotonGroup	3.8
Tabcorp Holdings	22.5	Alesco	11.9	Metcash	2.7
Fairfax (John) Holdings	22.3	HGL	11.9		

Table E

Year-on-year EBIT margin growth

The EBIT (earnings before interest and taxation) margin is one of the measures of a company's efficiency. So a rising margin is much to be desired, as it suggests that a company is achieving success in cutting its costs. This table does not include banks or insurance companies.

	%		%		%
Trust Company of Australia	160.6	Computershare	16.0	ARB Corporation	-2.8
Kingsgate Consolidated	101.5	CSL	15.0	Hills Industries	-2.9
SDI	101.3	Rural Press	13.7	Billabong International	-3.5
Rio Tinto	69.2	Coates Hire	12.4	CMI	-4.8
Ausdrill	55.0	Australian Stock Exchange	11.8	Corporate Express Australia	-5.2
Macarthur Coal	54.7	Oakton	9.9	CSR	-5.4
STW Communications	53.5	Blackmores	9.8	Crane Group	-5.8
Coles Myer	50.7	Hunter Hall International	9.4	Treasury Group	-6.0
National Can Industries	47.0	Infomedia	9.3	Technology One	-6.2
Troy Resources	42.1	Woodside Petroleum	8.8	Flight Centre	-6.6
Seven Network	40.1	Jubilee Mines	8.1	GWA International	-6.9
CVC	35.1	Adelaide Brighton	6.8	Select Harvests	-7.4
Rinker Group	34.3	OneSteel	6.5	Programmed Maint. Services	-7.8
Gazal Corporation	32.2	United Group	5.3	Orica	-8.5
BHP Billiton	31.5	Tabcorp Holdings	5.1	GUD Holdings	-9.9
Candle Australia	31.1	Cochlear	4.3	Boral	-10.4
Santos	29.8	Institute of Drug Technology	4.3	Gunns	-10.7
Beach Petroleum	29.6	Perpetual	4.2	Leighton Holdings	-11.0
Monadelphous Group	28.0	Reece Australia	3.9	OrotonGroup	-12.5
Lend Lease Corporation	27.7	HPAL	3.5	K&S Corporation	-13.5
Skilled Group	27.6	WHK Group	2.9	Commander Communications	-16.1
Cabcharge Australia	26.6	Harvey Norman Holdings	2.4	Housewares International	-16.5
Campbell Brothers	21.5	Primary Health Care	2.2	MaxiTRANS Industries	-17.2
Count Financial	21.3	Pro Medicus	1.2	Adcorp Australia	-19.9
David Jones	20.6	Sonic Healthcare	1.2	Colorado Group	-21.6
Wesfarmers	20.1	Metcash	1.0	Fantastic Holdings	-23.0
Alesco	20.0	Downer EDI	0.5	Objective Corporation	-24.3
Brambles Industries	19.6	Publishing & Broadcasting	-0.6	Sims Group	-28.7
IRESS Market Technology	18.0	Origin Energy	-0.8	Great Southern Plantations	-28.9
Fleetwood Corporation	17.6	Amalgamated Holdings	-2.2	HGL	-29.6
Rebel Sport	16.8	Fairfax (John) Holdings	-2.2	Magna Pacific	-41.7
OAMPS	16.3	Tasmanian Perpetual Trustees	-2.4		

Table F

After-tax profit

This table ranks all the companies according to their most recent full-year after-tax profit.

	$mn		$mn		$mn
BHP Billiton	13933.3	Metcash	127.9	Fleetwood Corporation	20.7
Rio Tinto	6497.0	Perpetual	122.4	Programmed Maint. Services	20.2
Commonwealth Bank	3928.0	Rural Press	113.4	IRESS Market Technology	19.6
National Australia Bank	3761.0	Bendigo Bank	108.3	Ausdrill	19.0
ANZ	3018.0	Seven Network	107.7	K&S Corporation	18.4
Westpac Banking	2818.0	Jubilee Mines	103.4	Trust Company of Australia	18.0
QBE Insurance	1091.0	Adelaide Bank	94.4	Count Financial	17.6
Woodside Petroleum	1037.7	Coates Hire	93.6	HPAL	17.2
Rinker Group	1036.3	Bank of Queensland	91.7	Kingsgate Consolidated	16.7
Macquarie Bank	945.0	Adelaide Brighton	87.8	Infomedia	16.5
Suncorp-Metway	916.0	Gunns	87.2	Housewares International	16.1
St George Bank	891.0	Reece Australia	86.9	Troy Resources	16.1
Wesfarmers	869.4	David Jones	81.1	ARB Corporation	15.8
Coles Myer	787.3	Flight Centre	79.9	Blackmores	14.5
Santos	762.1	United Group	78.7	Wide Bay Australia	14.5
Publishing & Broadcasting	619.2	Cochlear	78.2	Fantastic Holdings	14.4
Brambles Industries	573.5	Corporate Express Australia	66.0	Oakton	14.4
Tabcorp Holdings	543.4	GWA International	60.1	National Can Industries	13.9
AXA Asia Pacific	542.0	Amalgamated Holdings	57.0	Treasury Group	13.9
Lend Lease Corporation	415.2	Hills Industries	48.2	Hunter Hall International	12.7
Boral	362.4	Primary Health Care	47.5	Technology One	12.3
CSL	350.9	Beach Petroleum	44.0	Candle Australia	11.8
Orica	334.9	Alesco	42.1	Gazal Corporation	11.5
Origin Energy	331.9	Crane Group	41.8	CMI	11.2
Leighton Holdings	276.1	GUD Holdings	40.2	MaxiTRANS Industries	10.7
CSR	249.8	OAMPS	39.7	HGL	9.2
Fairfax (John) Holdings	234.3	Cabcharge Australia	38.0	Tasmanian Perpetual Trustees	7.5
Harvey Norman Holdings	229.6	Colorado Group	35.6	Objective Corporation	7.2
Sims Group	196.6	Campbell Brothers	34.3	Pro Medicus	6.1
Computershare	182.6	STW Communications	32.2	SDI	5.1
Sonic Healthcare	172.0	Monadelphous Group	29.4	Rock Building Society	4.6
OneSteel	171.6	Select Harvests	26.5	Magna Pacific	3.7
Macarthur Coal	149.6	Commander Communications	26.0	Adcorp Australia	3.6
Billabong International	145.9	Skilled Group	24.0	Institute of Drug Technology	3.6
Downer EDI	137.8	CVC	23.3	OrotonGroup	3.1
Australian Stock Exchange	137.1	Rebel Sport	22.0		
Great Southern Plantations	132.9	WHK Group	21.8		

Table G

Year-on-year EPS growth

The earnings-per-share (EPS) figure is a crucial one. It tells you – the shareholder – what your part is of the company's profits, for each of your shares. So investors invariably look for EPS growth in a stock. The YOY EPS growth figure is often one of the first ratios that investors look to when evaluating a stock.

	%		%		%
STW Communications	264.8	Wesfarmers	26.7	Downer EDI	7.7
Ausdrill	121.5	Perpetual	26.0	Institute of Drug Technology	7.7
Trust Company of Australia	118.8	WHK Group	25.2	Crane Group	7.6
Santos	113.8	Tabcorp Holdings	23.5	Infomedia	6.8
Rio Tinto	110.0	Alesco	22.0	Hills Industries	6.4
Macarthur Coal	108.8	Campbell Brothers	21.6	ANZ	4.3
Troy Resources	107.8	Sonic Healthcare	20.0	ARB Corporation	4.1
Kingsgate Consolidated	97.7	Harvey Norman Holdings	19.9	Flight Centre	3.9
Seven Network	91.6	Bendigo Bank	18.4	GUD Holdings	3.4
Lend Lease Corporation	84.0	Select Harvests	18.1	Orica	3.1
SDI	76.0	AXA Asia Pacific	18.0	National Australia Bank	2.6
Beach Petroleum	72.5	Publishing & Broadcasting	17.4	Adelaide Bank	2.2
Monadelphous Group	72.5	CSR	17.3	Suncorp-Metway	1.9
BHP Billiton	65.8	QBE Insurance	17.0	Origin Energy	-0.4
CSL	61.0	Primary Health Care	16.4	GWA International	-6.0
Skilled Group	58.5	Technology One	16.4	Adcorp Australia	-6.3
Oakton	54.9	Billabong International	16.2	Amalgamated Holdings	-7.3
Woodside Petroleum	54.1	Wide Bay Australia	16.1	Boral	-7.4
Gazal Corporation	53.7	David Jones	15.7	Great Southern Plantations	-8.7
Rinker Group	53.6	Reece Australia	14.6	Fairfax (John) Holdings	-9.8
National Can Industries	53.2	St George Bank	14.4	Objective Corporation	-10.3
Count Financial	48.5	Commonwealth Bank	14.2	CVC	-11.1
IRESS Market Technology	46.8	Metcash	14.0	Rock Building Society	-12.1
Hunter Hall International	44.3	HPAL	13.9	Gunns	-13.1
Cabcharge Australia	39.5	OAMPS	13.6	OrotonGroup	-13.1
Brambles Industries	39.3	Coles Myer	12.0	MaxiTRANS Industries	-14.2
United Group	39.1	Rural Press	12.0	CMI	-14.7
Candle Australia	38.1	Treasury Group	11.5	HGL	-14.7
Computershare	36.6	Pro Medicus	11.3	Housewares International	-16.1
Rebel Sport	35.6	OneSteel	11.0	K&S Corporation	-18.2
Jubilee Mines	34.4	Adelaide Brighton	10.7	Sims Group	-19.4
Leighton Holdings	33.1	Westpac Banking	10.7	Colorado Group	-21.1
Cochlear	32.8	Tasmanian Perpetual Trustees	9.6	Fantastic Holdings	-24.5
Bank of Queensland	29.4	Corporate Express Australia	9.5	Commander Communications	-27.8
Coates Hire	29.0	Fleetwood Corporation	8.3	Magna Pacific	-46.0
Australian Stock Exchange	27.7	Programmed Maint. Services	8.1		
Blackmores	27.4	Macquarie Bank	7.9		

Table H

Return on equity

Shareholders' equity is the company's assets minus its liabilities. It is, in theory, the amount owned by the shareholders of the company. Return on equity is the after-tax profit expressed as a percentage of that equity. Thus, it is the amount of profit that the company managers made for you – the shareholder – from your assets. For many investors it is one of the most important gauges of how well a company is doing. It is one of the requirements for inclusion in this book that all companies have a return on equity of at least 10% in their latest financial year.

	%		%		%
Count Financial	86.2	CSR	23.7	Seven Network	15.5
Hunter Hall International	72.8	Tasmanian Perpetual Trustees	23.6	Sonic Healthcare	15.4
Monadelphous Group	54.3	Macquarie Bank	23.5	STW Communications	15.4
IRESS Market Technology	53.0	Orica	23.2	Downer EDI	14.9
Jubilee Mines	52.9	Sims Group	22.9	MaxiTRANS Industries	14.9
BHP Billiton	50.0	Coles Myer	22.5	Lend Lease Corporation	14.8
Macarthur Coal	47.7	Skilled Group	22.4	Adelaide Brighton	14.6
Pro Medicus	47.0	David Jones	22.2	GWA International	14.6
Oakton	44.7	Beach Petroleum	22.0	CVC	14.4
Cochlear	43.8	Billabong International	21.6	Adcorp Australia	14.2
Blackmores	42.9	Computershare	21.2	Boral	14.1
Australian Stock Exchange	41.0	Suncorp-Metway	20.5	Bank of Queensland	13.9
Perpetual	40.8	Flight Centre	20.4	National Australia Bank	13.9
Treasury Group	39.4	K&S Corporation	20.1	WHK Group	13.7
Infomedia	37.4	OAMPS	19.7	Adelaide Bank	13.5
Rio Tinto	36.6	Fleetwood Corporation	19.1	Trust Company of Australia	13.5
Objective Corporation	35.3	Commonwealth Bank	18.8	Bendigo Bank	13.4
Fantastic Holdings	33.9	Coates Hire	18.5	Kingsgate Consolidated	13.4
Woodside Petroleum	33.1	St George Bank	18.5	Gunns	13.3
Corporate Express Australia	32.5	United Group	18.5	HGL	13.2
Technology One	31.7	SDI	18.2	CMI	13.0
Troy Resources	31.2	Candle Australia	18.0	Alesco	12.9
Wesfarmers	29.4	Harvey Norman Holdings	18.0	Amalgamated Holdings	12.8
GUD Holdings	29.2	Westpac Banking	18.0	Primary Health Care	12.8
Santos	28.6	Great Southern Plantations	17.8	Institute of Drug Technology	12.7
Rinker Group	28.3	CSL	17.1	Origin Energy	12.7
Select Harvests	27.9	Campbell Brothers	17.0	OneSteel	12.4
ARB Corporation	27.8	Ausdrill	16.9	OrotonGroup	12.1
HPAL	27.7	Wide Bay Australia	16.9	Rock Building Society	12.1
Leighton Holdings	27.7	Gazal Corporation	16.7	National Can Industries	11.7
Colorado Group	27.3	Programmed Maint. Services	16.5	Magna Pacific	11.4
Rural Press	27.1	Tabcorp Holdings	16.4	Commander Communications	11.0
Cabcharge Australia	25.6	AXA Asia Pacific	16.3	Fairfax (John) Holdings	10.9
Metcash	24.7	ANZ	16.2	Housewares International	10.3
Reece Australia	24.6	Brambles Industries	16.1	Crane Group	10.0
Rebel Sport	24.4	Hills Industries	16.0		
QBE Insurance	23.9	Publishing & Broadcasting	16.0		

Table I

Year-on-year return on equity growth

Company managers have a variety of strategies they can use to boost profits. It is much harder to lift the return on equity (ROE). Find a company with a high ROE figure, and one that is growing year by year, and the chances are that you have found a real growth stock.

	%		%		%
STW Communications	280.7	Commonwealth Bank	16.3	Downer EDI	-0.8
Seven Network	133.2	Hunter Hall International	13.7	Reece Australia	-0.8
Santos	119.9	Technology One	12.8	Tabcorp Holdings	-0.8
Kingsgate Consolidated	104.1	Leighton Holdings	11.7	Suncorp-Metway	-1.3
Trust Company of Australia	102.5	WHK Group	11.2	Corporate Express Australia	-1.5
Gazal Corporation	83.7	Wide Bay Australia	10.8	GWA International	-4.1
Lend Lease Corporation	80.3	Harvey Norman Holdings	10.6	Adelaide Bank	-4.6
Ausdrill	67.3	Blackmores	10.1	Campbell Brothers	-5.1
Troy Resources	65.5	Cochlear	8.1	Hills Industries	-5.6
SDI	64.8	Count Financial	7.8	Origin Energy	-5.8
Rio Tinto	60.9	Coates Hire	7.4	Adcorp Australia	-6.0
Macarthur Coal	54.3	OneSteel	6.9	Primary Health Care	-6.8
CSL	52.6	Institute of Drug Technology	6.7	ARB Corporation	-8.8
National Can Industries	46.3	Crane Group	6.5	ANZ	-9.1
Rural Press	43.3	Bank of Queensland	5.8	Fairfax (John) Holdings	-10.0
Rinker Group	39.8	Select Harvests	5.8	Macquarie Bank	-11.0
Monadelphous Group	39.2	Flight Centre	5.7	Rock Building Society	-12.6
Skilled Group	37.9	Adelaide Brighton	5.2	Housewares International	-13.7
Beach Petroleum	37.8	Billabong International	5.1	Boral	-13.9
Oakton	37.2	Jubilee Mines	4.9	Amalgamated Holdings	-16.5
David Jones	34.1	St George Bank	4.5	Great Southern Plantations	-16.8
OrotonGroup	29.1	HPAL	4.3	CMI	-17.4
AXA Asia Pacific	28.3	Fleetwood Corporation	3.7	Treasury Group	-18.3
Woodside Petroleum	28.2	National Australia Bank	3.4	MaxiTRANS Industries	-19.3
Wesfarmers	27.4	GUD Holdings	2.8	Colorado Group	-23.0
Candle Australia	25.5	QBE Insurance	2.5	HGL	-23.3
IRESS Market Technology	25.3	Westpac Banking	2.5	K&S Corporation	-28.4
Brambles Industries	25.1	Sonic Healthcare	2.3	CVC	-28.9
BHP Billiton	24.6	Pro Medicus	2.2	Fantastic Holdings	-29.5
Perpetual	24.5	Tasmanian Perpetual Trustees	2.2	Gunns	-32.3
Rebel Sport	23.3	Australian Stock Exchange	1.8	Objective Corporation	-33.6
Cabcharge Australia	23.0	Bendigo Bank	1.8	Commander Communications	-36.7
CSR	22.0	OAMPS	1.2	Magna Pacific	-42.8
Coles Myer	21.7	Alesco	1.0	Sims Group	-43.8
Publishing & Broadcasting	20.5	Orica	0.1	Metcash	-53.8
Infomedia	18.7	Programmed Maint. Services	-0.1		
Computershare	16.8	United Group	-0.6		

Table J

Debt-to-equity ratio

A company's borrowings as a percentage of its shareholder's equity is one of the most common measures of corporate debt. Many investors will be wary of a company with a ratio that is too high. However, a company with a steady business and a regular income flow – such as an electric power company or a large supermarket chain – is generally considered relatively safe with a high level of debt, whereas a small company in a new business field might be thought at risk with even moderate debt levels. Much depends on surrounding circumstances, including the prevailing interest rates. Of course, it is often from borrowing that a company grows, and some investors are not happy buying shares in a company with little or no debt.

There are various ways to calculate the ratio, but for this book the net debt position is used. That is, a company's cash has been deducted from its borrowings. For inclusion in this book no company was allowed a debt-to-equity ratio of more than 70%. Some of the companies had no net debt – their cash position was greater than the amount of their borrowings – and so have been assigned a zero figure in this table. The ratio has no relevance for banks, so they have been excluded.

	%		%		%
Adcorp Australia	0.0	Colorado Group	0.1	Publishing & Broadcasting	42.1
Australian Stock Exchange	0.0	HGL	1.9	OneSteel	42.5
AXA Asia Pacific	0.0	Skilled Group	2.8	Woodside Petroleum	43.4
Beach Petroleum	0.0	Institute of Drug Technology	4.1	SDI	44.0
Candle Australia	0.0	ARB Corporation	7.0	Rural Press	44.1
Count Financial	0.0	QBE Insurance	7.3	Wesfarmers	45.9
CVC	0.0	Cabcharge Australia	8.1	Alesco	46.5
Fantastic Holdings	0.0	Blackmores	9.5	Santos	46.8
Flight Centre	0.0	Lend Lease Corporation	9.5	MaxiTRANS Industries	48.0
HPAL	0.0	WHK Group	13.2	Downer EDI	49.7
Hunter Hall International	0.0	Rinker Group	13.5	Harvey Norman Holdings	50.6
Infomedia	0.0	Coles Myer	14.4	Cochlear	51.9
IRESS Market Technology	0.0	Corporate Express Australia	14.7	CSR	51.9
Jubilee Mines	0.0	CSL	15.3	Metcash	52.5
Kingsgate Consolidated	0.0	Great Southern Plantations	16.0	Orica	54.3
Leighton Holdings	0.0	Rio Tinto	18.4	CMI	56.2
Macarthur Coal	0.0	Fleetwood Corporation	20.3	Sonic Healthcare	57.0
Magna Pacific	0.0	Sims Group	24.0	Brambles Industries	57.2
Monadelphous Group	0.0	STW Communications	27.1	Boral	57.3
National Can Industries	0.0	Billabong International	27.5	Computershare	57.7
Oakton	0.0	Ausdrill	29.4	Coates Hire	58.1
OAMPS	0.0	Primary Health Care	31.1	Gunns	58.8
Objective Corporation	0.0	United Group	31.7	Programmed Maint. Services	59.0
Perpetual	0.0	Campbell Brothers	33.4	Commander Communications	59.4
Pro Medicus	0.0	BHP Billiton	33.7	David Jones	60.8
Rebel Sport	0.0	GWA International	34.2	OrotonGroup	65.4
Reece Australia	0.0	K&S Corporation	34.8	Tabcorp Holdings	65.8
Select Harvests	0.0	Hills Industries	36.7	Origin Energy	66.1
Tasmanian Perpetual Trustees	0.0	GUD Holdings	38.2	Fairfax (John) Holdings	68.1
Technology One	0.0	Amalgamated Holdings	39.6	Gazal Corporation	69.0
Treasury Group	0.0	Adelaide Brighton	40.4	Seven Network	69.5
Troy Resources	0.0	Housewares International	40.5		
Trust Company of Australia	0.0	Crane Group	41.2		

Table K

Current ratio

The current ratio is simply the company's current assets divided by its current liabilities. Current assets are cash or assets that can, in theory, be converted quickly into cash. Current liabilities are normally those payable within a year. The current ratio measures the ability of a company to repay in a hurry its short-term debt, should the need arise. Banks are not included.

Jubilee Mines	12.8	HGL	2.0	Computershare	1.3
Pro Medicus	8.0	Brambles Industries	1.9	Corporate Express Australia	1.3
CVC	5.7	CMI	1.9	Gazal Corporation	1.3
Trust Company of Australia	4.7	Hills Industries	1.9	Sonic Healthcare	1.3
Tasmanian Perpetual Trustees	4.5	OrotonGroup	1.9	United Group	1.3
National Can Industries	4.4	Reece Australia	1.9	Commander Communications	1.2
Institute of Drug Technology	3.9	Rinker Group	1.9	David Jones	1.2
GWA International	3.8	Adelaide Brighton	1.8	Downer EDI	1.2
Treasury Group	3.8	ARB Corporation	1.8	Fleetwood Corporation	1.2
Troy Resources	3.6	Ausdrill	1.8	Gunns	1.2
Technology One	3.4	Coates Hire	1.8	Monadelphous Group	1.2
Objective Corporation	3.3	MaxiTRANS Industries	1.8	OAMPS	1.2
IRESS Market Technology	3.1	OneSteel	1.8	Perpetual	1.2
Housewares International	3.0	Santos	1.8	Publishing & Broadcasting	1.2
Infomedia	2.9	Select Harvests	1.8	Rio Tinto	1.2
SDI	2.8	Seven Network	1.8	Skilled Group	1.2
Hunter Hall International	2.7	Sims Group	1.8	Wesfarmers	1.2
Magna Pacific	2.7	GUD Holdings	1.7	Lend Lease Corporation	1.1
Programmed Maint. Services	2.7	Boral	1.6	BHP Billiton	1.0
Billabong International	2.6	Crane Group	1.6	Coles Myer	1.0
Macarthur Coal	2.6	HPAL	1.6	Great Southern Plantations	1.0
Oakton	2.5	Australian Stock Exchange	1.5	K&S Corporation	1.0
Blackmores	2.4	Rural Press	1.5	Origin Energy	1.0
Cabcharge Australia	2.4	Alesco	1.4	STW Communications	1.0
Rebel Sport	2.4	Cochlear	1.4	Beach Petroleum	0.9
CSL	2.3	CSR	1.4	Primary Health Care	0.9
Campbell Brothers	2.2	Flight Centre	1.4	Woodside Petroleum	0.8
Colorado Group	2.2	Metcash	1.4	Kingsgate Consolidated	0.6
Fantastic Holdings	2.2	Orica	1.4	Amalgamated Holdings	0.4
WHK Group	2.1	QBE Insurance	1.4	Fairfax (John) Holdings	0.4
Count Financial	2.0	Adcorp Australia	1.3	Tabcorp Holdings	0.3
Harvey Norman Holdings	2.0	Candle Australia	1.3		

Table L

Price-earnings ratio

The PER – the current share price divided by the earnings-per-share figure – is one of the best-known of all sharemarket ratios. Essentially it expresses the amount of money investors are ready to pay for each cent or dollar of a company's profits, and it allows you to compare the share prices of different companies with widely different profits. A high PER suggests the market has a high regard for the company and its growth prospects; a low one may mean that investors are disdainful of the stock. The figures in this table are based on share prices as of 5 September 2006.

CMI	3.9
Macarthur Coal	5.7
Magna Pacific	6.2
Great Southern Plantations	6.3
CVC	7.9
National Can Industries	8.4
Ausdrill	8.7
Santos	8.7
Troy Resources	8.7
MaxiTRANS Industries	8.8
Adcorp Australia	9.4
HGL	10.5
Amalgamated Holdings	10.6
GUD Holdings	10.6
HPAL	10.6
Gunns	11.1
Rural Press	11.5
Boral	11.6
CSR	11.8
Downer EDI	11.8
Sims Group	11.8
Housewares International	12.0
BHP Billiton	12.1
Colorado Group	12.2
Jubilee Mines	12.2
Suncorp-Metway	12.7
Rebel Sport	12.9
K&S Corporation	13.1
Gazal Corporation	13.6
Candle Australia	13.7
Corporate Express Australia	14.1
OneSteel	14.1
ARB Corporation	14.3
GWA International	14.3
Wesfarmers	14.4
Tabcorp Holdings	14.5
Adelaide Brighton	14.6
Flight Centre	14.8
Alesco	14.9
Coates Hire	14.9
Commonwealth Bank	15.0
Infomedia	15.0
Lend Lease Corporation	15.1
National Australia Bank	15.1
Adelaide Bank	15.2
Westpac Banking	15.3
Crane Group	15.4
Origin Energy	15.5
STW Communications	15.5
Fleetwood Corporation	15.6
Programmed Maint. Services	15.6
Commander Communications	15.7
Beach Petroleum	15.8
Rio Tinto	15.8
Fairfax (John) Holdings	15.9
Macquarie Bank	15.9
Blackmores	16.1
Wide Bay Australia	16.1
Harvey Norman Holdings	16.2
ANZ	16.5
Bank of Queensland	16.6
Hills Industries	16.6
Hunter Hall International	16.8
OAMPS	16.8
QBE Insurance	16.8
SDI	17.5
Treasury Group	17.5
St George Bank	17.6
Bendigo Bank	17.7
Institute of Drug Technology	17.7
Monadelphous Group	17.7
Rinker Group	17.7
Technology One	18.2
Orica	18.5
OrotonGroup	18.5
Reece Australia	18.7
Seven Network	19.1
Tasmanian Perpetual Trustees	19.1
David Jones	19.2
Fantastic Holdings	19.2
Rock Building Society	19.6
Objective Corporation	19.8
WHK Group	19.9
Leighton Holdings	20.1
Select Harvests	20.1
Metcash	20.2
Publishing & Broadcasting	20.2
Oakton	20.3
Billabong International	20.6
Trust Company of Australia	20.6
Pro Medicus	21.1
Sonic Healthcare	21.4
AXA Asia Pacific	21.5
Coles Myer	21.9
United Group	22.1
Cabcharge Australia	22.4
Perpetual	22.4
Skilled Group	24.0
Campbell Brothers	25.0
Computershare	25.3
Australian Stock Exchange	25.4
Woodside Petroleum	25.9
CSL	26.6
Kingsgate Consolidated	27.4
Count Financial	28.7
Primary Health Care	28.7
IRESS Market Technology	33.6
Brambles Industries	35.0
Cochlear	36.2

Table M

Price-to-NTA-per-share ratio

The NTA-per-share figure expresses the worth of a company's net tangible assets – that is, its assets minus its liabilities and intangible assets – for each share of the company. Intangible assets, such as goodwill or the value of newspaper mastheads, are excluded because it is deemed difficult to place a value on them (though this proposition is debatable), and also because they might not have much worth if separated from the company. The price-to-NTA-per-share ratio relates this figure to the share price.

A ratio of one means that the company is valued exactly according to the value of its assets. A ratio below one suggests that the shares are a bargain, though usually there is a good reason for this. Profits are more important than assets.

In some respects this is an 'old economy' ratio. For many high-tech companies in the 'new economy' the most important assets are human ones whose worth does not appear on the balance sheet.

Eight companies – Alesco, Commander Communications, Computershare, John Fairfax Holdings, Metcash, Seven Network, Sonic Healthcare and Tabcorp – with a negative NTA-per-share figure, as a result of having intangible assets valued at more than their remaining net assets, have been omitted from this table.

CMI	0.8	Origin Energy	3.5	Blackmores	6.7
National Can Industries	1.0	OrotonGroup	3.5	Fantastic Holdings	6.7
CVC	1.1	STW Communications	3.5	Cabcharge Australia	6.8
Great Southern Plantations	1.2	Suncorp-Metway	3.6	Rinker Group	7.3
Magna Pacific	1.2	Adcorp Australia	3.7	Select Harvests	7.4
Gunns	1.3	GUD Holdings	3.7	Wesfarmers	7.4
Amalgamated Holdings	1.4	Kingsgate Consolidated	3.7	Coles Myer	7.5
Ausdrill	1.4	Trust Company of Australia	3.7	Technology One	7.5
Boral	1.8	Sims Group	3.8	Woodside Petroleum	7.5
HGL	1.8	Hills Industries	4.0	Tasmanian Perpetual Trustees	7.9
OneSteel	2.0	Orica	4.0	CSL	8.0
Adelaide Bank	2.1	Westpac Banking	4.0	Campbell Brothers	8.1
Santos	2.1	ARB Corporation	4.2	Monadelphous Group	8.8
MaxiTRANS Industries	2.3	Downer EDI	4.2	Corporate Express Australia	9.4
Bendigo Bank	2.4	Fleetwood Corporation	4.2	Infomedia	10.1
Institute of Drug Technology	2.4	Gazal Corporation	4.3	Perpetual	10.3
Macarthur Coal	2.4	Reece Australia	4.4	Australian Stock Exchange	10.5
Rock Building Society	2.4	Commonwealth Bank	4.5	Pro Medicus	10.7
Troy Resources	2.4	David Jones	4.6	Candle Australia	11.1
K&S Corporation	2.5	QBE Insurance	4.7	Hunter Hall International	11.1
Housewares International	2.6	SDI	4.8	Publishing & Broadcasting	11.5
Wide Bay Australia	2.6	St George Bank	4.8	OAMPS	12.4
Adelaide Brighton	2.7	Colorado Group	5.0	GWA International	12.6
Coates Hire	2.7	Rio Tinto	5.2	WHK Group	14.9
Harvey Norman Holdings	2.8	BHP Billiton	5.3	Oakton	18.6
National Australia Bank	2.8	Leighton Holdings	5.3	Skilled Group	20.1
Programmed Maint. Services	2.8	Flight Centre	5.5	IRESS Market Technology	21.2
Beach Petroleum	2.9	Jubilee Mines	5.6	Count Financial	21.8
Crane Group	2.9	AXA Asia Pacific	5.8	Rural Press	25.7
Lend Lease Corporation	2.9	Macquarie Bank	5.9	Billabong International	53.7
Rebel Sport	3.0	Objective Corporation	6.3	United Group	54.4
Bank of Queensland	3.1	Brambles Industries	6.5	Primary Health Care	55.1
CSR	3.2	HPAL	6.5	Cochlear	1235.8
ANZ	3.4	Treasury Group	6.6		

Table N

Dividend yield

Many investors buy shares for income, rather than for capital growth. They look for companies that offer a high dividend yield (the dividend expressed as a percentage of the share price). This table ranks the companies in this book according to their historic dividend yields. Note that the franking credits available from some companies can make the dividend yield substantially higher if you are in an appropriate tax bracket. The figures in this table are based on share prices as of 5 September 2006.

	%		%		%
Adcorp Australia	10.7	David Jones	4.5	Coates Hire	3.2
CMI	10.0	National Australia Bank	4.5	Publishing & Broadcasting	3.2
GUD Holdings	8.5	Perpetual	4.5	Sonic Healthcare	3.2
Macarthur Coal	8.2	St George Bank	4.5	Orica	3.1
Housewares International	8.1	Tasmanian Perpetual Trustees	4.5	Pro Medicus	3.1
Magna Pacific	8.1	Technology One	4.5	United Group	3.1
MaxiTRANS Industries	7.7	Treasury Group	4.5	Billabong International	3.0
HPAL	7.3	Wide Bay Australia	4.5	Cabcharge Australia	3.0
Alesco	6.3	Adelaide Brighton	4.4	Coles Myer	3.0
Wesfarmers	6.3	Adelaide Bank	4.3	Fleetwood Corporation	3.0
Tabcorp Holdings	5.9	Westpac Banking	4.3	IRESS Market Technology	3.0
GWA International	5.8	Flight Centre	4.2	Rinker Group	3.0
National Can Industries	5.7	Rebel Sport	4.2	QBE Insurance	2.9
Gunns	5.6	Bank of Queensland	4.1	Seven Network	2.9
Gazal Corporation	5.5	CVC	4.1	Count Financial	2.8
Great Southern Plantations	5.5	Jubilee Mines	4.1	Origin Energy	2.8
Hunter Hall International	5.5	ANZ	4.0	Troy Resources	2.8
Crane Group	5.4	OAMPS	4.0	Reece Australia	2.7
Hills Industries	5.4	OneSteel	4.0	Campbell Brothers	2.6
Institute of Drug Technology	5.4	Lend Lease Corporation	3.9	Metcash	2.6
HGL	5.3	Bendigo Bank	3.8	WHK Group	2.4
Infomedia	5.3	K&S Corporation	3.8	Harvey Norman Holdings	2.3
STW Communications	5.3	Programmed Maint. Services	3.8	Woodside Petroleum	2.3
Candle Australia	5.1	Downer EDI	3.7	AXA Asia Pacific	2.1
Colorado Group	5.1	Monadelphous Group	3.7	Brambles Industries	2.1
Sims Group	5.1	OrotonGroup	3.7	Commander Communications	2.1
Amalgamated Holdings	5.0	Primary Health Care	3.7	Objective Corporation	2.1
Commonwealth Bank	4.9	Ausdrill	3.6	Cochlear	1.9
Fairfax (John) Holdings	4.9	Corporate Express Australia	3.6	Kingsgate Consolidated	1.9
Rock Building Society	4.9	Fantastic Holdings	3.6	BHP Billiton	1.7
Rural Press	4.9	Trust Company of Australia	3.6	Computershare	1.7
Blackmores	4.7	Australian Stock Exchange	3.5	Rio Tinto	1.4
Boral	4.7	ARB Corporation	3.4	CSL	1.3
Oakton	4.7	Santos	3.4	Beach Petroleum	1.0
Select Harvests	4.7	Skilled Group	3.4	SDI	0.8
CSR	4.6	Leighton Holdings	3.3		
Suncorp-Metway	4.6	Macquarie Bank	3.3		

Table O

Year-on-year dividend growth

Most investors hope for a rising dividend, and this table tells how much each company raised (or lowered) its dividend in its latest financial year.

	%		%		%
Macarthur Coal	127.8	Metcash	21.1	ANZ	8.9
Rinker Group	100.0	Corporate Express Australia	20.0	Hills Industries	8.3
Monadelphous Group	68.4	CVC	20.0	Trust Company of Australia	7.9
Primary Health Care	68.0	GUD Holdings	20.0	Troy Resources	7.7
Oakton	67.5	Origin Energy	20.0	Great Southern Plantations	7.1
Woodside Petroleum	57.6	Wesfarmers	19.4	Lend Lease Corporation	7.0
Rebel Sport	50.0	OAMPS	19.2	MaxiTRANS Industries	6.3
Select Harvests	50.0	AXA Asia Pacific	19.1	Fairfax (John) Holdings	5.4
Candle Australia	47.8	Blackmores	19.0	Ausdrill	5.0
United Group	46.7	Campbell Brothers	19.0	Rural Press	4.9
Bank of Queensland	46.5	Skilled Group	18.8	Orica	4.4
CSL	44.7	Computershare	18.2	Rock Building Society	4.3
Kingsgate Consolidated	42.9	Infomedia	17.6	K&S Corporation	3.7
Adelaide Brighton	40.0	Seven Network	17.0	Flight Centre	3.0
Tasmanian Perpetual Trustees	36.4	Brambles Industries	16.3	Fleetwood Corporation	2.5
Cabcharge Australia	35.3	Westpac Banking	16.3	Rio Tinto	1.5
Macquarie Bank	33.5	IRESS Market Technology	16.1	Fantastic Holdings	0.2
Count Financial	33.3	Billabong International	15.8	Beach Petroleum	0.0
National Can Industries	33.3	Reece Australia	15.8	Boral	0.0
Leighton Holdings	32.0	Bendigo Bank	15.6	CMI	0.0
BHP Billiton	31.9	Santos	15.2	Colorado Group	0.0
QBE Insurance	31.5	Sonic Healthcare	13.9	Crane Group	0.0
Hunter Hall International	31.2	Commonwealth Bank	13.7	GWA International	0.0
Amalgamated Holdings	29.7	Publishing & Broadcasting	13.5	Housewares International	0.0
Gunns	28.0	HGL	13.3	Institute of Drug Technology	0.0
Coates Hire	26.7	Programmed Maint. Services	13.3	National Australia Bank	0.0
Australian Stock Exchange	26.3	Objective Corporation	12.5	Pro Medicus	-5.9
Coles Myer	26.3	St George Bank	12.3	Adcorp Australia	-11.1
OneSteel	25.9	HPAL	12.2	Jubilee Mines	-11.1
Perpetual	25.4	WHK Group	12.0	Gazal Corporation	-12.5
Cochlear	25.0	Suncorp-Metway	11.5	Sims Group	-25.0
CSR	25.0	Downer EDI	11.1	Commander Communications	-33.3
Treasury Group	25.0	Technology One	10.0	SDI	-33.3
Alesco	24.4	Tabcorp Holdings	9.9	Magna Pacific	-43.3
David Jones	23.1	STW Communications	9.7	OrotonGroup	-60.0
Harvey Norman Holdings	23.1	ARB Corporation	9.5		
Wide Bay Australia	22.6	Adelaide Bank	9.4		

Table P

Five-year share price return

This table ranks the return to investors from a five-year investment in each of the companies in the book. It is the accumulated return, which means it incorporates not only capital gain but also reinvested dividends, bonus stock and rights issues.

	% pa		% pa		% pa
Ausdrill	97.1	Gunns	28.4	Publishing & Broadcasting	19.4
Beach Petroleum	94.4	Troy Resources	28.2	Crane Group	18.7
Monadelphous Group	90.3	BHP Billiton	27.7	ARB Corporation	18.5
Skilled Group	63.0	Bank of Queensland	27.5	Santos	18.3
Jubilee Mines	62.8	Woodside Petroleum	27.0	Macquarie Bank	17.9
Select Harvests	58.0	Primary Health Care	26.9	Suncorp-Metway	17.8
United Group	54.1	Objective Corporation	26.7	Commonwealth Bank	17.4
Coates Hire	54.0	Colorado Group	26.6	ANZ	16.8
Treasury Group	53.0	Housewares International	26.6	Tabcorp Holdings	16.5
Great Southern Plantations	50.1	Trust Company of Australia	26.6	Westpac Banking	16.1
Kingsgate Consolidated	49.0	Fantastic Holdings	26.1	GWA International	13.5
Oakton	46.1	Rural Press	26.1	Computershare	13.1
Hunter Hall International	45.7	Blackmores	26.0	Sonic Healthcare	12.9
Count Financial	45.0	IRESS Market Technology	26.0	National Australia Bank	12.5
Fleetwood Corporation	44.2	WHK Group	25.5	Gazal Corporation	11.4
Orica	43.8	AXA Asia Pacific	24.5	Lend Lease Corporation	10.8
GUD Holdings	42.5	Boral	24.3	Seven Network	10.7
OneSteel	41.6	Cabcharge Australia	23.6	Wesfarmers	10.7
Sims Group	39.9	National Can Industries	23.6	Fairfax (John) Holdings	10.3
SDI	38.1	Downer EDI	23.3	Pro Medicus	10.1
Campbell Brothers	38.0	Bendigo Bank	23.0	CMI	8.5
Candle Australia	38.0	Commander Communications	22.8	OrotonGroup	8.3
MaxiTRANS Industries	37.8	Rebel Sport	22.6	Brambles Industries	6.6
QBE Insurance	37.1	Adelaide Bank	22.1	Corporate Express Australia	6.3
Reece Australia	36.4	HGL	21.2	Technology One	6.0
K&S Corporation	36.0	Perpetual	21.0	Cochlear	5.3
Macarthur Coal	36.0	Rock Building Society	20.7	CSL	4.2
Alesco	35.0	CVC	20.5	Magna Pacific	4.1
Rinker Group	35.0*	Hills Industries	20.4	Harvey Norman Holdings	2.9
OAMPS	33.7	Billabong International	20.3	HPAL	-0.5
Tasmanian Perpetual Trustees	32.4	Programmed Maint. Services	20.1	STW Communications	-2.3
Metcash	31.9	CSR	20.0	Adcorp Australia	-2.6
Adelaide Brighton	31.7	Rio Tinto	19.8	Flight Centre	-4.6
David Jones	31.4	St George Bank	19.8	Infomedia	-9.3
Australian Stock Exchange	29.6	Coles Myer	19.7	Institute of Drug Technology	-14.4
Wide Bay Australia	29.3	Origin Energy	19.7		
Amalgamated Holdings	29.2	Leighton Holdings	19.4		

* 3-year return

Table Q

Non-interest income to total income

The final three tables rank the banks only. Most of the banks are working to diversify away from their traditional lending business into other operations, such as insurance and funds management. This table ranks them according to their success, showing how much of their income derives from non-interest sources.

	%
Macquarie Bank	86.5
Suncorp-Metway	84.8
National Australia Bank	48.9
Commonwealth Bank	47.0
Westpac Banking	40.4
Bank of Queensland	39.2
St George Bank	38.5
ANZ	38.0
Bendigo Bank	34.0
Wide Bay Australia	31.4
Rock Building Society	28.7
Adelaide Bank	19.8

Table R

Cost-to-income ratio

All the banks are working to reduce their high costs. The cost-to-income ratio – expressing costs as a percentage of operating income – is one of the measures commonly used by analysts to ascertain their success.

	%
St George Bank	45.5
Westpac Banking	46.6
ANZ	48.3
Commonwealth Bank	48.8
Adelaide Bank	51.8
National Australia Bank	53.4
Wide Bay Australia	56.7
Bank of Queensland	59.8
Macquarie Bank	70.7
Bendigo Bank	70.8
Rock Building Society	74.7
Suncorp-Metway	75.8

Table S

Return on assets

Banks have large assets, and the return on assets ratio – after-tax profit as a percentage of average total assets – is another popular measure of their efficiency.

	%
Suncorp-Metway	1.7
St George Bank	1.2
ANZ	1.1
Commonwealth Bank	1.1
Macquarie Bank	1.1
Westpac Banking	1.1
Bank of Queensland	0.9
National Australia Bank	0.9
Wide Bay Australia	0.9
Bendigo Bank	0.7
Adelaide Bank	0.4
Rock Building Society	0.4